EFFIGIES DEI

STUDIES

IN THE HISTORY OF RELIGIONS

(SUPPLEMENTS TO *NUMEN*)

EDITED BY

M. HEERMA VAN VOSS • R. J. Z. WERBLOWSKY

LI

EFFIGIES DEI

EFFIGIES DEI

ESSAYS ON THE HISTORY OF RELIGIONS

EDITED BY

DIRK VAN DER PLAS

E.J. BRILL

LEIDEN · NEW YORK · KØBENHAVN · KÖLN

1987

Library of Congress Catalog —
card number 87-26894

ISSN 0169-8834
ISBN 90 04 08655 2

PRINTED IN THE NETHERLANDS

CONTENTS

PREFACE

The essays on the history of religions collected here in this book are offered by members of the *NETHERLANDS ASSOCIATION FOR THE HISTORY OF RELIGIONS* on the occasion of its 40th anniversary. The Dutch organization is connected with the *INTERNATIONAL ASSOCIA-TION FOR THE HISTORY OF RELIGIONS*. It numbers 140 members, specialized in quite different branches and aspects of the discipline. Twice a year they assemble to listen to some lectures and to discuss the subjects from their own point of view. This presupposes that the papers are offered in such a way that they are intelligible and interesting even for colleagues who are specialized in an other field. The collection was put together according to the same principle, in the hope that colleagues working on the history of religions will be interested in all of the essays. The authors were asked to fill in the theme *EFFIGIES DEI* in their own way, being free to choose a subject from their own special interests, whether it be a literal interpretation of the title of this book, or a figurative one. The result is this booklet with an anthology of Dutch research in the history of religions, which I hope is just as many-coloured as the *EFFIGIES DEI*. And also that this 'bouquet' may contribute to the flourishing of the *NETHERLANDS ASSOCIATION FOR THE HISTORY OF RELIGIONS*.

August 1987   Dirk van der Plas

THE VEILED IMAGE OF AMENAPET

Dirk van der Plas

Representations of gods from Ancient Egypt are well-known, even to scholars who are not specialized in Egyptian religion. The one of Amun of Luxor, that forms the subject of the present article, is less familiar. Unusual in some respects, it has been studied by several Egyptologists[1].

The Egyptians have been quite explicit how they conceived of the cult-images of their gods, both statues and two-dimensional representations in the ritual scenes on the temple walls. They believed that their gods were bodily present in their images. Statues, after being manufactured by sculptors in an apartment of the temple called 'Goldhouse' became animated, *i.e.* received the means to use their senses and to perform their vital functions, by a ceremony which the Egyptians, since the Old Kingdom, called 'Opening the Mouth'[2]. By this ritual the statues became 'living images'. In this respect the title of the sculptors in the New Kingdom is meaningful. They were called 'those who make alive (animated)'[3]. In the temple-service the statues were treated in accordance with this. Each morning the statues, which where locked up inside the sanctuary, had to be awakened, refreshed by washing and anointment, dressed, fed and censed by the priests.

Yet the Egyptians did not identify the gods with their images. This appears clearly from texts of the New Kingdom and especially from the inscriptions of the temples of the Graeco-Roman period. Being in heaven himself, god comes down on earth through his *Ba*[4] to take possession of his statue, which is his body, in the same way as the *Ba* of the dead, represented by a bird with human head, flies up to heaven during the day to join the gods, and returns to the mummy and his images in the grave by night. In a text from the Eighteenth Dynasty (1550-1291 B.C.[5]) it is said:

'May my *Ba* come down on my statues of the monuments
which I have made'[6].

The text which is being adduced traditionally in this context is to be found on the famous Shabaka stone (British Museum, *No. 498*). This cultic-theological text, which was carved on stone by order of king Shabaka in the Twenty-fifth Dynasty (775-653 B.C.), because the original was found to be wormeaten, probably goes back to the New Kingdom[7]. In this text the god Ptah of Memphis is said to have created all things by planning them in his heart and calling them into existence by his speech. So the gods, their temples and cults came into being too:

'Truly, he created the gods.
He made all the cities and founded the nomes.
He placed the gods in their shrines and established
their offerings.
He founded their shrines and made their bodies in
agreement with the wishes of their heart.
And so, the gods entered into their bodies of every kind
of wood, every kind of stone, every kind of clay, of
everything that grows on him (*i.e.* Ptah as earth-god),
and in which they want to assume a shape'[8].

But not only the cult-statues appear to be the animated 'bodies' of the gods, the same concept applies to their images in the reliefs. A text from the room of the god Osiris in the temple of Dendara (Graeco-Roman period) states:

'Osiris (...) comes like a spirit to unite himself with
his shape in his sanctuary.
He comes down from heaven flying like a sparrow with
gleaming feathers, and the *Bas* of the gods with him.
He swoops down like a falcon to his room in Dendara.
(...)
He enters his beautiful room peacefully, together with
the gods that are around him.
He sees his secret shape which is pictured at its place,
his figure which is engraved on the walls.
Then he enters his secret image,
he comes down on his statue (...),
and the *Bas* of the gods take their seats at his
side'[9].

However, gods do not always live in their statues and images. They need the cult, in which the union between their *Bas* and bodies is being realized daily and annually by the performance of ritual ceremonies. These could be enacted by priests only; for daily service of the gods in the temple could not be attended by common people. They met their gods during the festivals, when the cult-statues left the hidden part of the temple for a procession. Apart from the daily service, which aimed at the maintenance of the cosmic order, these processions of the gods form an essential element both in official cult and in popular piety. On these occasions a god could interfere in the life of individuals through miracles and oracles. The usual procedure was that the god appeared in his processional bark, which was lifted up by priests and carried around on their shoulders. Yet the cult-statue remained hidden in the bark- shrine[10]. At the same time, there was a veil at both sides of the shrine itself, which removed it partly from the eyes of people (*Fig. 1*). Only few exceptions are known[11]. One of them is the processional image of Amenapet of Djeme[12].

Djeme is the name, already attested in the Twenty-first Dynasty (1075-945 B.C.), of the small temple of Medinet Habu. This temple, located on the west bank of the Nile, across Thebes, seems to be built in close relation with the temple of Luxor[13]. According to a tradition appearing in texts of the Late Dynastic Period (1075-332 B.C.), the small temple of Medinet Habu was looked upon as a necropolis. The primeval snake 'Kem-atef' (litt. 'The one who completed his time'), manifestation of the god Amun of Thebes, would be buried there together with the eight primeval deities brought forth by his son, the snake 'Ir-ta' (litt. 'The one who made the earth'), who are being said to have created the light. They received a funerary cult which was organized by the temple of Luxor.

The Luxor temple was called 'Opet (sanctuary) of the South'. Here, another manifestation of Amun of Thebes, called Amenapet, was worshipped. This god was a synthesis of Amun-Re and the god of fertility and generating force, Min of Koptos (*Fig. 2*). From the latter Amenapet took his ithyphallic shape, lifting up his right arm squarely from the elbow and holding a flail. Texts from the Theban temples characterize him as a primeval god who regenerates himself. He is said to be his own father, even his own grandfather, the one who created all gods:

'Amenapet, bull who lifts his arm, who gives birth to the
gods, great living god, chief of the gods. He is the
image of Re'[14].
'King of Northern and Southern Egypt, who gave birth to
the primeval gods. Kamutef (litt. "bull of his mother"),
who begot his father. [...] Who created the Ogdoad, the
Father of fathers of the eight primeval gods. Who rises
in [...]. Everyone lives by seeing his rays. Who appears

continuously from the (primeval) lotus in order to be
king at the beginning of the decade: Amenapet of Djeme,
great living god, chief of all gods, Lord of heaven,
earth and netherworld'[15].

Thus, according to the texts of the Late Dynastic and Ptolemaic Period (310-30 B.C.), Amun of Luxor is both the father of the primeval gods who were buried in the small temple of Medinet Habu (Kem-atef) and his son (Ir-ta). He is both the begetter and the begotten. In other words, he is self-renewing. He embodies the cycle of life and death.

A son has to take care of the funerary cult for his parents. In the second text, which dates from the time of Ptolemy IV (221-203 B.C.), 'Amenapet of Djeme' is the name for Amun of Luxor viewed as this son. But it also refers to a separated and individual deity.

The data about Amenapet of Djeme characterizes him as a king who travels to Djeme at the beginning of each decade[16] to bring offerings, especially libations, to the ancestral gods who are buried in the small temple of Medinet Habu[17]. As an individual god, the ithyphallic Amenapet of Djeme is being represented in two ways: (unveiled) standing as usual[18] and (with veiled body) sitting(?[19]) in a litter. In the latter shape he appears for the first time on a bronze mirror which dates from the time of Psammetichos II (Twenty-sixth Dynasty, 595-589 B.C.) together with Amun of Luxor (*Fig. 3*)[20]. This veiled god with unveiled face is an unusual representation in Egyptian religion and iconography.

On stele *E 20363* of the Louvre museum in Paris (*Fig. 4*), at the right side, a priest and four assistants are depicted bringing praise and offerings to a god whose name is, according to the inscription at the top, 'Amenapet of Djeme'. They are standing in front of a litter, placed on a sort of low table. On the side of the litter two animals are represented: on the top of the poles on which the stool is carried, a lion, and above him a sphinx, wearing the double crown of Northern and Southern Egypt on his head. The litter is made in the shape of a portable shrine on which a throne is placed. In front of the shrine, two birds with human heads (*Ba*-birds) are sitting. In this type of litter, kings were carried around (*Fig. 5*). The statues of the deified king Amenophis I (Eighteenth Dynasty, 1525-1504 B.C.), patron of the royal necropolis and of its artisans, used to visit in it the necropolis of Thebes on the western bank of the Nile during some festivals[21]. Behind the litter, Isis-Hathor, with the sign of life in her left hand, stands to protect the god. Before the litter, facing the priestly figures, the young god Chonsu seems to be worshipped as well[22].

Amenapet of Djeme himself is in the litter. His face has disappeared, but his chin and beard, a necklace with a pectoral in the shape of a shrine, and the two ostrich feathers of his diadem are still visible. Behind his head, contours of a protuberance are visible, above a mass which corresponds to the body. This image has been misinterpreted in different ways, e.g. as an 'aniconic form of Amun' or a 'magical Amun-throne'[23]. But Miss Marianne Doresse, who collected twenty-one examples of this representation of Amenapet of Djeme and examined them very thoroughly together with the relevant texts, has clearly shown that the body of Amenapet of Djeme is veiled by a sort of cloak. Traces of some figures are discernible on it: a crocodile, a squatting god and a cruciform-shaped sign. On the shoulder, a rectangular motive is outlined. The protuberance turned out to be the right arm of the god, lifted up squarely from the elbow with the flail, covered by the veil[24]. This interpretation seems to fit the data provided by the texts that accompany the veiled images of Amenapet of Djeme. Twice he is described explicitly as being the one 'with lifted arm'. And a lot of other epithets prove that the god in the litter, whose body is hidden by a veil, is in essence no other than the standing ithyphallic Amenapet of Djeme. Both appearances of Amenapet of Djeme are manifestations of an aspect of the self-generating god Amun of Luxor. They both have in common that they travel to Djeme to take care of the funerary cult of their divine ancestors.

One of the most characteristic features of Egyptian culture is, what can be called, the 'aspective mode of thinking'[25]. According to this approach of reality, a phenomenon is analyzed in parts that are looked upon as the essential aspects of the whole. The various aspects do not contradict each other, but are complementary[26]. For this reason Egyptian religion cannot adequately be described in the usual way, using terms like 'polytheism' for most of history and 'monotheism' only for the short Amarna period (1369-1353 B.C.). The Egyptian conception of god can best be characterized with the words 'The One and the Many'[27]. Two well-known examples of this mode of thinking are the coexistence and mingling of several creation myths[28], and the way the human body is portrayed. Different phases of a process, action or motion are represented as separated pictures too[29].

The various manifestations of Amun of Luxor, referred to above, should be understood in the light of this aspective mode of thinking as well. They are 'frozen moments' in the (repeated) life-cycles of this self generating god, appearing as distinct characters. Thus, Amenapet of Djeme illustrates the son who takes care of the ancestral funerary cult. This takes place when he goes in procession to Djeme, in a royal litter and veiled except his head.

To the Egyptians, going out in procession, whether it may be a god or a king (for the reigning monarch has been transformed through the coronation ceremony into a god himself) has always been connected with the idea of the renewal of life. For to ascend or to be lifted up symbolizes resurrection. This is clearly shown by the fact that the Egyptians used the same word for the rising of the sun in the morning, the king's accession to the throne, and the appearance of gods in their processional bark during the festivals[30]. Though we should be careful because of the scarce data, it seems that for this reason the veiled Amenapet of Djeme is being characterized by the epithets 'Kamutef', the 'Bull that lifts the arm', the 'Lord of the double plumes' and 'Saviour'[31]. None of them occur for the unveiled standing Amenapet of Djeme. More over, only the former is said 'to appear as a young child', 'to protect Luxor against the rebels of Re', and 'to wreak havoc among her (i.e. Luxor's) enemies'[32]. But not only these words underline the 'frozen' regenerative moment of the veiled Amenapet of Djeme, it is also illustrated by the symbolism of the throne on which he is carried[33].

As shown above, gods usually go out in procession hidden in the shrine of their processional bark. In one text it is said of the unveiled Amenapet of Djeme that he appears from Luxor at the beginning of the decade in order to be seen as the 'King of the gods'[34]. Might this perhaps refer to the appearance of the veiled god in his procession? For the Kamutef embodies the unity of essence of a divine father and a divine son, i.e. of Amun and the king, and the continuous renewing and incarnation of the divine-human dynasty[35]. As 'Kamutef' and 'King of the gods' he would have to appear in a litter rather than a bark.

As to the veil, Marianne Doresse considers that it was meant to hide the god from profane eyes[36]. Though hiding (parts of) sacred objects is not uncommon in religion to protect people against overwhelming holiness rather than the inverse, as Doresse seems to have in view, it remains here unsatisfactory, for the simple reason that the face of Amenapet of Djeme remains unveiled. For this reason two other explanations may be considered here shortly.

It is worth noting that the ancient Egyptians did not comment on the veil covering the body of Amenapet of Djeme as they did for his uplifted right arm. That would imply that the veil was not one of his characteristics. As we have already seen, Egyptian gods were dressed every morning by priests. This is well-known from the daily temple ritual. A scene in the temple of Abydos shows the god Amun-Min wearing a veil or cloak on his shoulders, which is being offered to him by a priest (*Fig. 6*)[37]. One may suppose that a god, leaving his sanctuary after being dressed, would still wear this garment when he is hidden in the shrine. This might be the case of the veil that Amenapet of Djeme wears in his litter. The meaning of the veil would first of all be functional: *i.e.* to clothe the god rather than to hide or to protect him[38].

Another possibility appears when one notices the similarity of the veiled image of Amenapet of Djeme to the image of another god. Amenapet of Djeme was linked with the underworld, the realm of the dead. It has been explained already that Djeme was considered as a necropolis. It is there that life is regenerated and renewed. Common people did expect to receive abundance of food in this life, and prosperity in the hereafter, from this popular god[39], who embodied renewing of life himself. That is congruent with the very 'frozen moment' of Amenapet of Djeme lifted up in his litter. The way he is depicted recalls the image of the god Sokaris. The latter is a god of the dead in the necropolis of Memphis, and was worshipped by the craftsmen in its mortuary workshops[40]. He is portrayed as a mummy with a falcon's head. From the New Kingdom on, he has also been represented squatting in a chapel in the middle of his Henu-bark, his head emerging from what is named a 'conical object' (*Fig. 7*)[41], but looks more like a veil of ample proportions. Could the veil of Amenapet of Djeme be, as well as Sokaris's, a sort of shroud[42], the function of which might be to symbolize the regeneration of the god? The long wide cloak which is worn by a deceased on a mythological papyrus from the Twenty-first Dynasty (1075-945 B.C.; *Fig. 8*) should probably be interpreted in the same way[43]. This shroud would then appear as a symbol for the renewal to come of the dead, an idea very familiar to the ancient Egyptians.

NOTES

1   *E.g.* M.G. Daressy, *Annales du Service des Antiquités de
     l'Egypte*, 9 (1908) 64-69; G.A. Wainwright, *Ibid.*, 28 (1928)
     175-189; K. Sethe, *Amun und die acht Urgötter von Hermopolis*,
     Berlin 1929. For the articles on this subject by M. Doresse, see
     below note 12.
2   E. Otto, *Ägyptische Mundöffnungsritual* I-II, Wiesbaden 1960.
     French translation: J.-Cl. Goyon, *Rituels funeraires de l'ancienne
     Egypte*, Paris 1972, 85-187.
3   *Wörterbuch der Ägyptischen Sprache*, IV, 47.17.
4   The Egyptian word *Ba* cannot be translated in terms of our modern
     languages which are to much influenced by dualistic body-soul
     thinking. The *Ba* is to been seen as a mode of being in which the
     fullness of both physical and psychic individuality (powerful) can
     be perceived. Cf. *Lexikon der Ägyptologie* I, 588-590. For this
     and other modes of existence, see also H. Brunner, *Grundzüge
     der altägyptischen Religion*, Darmstadt 1983, 138-143.
5   All approximating dates in this article are based on J. von
     Beckerath, *Handbuch der Königsnamen*, München 1984.
6   W. Helck, *Urkunden der 18. Dynastie*, Berlin 1957, 1526, 11-15.
7   R.B. Finnestad, 'Ptah, Creator of the Gods', *Numen*, 23 (1976)
     111, note 80. J. Assmann, *Mitteilungen des Deutschen
     Archäologischen Instituts, Abteilung Kairo*, 28 (1973) 126-127.
8   *Denkmahl Memphitischer Theologie*, Zeile 59-61.
9   H. Junker, *Die Stundenwachen in den Osiris Mysterien*, Wien 1910,
     6. See for the Egyptian conceptions of images, S. Morenz,
     Ägyptische Religion, Stuttgart 1960, 158-161.
10   S. Morenz, *op. cit.*, 94, 105. The question of whether people did
     see god at the culmination of the festivals is still being discussed
     and needs more investigation. See H. Bonnet, *Reallexikon
     der Ägyptischen Religionsgeschichte*, Berlin 1952, 411. For the wish
     of the dead in the necropolis to behold god, see S. Schott, *Das
     schöne Fest vom Wüstentale*, Wiesbaden 1952, 94-96.
11   E. Hornung, *Der Eine und die Vielen*, Darmstadt 1971, 125, note
     76. For processions with visible statues carried by priests, see H.
     Bonnet, *op. cit.*, 613.
12   See for this subject M. Doresse, 'Le dieu voilé dans sa châsse et
     la fête du début de la décade', *Revue d'Egyptologie*, 23 (1971)
     113-136, 25 (1973) 92-135, 31 (1979) 36-65.
13   *Lexikon der Ägyptologie*, III, 1255.
14   Graffito Luxor temple, *apud* Doresse, *op. cit.*, [174].
15   Karnak temple, *apud* Doresse, *op. cit.*, [175].
16   The Egyptian year was divided into 36 decades; 3 seasons of 4
     months of 30 days each, *i.e.* 360 days rounded off to 365 days by
     the addition of the 5 so-called epagomenal (*i.e.* 'added') days. The
     first day of each decade being a holiday.
17   Goyon, *op cit.*, 52, note 3. For the ritual performed there, see
     F.-R. Herbin, 'Une liturgie des rites décadaires de Djemê, Papyrus
     Vienne 3865', *Revue d'Egyptologie* 35 (1984) 105-126.
18   First example: Ptolemy III (246-221 B.C.), see Doresse, *op. cit.*,
     [168].
19   A sitting ithyphallic deity is rather unusual in Egyptian
     iconography. Only one example seems to be found, which is badly
     damaged. Cf. H. Ricke, *Das Kamutef Heiligtum Hatschepsuts und
     Thutmoses III. in Karnak*, Cairo 1954, 6, Fig. 3.

20 Cairo museum, temp. reg.: *27.11.26.3*. See Wainwright, *op. cit.*,
    177-178, and Doresse, *op. cit.*, [146-148].
21 Doresse, *op. cit.*, [157].
22 Chonsu was in this temple the child-god in a triad together with
    Amun and Mut. He is said to bring foodofferings to Djeme each
    day (Goyon, *op. cit.*, 315). See also *Lexikon der Ägyptologie* I,
    962, note 26, and Doresse, *op. cit.*, [142], note 6.
23 Doresse, *op. cit.*, [158]-[159]. *Lexikon der Ägyptologie* I, 239.
24 Doresse, *op. cit.*, [159]-[160]. That the elevation of the right arm
    of the veiled god seems less than usual in the case of 'Min-figures'
    does not take away from the correctness of her opinion.
25 Cf. *Lexikon der Ägyptologie*, I, 474-488. See for this subject the
    epilogue 'Aspective' by Emma Brunner-Traut in Heinrich-Schäfer,
    Principles of Egyptian Art, Oxford 1980, 421-446 (translation by
    John Baines).
26 H. Frankfort e.a., *Before Philosophy*, Pelican Book A 198, Balti-
    more 1963 (repr.), 54. H. Frankfort, *Kingship and the Gods*,
    Chicago 1965, Chap. 3, note 15: 'Multiplicity of approaches'.
27 Hornung, *Der Eine und die Vielen*, Darmstadt 1971.
28 See for them, S. Sauneron and J. Yoyotte, 'La naissance du monde
    selon l'Egypte ancienne', *Sources Orientales*, I, Paris 1959,19-91.
29 *Lexikon der Ägyptologie*, I, 478.
30 *Wörterbuch der Ägyptischen Sprache*, III, 239.7, 15; 240.5.
31 Doresse, *op. cit.*, [173].
32 Doresse, *op. cit.*, [142]-[143].
33 For the symbolism of the throne, see W.B. Kristensen, *The Mean-
    ing of Religion*, The Hague 1968², 375f.
34 Doresse, *op. cit.*, text E¹ [170]. 'King of Northern and Southern
    Egypt' as title of the unveiled Amenapet of Djeme in texts D¹ and
    E¹ [170]. 'King of the gods': text C [169] and E [170].
35 For the 'Kamutef', see *Lexikon der Ägyptologie*, III, 308-309. It is
    worth noting that the Luxor temple, by which the procession to
    Djeme was organized, officiated from the New Kingdom to the
    Roman period as the center of the cult of the royal 'Ka', *i.e.* the
    divine aspect of the king, linking him both with the (primeval)
    gods and his royal predecessors, and transferred to him by the
    Kamutef. See L. Bell, 'Luxor temple and the cult of the royal Ka',
    Journal of Near Eastern Studies, 44 (1985) 251-294.
36 Doresse, *op. cit.*, 115; cf. [180]: to conceal his form.
37 A. Mariette, *Abydos*, I, Paris 1869, 44.
38 Being functional as dress, clothes of gods may have symbolic
    value.
39 Doresse, *op. cit.*, [180].
40 *Lexikon der Ägyptologie*, V, 1056-1057.
41 Bonnet, *op. cit.*, 723; *Lexikon der Ägyptologie* V, 1067.
42 *Lexikon der Ägyptologie*, III, 995-996. The veil of *Fig. 6* is named
    'djamet', *Wörterbuch der Ägyptischen Sprache*, V, 354.17-18:
    'Binde als Hülle des Götterbildes; Mumienbinde'. Cf. A. Moret, *Le
    rituel du culte divin journalier en Egypte*, Paris 1902, 188. In the
    Ptolemaic dedication text of the temple of Medinet Habu this word
    is used for the etymology of the name Djeme. (K. Sethe, *Amun
    und die acht Urgötter von Hermopolis*, Berlin 1929, 54, note 1).
    Though the name Djeme has been known from the Twenty-first
    Dynasty (1075-945 B.C.) on, the first representation of the veiled
    Amenapet of Djeme dates from the Twenty-sixth Dynasty (664-610
    B.C.). A relation between the name of the necropolis of Medinet
    Habu and the veil of the god should be precluded for this reason.
43 A. Piankoff and N. Rambova, *Mythological Papyri*, Chicago 1957,
    Pl. 19, scene 7, and p. 162: 'The deceased stands wrapped in a

long cloak on which is depicted the head of a lion'. 'This figure symbolizes the regeneration and rising of the deceased' (*Ibidem*, note 11). The so called *wesekh*-collar is also worn by the veiled Amenapet of Djeme. See Doresse, *op. cit.*, [160]. For the lion as symbol of resurrection, see C. de Wit, *Le rôle et le sens du lion dans l'Egypte ancienne*, Leiden 1951, 158-172.

Fig. 1

Fig. 2

Fig. 3

Fig. 4

Fig. 5

Fig. 8

Fig. 6

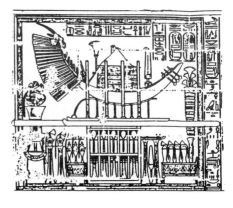

Fig. 7

THE SUN GOD OF HEAVEN
THE ASSEMBLY OF GODS AND THE HITTITE KING

Philo H.J. Houwink ten Cate[*]

1. In 1943 H.G. Güterbock recognized that the God of relief no 34 of Yazilikaya whose name is written with HH no 191 and who follows the Moon God (no 35: now, in the Hurrian interpretation of this gathering of Gods and Goddesses, Kusuh) needed to be identified as a male Sun God, and thus in the current Hurrian interpretation represents Simegi. Before that time the figure had been interpreted as a deified King[1]. After an earlier treatment of the Hittite word for 'lituus', based on a large number of passages from Hittite Festival texts in which S. Alp (1947) extensively dealt with representations in Hittite art of both the King and the Sun God from Empire times and the later period of the Syro- Hittite States which confirmed Güterbock's identification and supported his own linguistic equation[2], the same Turkish scholar decisively established the function of the accompanying logogram HH no 182 in 1950 as signifying 'Heaven'[3]. The inscription accompanies the figure of a God clad in the togalike attire of a Hittite King carrying the lituus, held down, in his right, and making a 'speaking gesture' with his left hand. The God wears the hemispherical cap, also characteristic of royal representations, to which the winged sun disc (HH no 190) has been attached. Güterbock remarked: "Während Mond und Sonne hier genau an der Stelle stehen, wo sie in den churritischen Götterlisten aufgeführt sind, stösst sich die interpretatio hurritica hier an dem Umstand, dass man beim churritischen Sonnengott den Zusatz "des Himmels" nicht kennt, während das Beiwort im hethitischen Göttersystem geläufig ist"[4]. It has more than once been noted that the customary title of Hittite 'Great Kings' residing in Hattusa, in Empire times, 'My Sun', in earlier periods and presumably already in the time of Hattusilis 1, 'Our Sun'[5], may help to explain the resemblance in representation between the Sun God of Heaven and the Hittite King[6]. It has also repeatedly been noted that the similarity is not complete: the Sun God carries the winged sun disc on his head, while it crowns the customary aedicula or cartouche giving the name and titles of a Hittite King[7].

Already in the period before Güterbock's highly important discovery, one of his fundamental discoveries in regard of the Yazilikaya Gallery of

Deities, A. Goetze (1933) remarked about the Hittite Sun God of Heaven that this God would seem to convoke 'the Assembly of the Gods', the well-known 'thousand Gods' of the Hittites, in the same manner in which the Hittite King convokes his 'Great Ones' for consultation[8]. The text-passage which induced Goetze to make this remark, is quoted below sub 4. But before I set out to specify the subjects to be summarily treated in this contribution, a few further remarks need to be made.

The first concerns the antiquity of the iconographical similarity. Th. Beran and, in the sequel, also W. Orthmann dealt with a possible forerunner of the Empire representation of the Sun God of Heaven. In his study Beran (1967) remarked about the 2nd scene of the seal impression 384/o (his no 136 stemming from Old Hittite times), a presentation scene in which the Sun God is introduced before the Tutelary God of the Steppe: "Vor den Tisch tritt eine Figur im halboffenen Mantel, mit Nackenzopf, und mit einer flachen Kappe, an der etwas wie Flügel befestigt sind, vermutlich wohl eine geflügelte Sonnenscheibe, die eine Hand ist im Sprachgestus erhoben, die andere hält etwas wie ein Bündel von an ihren Enden eingerollten Stäben, vielleicht auch als Flammenbündel aufzufassen"[9]. Orthmann gave some support to Beran's forerunner by noting that the Shamash-representations in the so-called "Anatolian Group of Cylinder Seal Impressions" published by N. Özgüç (1965, AG Plates I-III nos 1-8), showing a form which is clearly different from the later traditional type, might resemble the figure of Beran's scene[10]. N. Özgüç remarked about the Sun God type of these impressions: "On the seals of the native style, the Sun God of each of the three types appears before a seated deity and among other gods. There is no instance of Shamash being worshipped himself"[11]. The most convincing parallel in my personal opinion must be Plate II no 5 which shows the Sun God with rays issuing from his shoulders and wearing the horned tall conical hat, with a disc at the crown, so that the similarity would actually be limited to his mantle and his general posture. Also in this example the God makes a 'speaking gesture'. If Beran's description, in particular the detail concerning the winged sun disc, should prove to be correct, the example from Boghazköy might be thought to represent some sort of in essence related forerunner, which, as far as the mantle and the general posture are concerned, might be compared to the earlier example AG, Plate II no 5. From the viewpoint of the text-passages treated below, the most interesting point would be that in both seal impressions, and, as far as the seal impressions of the

'Anatolian Group' of Kültepe showing the Sun God of Heaven are concerned, in all of the examples the Sun God would seem to be admitted
into the company of another Deity.

The second point concerns the Antiquity of the type of Solar Deity,
in later texts referred to as 'the Sun God of Heaven'. The Hittite texts
mention a number of 'types' or 'hypostases' of the Solar Deity in addition to the use of 'the Sun' to denote the celestial body of the sun as
such, possibly without religious and certainly without 'theological'
connotations, and the use, already referred to, in order to designate
the 'living embodiment' of the first King T/Labarnas, either as spoken
by the King himself or as used by his subjects. I shall only deal with
likely older examples referring to the Sun God of Heaven and with
younger ones which clearly use the genitival adjunct 'of Heaven'[12].
This should not be interpreted to mean that the other 'types', especially the Sun Goddess of the Earth and, to exactly the same degree, the
Sun Goddess of Arinna would not be connected with the Hittite ideology
of Kingship. The opposite is true[13]. In addition to the possibly relevant iconographical evidence mentioned above, I may perhaps quote the
words of E. Laroche, the main authority on Anatolian religion. In his
treatment of the identifications of the various Netherworld Goddesses,
Sumerian Ereshkigal, Akkadian Allatum, Hurrian Allani, Hattic Lelwani
and the Hittite Sun Goddess of the Earth, Laroche remarked: "J'imagine
qu'en opposant et liant leur Soleil du ciel (nepisas Istanus), masculin, à
un Soleil terrestre féminin, les Hittites créaient un concept original, et
exprimaient leur propre conception théologique, d'ailleurs banale. ...
Mais l'opération Lelwani = Soleil de la terre a dû s'accomplir à très
haute époque; nous n'en saisons plus la genèse, nous en constatons
l'aboutissement"[14]. With respect to the evidence of the texts, one may
add that, after the hypothesis, first proposed by Sh. R. Bin-nun and
later also defended by E. Neu, that Siusummi, lit. 'our God', of the
'Text of Anitta' would represent the male Sun God of Old Hittite times
had been rather forcefully disposed off by F. Starke[15], the renewed
argumentation for a male Sun God Istanu as presented by G. Kellerman
has gained in strength[16]. In my personal opinion the Akkadian version
of the Annals of Hattusilis I now offers the earliest textual reference to
the Sun God of Heaven (see below sub 4).

The remarkable similarity in iconographical representation has sometimes led to the use of the adjective 'mystical' with respect to the
mutual relationship between the King and the Sun God of Heaven. In

view of the likelihood that Goetze's remark of 1933 was correct, I will
deal with a hopefully not too small, group of passages which mention
'Divine Meetings' and more in particular with 'the Assembly of the Gods'
as convoked by the Sun of Heaven, for practical reasons restricting the
term 'Divine meeting' to Old Hittite precursors of the idea mentioned
sub 2, and using the term 'Assembly of the Gods' for the Hittite variant of a more general Ancient Near Eastern concept which would seem
to have been introduced in Empire times, concisely treated sub 3.
Finally, I shall try to explain the character of the special relationship
between the Hittite King and the Sun God of Heaven (sub 4).

2. A 'Divine meeting' is probably mentioned in the Ritual in which
the 1st version of the Telebinu Myth (main copy KUB 17.10 = OH/MS)
is embedded. The passage III 28-34 refers to 'all of the Gods'(30). The
enumeration starts out with [Papaya] (restoration by Güterbock) and
Isdustaya, known from the in origin Old Hittite Building Ritual KUB
29.1 [17] I 50-II 10 to be 'primeval Netherworld Goddesses' (of Hattic
origin and thus belonging to the circle of Lelwani), who in that passage
are described 'sitting bowing down' (II 2-4), 'holding a spindle and full
distaffs' (II 6-7) while 'they are spinning the King's years of which
there is no limit or counting' (II 8-10), thus functioning as Hattic
Parcae in Güterbock's translation and interpretation[18]. The enumeration
continues with the Hittite Goddesses of Fate and Birth, the Gods of
Fertility Halki, Miyatanzipa and Telebinu and the Tutelary Gods LAMMA
and Hapantaliya. The meeting-place would seem to be below (or: near?)
a bush consisting of a plant or a tree, assumed to be the hawthorn[19].

While the technical term *tuliya-* is partly restored in this first example (III 28), another example from Bo 6483, published in textcopy and
commented upon by H. Otten, JKF 2 (1952/3), 69-70 and included in
Laroche's text-edition, offers complete certainty (II or III? 10'-11' and
12'). This enigmatic mythological fragment, which has not yet been
translated, shows older language forms and a notable sentence conective
a-, known from Luwian and Palaic but not elsewhere attested in Hittite
(ll. 8' and 12'). Perhaps it is one of the rare texts which display
dialect forms. The text mentions the old Anatolian Deities Katahha
(written logographically ^{D}SAL.LUGAL-*a-*), Pirwa/Perwa and Ilali (in
texts in Old Ductus usually Ilali(y)ant-) and the Place-name
Hassi/Hassuwa[20]. Otten, *l.c.*, surmised that the fragment might form
the Hittite part of a bilingual text. Whatever the real character and the
ultimate origin of the fragment may turn out to be, it offers clear proof

of the antiquity of the notion of a 'Divine meeting' in the Anatolian past.

Another type of gathering of the Gods which is referred to as a 'Feast' or a 'Festival', is regularly mentioned in the mythological parts of the Rituals of the 'vanished God' type[21]. It is an occasion at which the Gods eat and drink, as is also the habit when serious matters are discussed or an 'Assembly of the Gods' is in progress (see below sub 3). Curiously enough, these 'Feasts' (EZEN-a-) are convoked by the Sun God instead of by the Storm God (of Heaven), ussually assumed to have been from the beginning onwards the main male God of the Pantheon. The 'Feast' takes place at a turning-point in the story. The disappearance of an angry God has disrupted the normal course of nature, a fact which is extensively described in apparently fixed turns of speech. After the Gods who have been summoned by the Sun God, presumably the Sun God of Heaven, have not been satisfied by their eating and drinking, one of the guests, the father of the 'vanished God', notices the absence of his son. The search may begin. I quote a passage from the 1st version of the Telebinu Myth: "The humans and the Gods perish by hunger. The Great Sun God held a "Feast" and he summoned "the thousand Gods". They ate and did not become satiated. They drank and did not quell their thirst. And the Storm God became aware of Telebinu, his son, (saying) "Telebinu, my son, is not present! He has become enraged and took along everything good!" The Great Gods (and) the Small Gods set out to search for Telebinu. The Sun God dispatched the swiftly flying eagle" (KUB 17.10 I 18-24)[22].

The 2nd version of the Telebinu Myth describes the guests at the Feast immediately as 'the Great Gods (and) the [Small] God[s]', thus not using the stock-phrase 'the thousand Gods' of the 1st version and the Empire examples referring to the 'Assembly of the Gods' but the parallel Myth concerning the 'vanished' Storm God again uses both the stock- phrase and the characteristic verb halzai-/halziya-, 'to summon', of the 1st Telebinu version and the later occurrences[23].

There is no need for concern, I think, that the second type of Divine gathering is referred to as a 'Feast', since the same term is used in KUB 36.97 III 3'-5' (dassus EZEN-as), the pivotal clause of the literary and presumably also mythological fragment (embedded in a Ritual) adduced by H.Otten as a possible Hittite parallel to the gathering of the Babylonian Gods which formed the climax of the New Year Festival in Babylon[24]. However, there also are differences: the Old

Hittite examples of *tuliya-* and EZEN-type would seem to describe *ad hoc* meetings. KUB 36.97 depicts a regular Festival in the beginning of the year. The 'Feasts' rather than 'Festivals' of the mythological passages mention the God who organized the meeting in question. KUB 36.97 mentions the location of the Festival, 'the House' or 'the Temple of the Storm God'. On account of the regular character of the occasion, the meeting perhaps did not need to be convoked.

3. From Goetze, *Kleinasien*, 1933[1], 122-123 onwards, the customary description of the Hittite Pantheon takes its starting-point from the lists of 'the thousand Gods' summoned in the Treaties to act as the Divine witnesses with regard to their contents. Goetze was the first to note that these lists are systematically organized and present the Deities of the Empire period in a clearly recognizable typology[25]. A characteristic introductory formula runs as follows: "[And for this] oath [we] sum[moned] 'the thousand Gods' to the Assembly. [Let them all hear] and be [witnesses]", or, in an older example of a different type of Treaty, "Lo and behold, these matters I have placed for you under oath, and, see, for this purpose we have summoned 'the thousand Gods' to the Assembly". And in a final blessing for the faithful vassal in a third example, "these 'thousand Gods' whom I, "His Majesty", the Labarnas Muwattallis, "Great King", have summoned to the Assembly, the Gods of the Hittites (and) the Gods of Wilusa, ..."[26]. This, also for other parts of the Ancient Near East, wellattested phenomenon of an 'Assembly of the Gods' which rules over the course of events on Earth is fairly often alluded to in Hittite texts of the Empire period belonging to a variety of genres, Treaties, Instructions, Royal Prayers, Mythological texts of the type characterized by its editor E. Laroche as 'Mythologie d'origine étrangère', and in at least one important Ritual[27].

As has been noted by both O.R Gurney and G. Kestemont[28], the brief God-lists of the two Gasga Treaties CTH 138 and 139, to which may be added the replica of CTH 133[29], constitute as it were the precursors of the later examples in their classical form. Approximately in the same period in which the *pangus* began to lose its political importance[30], the notion of an 'Assembly of the Gods', which may have received an additional *impetus* through cultural borrowings from the East, began to acquire a fixed form. Of course Treaties in general required divine sanction. But, in the absence of convincing comparative material belonging to the same genre from elsewhere and thus merely reckoning with earlier evidence from Hittite sources, one might, with respect to the official Hittite variant of the more general Near Eastern idea of an 'Assembly of the Gods', formulate the tentative hypothesis that, in analogy with the manner in which the King used to convoke the *pangus* and at the same time employing the tradition that the all-seeing Sun God of Heaven was wont to convoke the Gods and to warn them in case of alarming events (see above sub 2, note 27 and below sub 4), a form was developed in which the Hittite King, starting out with his Divine Counterpart the Sun God of Heaven, approaches all the Deities of his Kingdom with the request to act as witnesses to the Treaty. I hope to show below that the concept was also applied to a few Royal Prayers.

An actual 'Assembly of the Gods' is described in the ritual KUB 4.1 (CTH 422). In his book on the Hittite Depositions in Court (German: Gerichtsprotokolle) R. Werner rightly characterized this ritual as being related to his subject of study since it constitutes a "description of (pseudo-)legal proceedings within a Divine Court of Justice"[31]. The part devoted to the accusation has been fully preserved. The performer of this ritual, to be enacted before a military campaign against Gasgaean territory, demands that all the Gods take a decision upon a law-suit which has been set into motion by the God Zithariya, while the text overtly says: "Lo and behold, O God of the Gasgaean country, we have summoned you to the Assembly! Thus, come and eat (and) drink!". This originally Middle Hittite text, preserved in two New Hittite copies, corroborates the well-known Hittite metaphor of warfare as a law-suit before a Divine Court of Justice. The ritual also offers valuable proof that the inclusion in the God-list of the Gods of the party with which a Treaty was concluded must have been highly functional from both a legal and a religious point of view: the presence of their own Gods forced the other party to abide by its stipulations, but apparently it also served to render these very same Gods accountable in the 'Assembly of the Gods' in case the Treaty was not kept. The wording of the accusation actually first blames the Gasgaean Gods for their trespasses against the property rights of the Hittite Gods and then mentions the acts perpretrated by the Gasgaeans themselves against the Hittites[32].

A passage from a later Hittite Royal Prayer can be adduced to strengthen the hypothesis that the 'Assembly of the Gods' sometimes dealt with the administration of justice. KUB 31.121 + 121 a + KUB 48.111 (CTH 379), comparatively late (one but last?) in the series of

Plague Prayers of Mursilis II stemming from the second decade of his
reign and probably addressed to the 'Assembly of the Gods' as a
whole[33], ends the God-list with the naming of the meeting-place itself,
"the place of the Assembly, the place of judgement of the Gods, to
whi[ch] pla[ce, the t]u[li]ya-, the Gods all step up" (I¹21'-22')[34].
There is little doubt, I think, that, in accordance with the first position usually assigned to the Sun God of Heaven in the God-lists of the
Treaties, also in KUB 31.121 I x + 1 [the Sun God of Hea]ven heads
the listing.

   This also applies to Muwattallis's 'Prayer to be Spoken in an Emergency' (CTH 381) with as main copies KUB 6.45 + KUB 30.14 and KUB
6.46, which, in my opinion, is also addressed to the, in this case very
fully enumerated, 'Assembly of the Gods'. This Prayer gives a list of
practically all the Hittite Gods and Goddesses of this period arranged
according to their cult centres. After a short description of offering
preparations[35], the King goes up to the roof (of the Palace or Temple?)
and "[spea]ks to the Sun God [of] Hea[ven]" who is the first God to
be invoked in the following line (KUB 6.45 + I 9-10 = KUB 6.46 I
9-11)[36]. At the end of the long list Muwattallis enumerates geographical
and atmospherical phenomena in the usual fashion also known from the
Treaty listings, ending with "the place of the Assembly, to which
place, the tuliya-, the Gods all step up" (KUB 6.45 + III 11-12 = KUB
6.46 III 50-51). The first God who is more fully addressed and who is
actually asked to take care that all the Gods convene is the Sun God of
Heaven (see below sub 4). However, there is a difference between the
two Prayers. The Mursilis II Prayer, which is the first one in its series
to mention "the tablet of the country of Egypt" (II¹ 6': Mursilis still
tries to exempt himself from responsibility, pointing to his own youth at
the time of the Amqa attack, the death of presumably Tutankhamun and
the marriageproposal of the Egyptian Queen-widow[37]), uses the
apposition "the place of Judgement of the Gods" which is lacking in the
'general' or 'open' Prayer of Muwattallis. This should serve as a warn-
ing that the specific circumstances under which a Prayer was spoken
may have influenced the viewpoint expressed with respect to the Assembly in question.

   Thus, with a slight modification of the earlier point of view, I would
like to posit now that, witness the mentioning of the Sun God of Heaven
in first position heading a trias which is more or less standard in the
God-lists of the Treaties, and, on account of the inclusion of 'the Place

of the Assembly' in the listing of geographical and atmospherical phe-nomena before the actual Prayer begins, both CTH 379 and 381 are likely to have been addressed to 'Assembly of the Gods'. Apparently in due course of time two types were developed, first a type which used the customary typological method of the God-lists of the Treaties (CTH 397), and later a second type which showed a geographical approach in which the Gods are enumerated according to the cult centres (CTH 381; see below). With respect to the latter type, CTH 378 IV, Mursilis II's Fourth Plague Prayer of the series edited by A.Goetze, may be said to function as a precursor. The Prayer mentions a short list of cult centres.

Both Prayers open the listing of the Gods with a traditional trias: "Sun God of Heaven", KUB 31.121 + continuing with "Storm God, K[ing of Heaven]", followed by "[Sun Goddess of Arin]na" (I x + 1-2'); CTH 381 "Sun God of Heaven", continuing with "Sun Goddess of Arinna, My Mistress, Queen of HATTI-land," followed by "Storm God, King of Heaven, my Lord," (KUB 6.45 + I 10-11). Muwattallis's 'list of summon-ing' in CTH 381 is interrupted by a short prayer in which the King adduces the reasoning behind his full enumeration of all the cult centres with their Deities: "You, Lords, Divine Lords, Sun Goddess of Arinna, My Mistress, and all the Gods of HATTI-land, Lords whose priest I am (and) who have expressed (lit., spoken) my rulership over HATTI-land in full measure (?)! Now, Oh Gods, listen to my word, my accounting of me who are your priest and servant! Forthwith I shall make an accounting with regard to you, my own Divine Lords, with regard to your Temples (and) your statues, (in order to show) to what extent (lit., how) the Gods of HATTI-land are worshipped and to which extent they are slighted!"[38] After the presumably exhaustive listing, follows the decisive passage quoted below sub 4.

The two Prayers from reign of Hattusilis III and Puduhepa addressed to the Sun Goddess of Arinna and her cirle, recently edited by D. Sürenhagen[39], both refer to discussions in the 'Assembly of the Gods' and, in doing so, amply attest that the idea that 'mortals may try to win support for their cause among the Gods' was a fairly general one: the Gods were supposed to transmit to their equals complaints which had reached them from human beings. (KUB 21, 19 + IV 14'-22' = CTH 383) "[If] those sins actually still are present before the Gods in one way or another, and (if) some God has been called upon with respect to that evil matter and (if) he pays heed to it, (then) as soon as the

Storm God and the Gods step up to the Assembly, if (at that time) someone mentions that evil affair in the Assembly, the Sun Goddess of Arinna and the Storm God of HATTI and the Gods should take to heart the matter of the *dahanga-* of the Storm God of Nerik!"[40] The phrase about the 'Assembly' (of the Gods) resembles the examples from CTH 379 and 381 and recurs in all likelyhood in KUB 21.27 + II 25-26 (CTH 384). In view of the possibility that the rock sanctuary of Yazilikaya may have played a role in the Festival of the Spring and perhaps in the Festival of the Autumn as well, it is not without interest that in the immediate context of the passage from KUB 21.19 + IV 14'-22' Hattusa would twice seem to be mentioned as the meeting-place of the 'Assembly': "And Hattusa should count for you (*i.e.* be reckoned with by you) as the [pla]ce [of] the Assembly of the Go[ds], Arinna as your (own) beloved ci[ty] and Nerik and Zippalanda as the cities of your son" (IV 25'-28' and comparably IV 10')[41]. The reference to the 'Assembly of the Gods' in the 1st Plague Prayer of Mursilis II (CTH 378 I), a third example of a Prayer in which the Assembly is mentioned at the end of the introductory God-list, actually brings the reader back to the examples from the Treaties mentioned above. Apparently the afore-mentioned Gods are the very same Deities who had been summoned to act as witnesses for the Oath forming part of the Instruction through which Tudhaliyas Junior had been designated to be the eventual successor of his father. The King Tudhaliyas was in fact succeeded by Suppiluliumas I, whose apparently irregular accession to power temporarily was deemed to have caused the Plague[42]. From the Hittite point of view, Instructions and Treaties form one and the same genre of texts, showing a similar introduction and structure.

4. It has long gone practically unnoticed that Goetze not only rightly discerned that the Sun God of Heaven usually is mentioned first in the God-lists of the Treaties, but also justly concluded from CTH 381 that the Sun God of Heaven used to convoke the Assembly of the Gods and also offered an explanation of this last prerogative. As early as 1933, Goetze noted the parallelism between the manner in which the Hittite King convokes the Assembly of his 'Great Ones' and the way in which the Sun God of Heaven 'summons' the Gods in order to meet for an Assembly[43]. Goetze tentatively suggested in this context that the Sun God would have wielded supreme authority in Heaven. This part of his explanation may need to be modified. The passage from Muwattallis's 'Prayer to be Spoken in an Emergency' which prompted Goetze to his

remark runs as follows: "Oh Sun God of Heaven, my lord, Shepherd of mankind[44], you, Oh Sun God of Heaven, rise up from the see and take your stand in Heaven. Oh Sun God of Heaven, my lord, daily, you, Oh Sun God, give judgement over man, dog, swine and the beasts of the steppe! Lo and behold, I, Muwattallis, King (and) Priest of the Sun Goddess of Arinna and of all the Gods, continuously render account to the Sun God of Heaven! And, Oh Sun God of Heaven, my lord, arouse (?) on this day the Gods! And those Gods whom *I have summoned* on this day in whatever (part of my) accounting through my speaking (lit., my tongue), Oh Sun God of Heaven, *you must summon* them, from Heaven (and) Earth, from the Mountains (and) the Rivers, from their Temples (and) their Thrones!"[45] As Goetze apparently surmised, it may be more than a mere coincidence that the King asks the God to summon those Deities who have been summoned by the King himself in the preceding long list of cult centres.

Not just the usage of the traditional Hittite title 'Our' and later 'My Sun' for the King and the similarity in representation of the Sun God of Heaven to a Hittite King in official attire, complete with both sun disc and lituus, in fact the shepherd's crook[46], but also a number of important text-passages stemming from a variety of literary genres of all periods warrant the close connection between the Sun God of Heaven and the Hittite 'Our' and 'My Sun'[47]. In the description in his Annals of Hattusilis I's most impressive military feats, his victories over Hassi and Hahhi which resulted in his setting both towns in flames, a military achievement which, as far as Hahhi was concerned, had been unique since Sargon, the famous Akkadian conqueror, had managed to cross the Euphrates (in the opposite direction) and in the sequel had defeated the army of Hahhi, but had not conquered Hahhi itself, it is noted with evident satisfaction that the King Hattusilis I had shown the smoke of the towns to the Sun God of Heaven and the Storm God[48]. The Old Hittite Ritual for the Royal Pair, preserved in a group of copies in 'Old Script', refers with respect to the King and the Queen in close proximity to both the Sun God of Heaven and the Sun Goddess of the Earth[49]. It is completely in line with the preceding evidence that, "When to the King dying is predetermined, whether he sees it in a dream, or whether it is announced by oracle extispicy or by oracle birds, or whether some evil omen signifying (lit. of) Death previously occurs (whit respect) to him"[50], and the ensuing Ritual precribes the installation of a 'Substitute King', the King prepares a substitute statue for the Sun

Goddess of the Earth, while he is replaced on Earth by this substitute King who is supposed to expel him from his Palace. At sunrise the replaced King daily kneels before the Sun God of Heaven, praying to be relieved from his now, as an ordinary mortal, inevitable future residence among the shades, saying: "Oh Sun God of Heaven, my lord, what have I done? You have taken the throne away from me and you have given it to another. ... But me you have assigned to the shades! I have made my appearance before the Sun God of Heaven, my lord: admit me to my Divine Fate, to the Gods of Heaven and [release] me [from] (my residence) among the shades!". The editor of the text, the late Professor H.M. Kümmel, explained that with these last lines the (real) King alludes already to his renewed installation on the throne which will enable him, in due time, 'to become God', as the Hittite stock-expression says[51].

There is not the slightest doubt that someone who 'becomes God' through, or at least after, his death must have been an ordinary mortal, although in his case a highly special one during his lifetime. The Hittite King was supposed to constitute a 'vital link' in the long 'chain', uninterrupted for several centuries, of living embodiments of the first T/Labarnas of the Old Hittite Kingdom, apparently destined to become, after his death, one of the Heavenly Gods. What actually was, as long as he functioned on earth, his special relationship with respect to the Sun God of Heaven, who apparently was thought to be able to depose and to reinstitute him? Both Muwattallis's Prayer and the first place in the God-list usually reserved for the Sun God of Heaven indicate that the Sun God functioned as an intermediary agent between the King who represented his people and the Divine World at large.

In his treatise on 'Hittite Kingship' O.R. Gurney dealt with a passage from a ritual which in his opinion "expresses the wish that the spirit of the Hittite monarch should become mystically fused with that of the sungod": "As marnuwan(t)- (a type of beer) and siessar (beer) have been blended for the 'Sun God of the Gods', while their 'soul' and their 'body' (viz. their essence and their substance) have become one, may they, the 'soul' and the 'body' of the 'Sun God of the Gods' and of the Labar[nas], (in the same manner) become one here (on earth)!" Seen in the light of evidence and comments, later published, the passage expresses rather, I think, the wish that the Labarnas may become like 'the Sun God of the Gods' in both mental attitude and physical appearance[52]. G. Kellerman devoted a special study to the subject,

"The King and the Sun-god in the Old Hittite Period", in which she convincingly argued that "in the Hittite Royal Rituals from the Old Hittite Period the Sun Deity is the male God Istanus", but added that the God's "image has a mystical connection with the image of the king". Also in this case I wonder whether the epithet 'mystical' needs to be added[53]. The curious phrase 'Sun God of the Gods' of Gurney's passage suggests, I think, a specific link with and, at the same time, an opposition to the Labarnas (or 'My Sun') who rules over the Hittites, mentioned next. The 'official contacts' between the human and the Divine World were, so it seems, transacted by and through the human and the Divine 'Sun (God)'[54].

This still leaves the question why the Sun God of Heaven was chosen for this role in the Hattusa variant of Kingship ideology, as contrasted to the Kanes/Nesa variant (1. note 15). In his highly convincing recent treatment of the solar symbols of the Hittites, E. Laroche gave a new analysis of the Ritual passage KUB 9.12 II 3-8, already adduced by A. Goetze[55]. The gist of the passage is that God supposedly has three pairs of eyes, one pair in order 'to see with', a second intended 'to appease' or 'to soothe' - in this respect the Ritual specifically mentions the King and the Queen, whose good relationship towards the God would seem to be warranted by this second pair of eyes -, and a third pair destined for 'rule, government'. It is this third pair of eyes which the Ritual connects with *hannessar*, 'lawsuit' or 'judgement'. This passage may provide the answer to the second question. In accordance with ultimately Mesopotamian traditions (cf. sub 3. note 27), the Hittite King in his function as law-giver and highest judge promulgating edicts, treaties and instructions, may have felt a special affinity with the Sun God of Heaven as God of Justice, at least on a par with his relationship with the Sun Goddess of Arinna whose Priest he was[56], or with the Storm God of Heaven for whom he functioned as 'Administrator'[57]. This perhaps explains the choice of the Sun God of Heaven and the customary presence in God-lists of many Treaties and Instructions and two Royal Prayers of an initial trias consisting of the Sun God of Heaven, the Sun Goddess of Arinna, the highest Goddess of the Pantheon, and the Storm God of Heaven, its male leader[58]. But even if the reverse should prove to be true, if the King imitated in his royal attire the conventual rendering of the Sun God of Heaven and the two components of the equation would need to be interchanged, the argumentation put forward above still remains valid: the King and the God share a common responsibility for justice and law-giving, cf. already O.R. Gurney, Schweich, 1977, 6 in his comments upon the Shamash-like character of the Sun God of Heaven.

It is not likely to be a mere coincidence that the famous bilingual of Karatepe, possibly one of the latest official Hittite texts in the general sense of the term[59], still refers to the Sun God of Heaven with regard to the concept of Kingship. In the final curse of a "King among Kings or other person" who might harm the inscription or the gates of the town, the two texts declare: "May Tarhunzas of Heaven (viz. the Luwian Storm God of Heaven), the Sun God of Heaven, Ea and all the Gods delete that Kingdom, and that man" and, in the Phoenician version, "then may Baal of Heaven and El, the creator of the Earth, and the Eternal Son and all the assembly (?) of the sons of Gods delete that Kingdom and that King and that man who (is) a man of name!" (Karatepe LXXIII)[60].

The curious phenomenon of a God being likened to the King in the classical iconographical representation of the Sun God of Heaven of Empire times and the subsequent period of the Syro-Hittite States, actually a sort of *effigies dei* in reverse through iconographical means, expresses (I agree with A. Goetze) their likeness in functioning as well as the resulting special affinity between them. The possibly relevant renderings of the Sun God referred to sub 1 and the text-passages quoted above sub 2 may indicate that the notion of the Sun God as a sort of 'organizing messenger' or 'reporting organizer' were originally Old Hittite. The classical iconographical representation of his functioning in this manner was developed in the Empire Period, when the Hurrian and Luwian influences from the southeastern parts of Anatolia were particularly strong. This might also explain the retention of the notion, evident from both iconography and the textual passage quoted above, up to the latest phase of the Syro-Hittite States.

NOTES

* The abbreviations used are basically those of the Hittite Dictionaries in progress. The more general treatment "Sonnengottheit und 'Königliche Sonne' bei den Hethitern" by Wolfgang Fauth, UF 11 (1979), 227-263 contains a wealth of material on both subjects in their intimate connection. This, in scope more restricted contribution will be focussed on the Sun God of Heaven and his function in relationship to the Hittite King, with a strong emphasis on the relevant data of the Empire Period. I hope to show that the opinion of the majority (?) of Hittitologists

that the Sun God is represented like the King - instead of the alternative possibility that the King would have been dressed in accordance
with the conventional representation of the Sun God - may be less
enigmatic than has hitherto been assumed.

1 H.G. Güterbock, *Belleten* 7, fasc. 26 (1943): 298-300; see for the
   earlier state of the question K. Bittel, *WVDOG* 61, 1941,
   Yazilikaya, 67-69; see already H.G. Güterbock, *SBo* II, 1942, 55
   (Nachträge).
2 S.Alp, *JCS* 1 (1947): 164-175 and *Belleten* 12, fasc. 46, 1948,
   320-324.
3 S.Alp, *ArchOr* 18.1-2, 1950: 1-8.
4 See K. Bittel, *Yazilikaya*, 1975, 138-139 (description) and Plates
   22.1 and 23.1; H.G. Güterbock, *idem* 174 together with notes
   35-36; E. Laroche, *RHA* 27, fasc. 84-85, 1969, 73-75. Laroche
   remarks: "En réalité "Soleil (du) Ciel" pour Simegi n'est qu'un
   aspect d'un problème beaucoup plus grave, et inséparable, posé par
   la représentation d'un dieu solaire sous les traits d'un roi-prêtre,
   affecté en outre de l'attribut 'disque solaire' = "Mon Soleil"." See,
   too, the perhaps more readily available reproductions in K. Bittel,
   Die Hethiter, 1976, 234 on p. 205 and M.N. van Loon, *Iconography
   of Religions* XV.12, Anatolia in the Second Millennium B.C., 1985,
   XXIX a, as well as the description and commentary on 22-23. In
   essence the problem to which, following a suggestion offered by A.
   Goetze, I am trying to apply the evidence of the texts, is as it
   were, the counterpart of another, related iconographical problem,
   the rationale of the manner in which in 13th century Art Hittite
   Kings and Queens are assimilated to the Deities whom they worship,
   cf. in first instance K. Bittel, *NHF*, 1964, 127[6], as followed by me
   in *Numen* 16, 1969, 91-92.
5 Cf. E. Neu, *StBoT* 18, 128-129 and Sh.R. Bin-Nun, *THeth* 5, 1975,
   151. This form of the title explains the 'mistake' in F. Sommer-A.
   Falkenstein, *HAB*, 1938, 8-9, II 44, a passage which is bound to
   mean 'the progeny of "Our Majesty"'.
6 See from the outset, H.G. Güterbock in his comprehensive treatment, 299.
7 See *e.g.* W. Orthmann, *Untersuchungen zur Späthethitischen
   Kunst*, 1971, 255, but again from the outset Güterbock, *l.c.*[2], 298.
8 A. Götze, *Kleinasien*[1], 1933, 129; A. Goetze, *Kleinasien*[2], 1957,
   138.
9 Th. Beran, *WVDOG* 76, 1967, 63[19] continued on 64 and the Plates
   10 and III.
10 W. Orthmann, *Untersuchungen* (cf. note 7), 1971, 255-256.
11 N. Özgüç, *The Anatolian Group of Cylinder Seal Impressions*, 1965,
   17/59, 35-36/75-76 and Pl. I-III nos 1-8.
12 In texts not only written in, but also originating from Hattusa, as
   far as both Neu's corpus of religious texts in Old Ductus and Old
   Hittite historical texts in New Hittite ductus are concerned, the
   name of the Sun God always precedes the name of the Storm God in
   enumerations in which both occur, whereas distinguishing adjuncts
   in genetival form concerning the Deity's sphere of influence, or
   his, *c.q.* her place of veneration, presumably often fulfilling a
   similar function, are comparatively rare. Apparently the context was
   deemed to offer sufficient indications as to which type of Solar
   Deity was meant; in a number of cases this is indeed the case,
   even for the modern reader. In addition to the passage quoted
   below sub 4, the Old Hittite Ritual for the Royal Pair (CTH 416)
   also refers to the Sun God of Heaven in Neu *StBoT* 25, 1980, no 5
   II 4. It is not unlikely that one should in fact deduce from the
   absence of the genitival adjunct 'of (the town of) Arinna' in Old

Hittite texts in Old Ductus that this Solar Goddess (see the subsequent note) had an important temple in the administrative centre of the Old Hittite Kingdom, Hattusa, itself.

13 Both the Sun Deity of$_7$ the Earth, a Goddess, as shown by H. Otten, *JCS* 4, 1950, 120^7, and the Sun God of Heaven were studied by E. Tenner in *ZA* 38 (NF 4), 1929, 186-190 and *KIF* 1, 1930, 387-392, respectively. Especially his remark in the former article, *l.c.*, 189, about the opposition between 'the road of the King' in KUB 17.10 IV 12 and 'the road of the Sun Goddess of the Earth' in *ibidem* IV 13, is of importance in the context of this study: it attests the fact that the regions above earth were common territory for the Hittite King and the Sun God of Heaven. See below sub 4 together with the notes 52 and 54 for an opposition between the latter two. Indications about the importance of the Sun Goddess of the Earth and the Sun Goddess of Arinna for the ideology of Kingship are given below 3 note 35 and sub 4 together with the notes 49 and 56. It is not to be excluded that these two types are related, cf. J.G. Macqueen, *AnSt* 9, 1959, 171-188 and especially 175-180 and H.G. Güterbock, *NHF*, 1964, 58-59 together with the relevant notes. A future monograph on the Sun Goddess of Arinna might also clarify her relationship to the Hattic Sun Goddess Estan, cf. O.R. Gurney, *Schweich*, 1977, 12.

14 Cf. E. Laroche, *FsGüterbock* 1, 185 in the fundamental study, *o.c.*, 175-185. Laroche's identification of the Hittite Sun Goddess of the Earth with the Hurrian Goddess Allani has been confirmed by the forthcoming Hurro-Hittite bilingual, cf. H. Otten, *Arch.Anz.* 1984, 373. Both in a form closely corresponding to her original Hurrian name and in her presumably derived Akkadian designation Allatum, the name of this Goddess occurs in historical texts describing events of the period of Hattusilis I and Mursilis I.

15 Cf. his major study "Halmasuit im Anitta-Text und die hethitische Ideologie vom Königtum", *ZA* 69, 1979, 47-120. It deserves to be stressed that, after Starke's intervention, the 'Anitta Text' merely offers support for the role of the Storm God of Heaven and of Halmas(s)uit(t)- in the Kanes/Nesa variant of Kingship ideology. One must reckon with the possibility - I believe - that, with respect to the subject dealt with in this study, local variations may have been of considerable importance, cf. note 12.

16 Cf. G. Kellerman, "The King and the Sun-god in the Old Hittite Period", *Tel Aviv* 5: (1978): 199-208.

17 G. Kellerman treated the text in her Paris Dissertation (1980), "Recherches sur les rituels de fondation Hittites", which will appear in the near future in a printed version.

18 Cf. H.G. Güterbock, *RHA* 14, fasc. 58 (1956); 22-23 and Hittite Mythology in S.N. Kramer (ed.), *Mythologies of the Ancient World*, 1961, 149, with a minor adaptation of the translation after H.A. Hoffner, *GsFinkelstein*, 1977, 108.

19 Cf. E Laroche, *Mythologie Anatolienne*, *RHA* 23, fasc. 77 (1965): 95/[35]-96/[36] and, as far as the 'hawthorn' is concerned, H. Ertem, *Flora*, 1974, 92-94 and H.A. Hoffner, *AlHeth*, 1974, 16 and 120. See G. Kellerman for an adstruction of the opinion that also the Ritual must needs go back to Old Hittite times: *FsGüterbock* 2, 1986, 115-117; see, too, E. Neu, *Hethitica* 6 (1985), 139-159 and especialy 148.

20 Cf. H. Otten, *JKF* 2 (1952/3): 69-70 and Laroche, *o.c.*, 174/[114]-175/[115]: Katahha occurs in ll. 2' and 4', Pirwa in ll. 3', 4', 6' and 10', Ilali (cf. Ilali(y)ant- in StBoT 26: 339) in I. 14'. See for this text, too, E. Neu, *StBoT* 5, 1968, 188 *sub voce 'wallu'*-, note 1; see H.A. Hoffner, *JNES* 31 (1972): 32 for the fact that this form

of the verbal stem is restricted to the old(er) texts.

21   See for this type of myth Güterbock, *Hittite Mythology* (note 18),
     143-148 together with the relevant notes; E. von Schuler, Klein-
     asien in H.W. Haussig (ed.), *Wörterbuch der Mythologie* I, 1965:
     207-208.

22   Laroche, *o.c.*, 90/[30] - 91/[31].

23   See Laroche, *o.c.*, 99/[39] (KUB 33.4 + I 4'-12') with respect to
     the 2nd version and *ibidem*, 113/[53] (KUB 33.24 + KBo 26.124 I
     14'- 23') and Güterbock, *Hittite Mythology*, 145 with regard to the
     Storm God version. KUB 33.25 and KUB 36.71, both belonging to
     copy C, were available to Laroche and Güterbock; this does not
     apply to KBo 26.124.

24   Cf. H.Otten, *OLZ* 51 (1956): 101-105 and, more recently, O.R.
     Gurney, *Schweich*, 1977, 39. Gurney's 3rd example is disputed by
     the editors of the text: Bo 2326(= KUB 53.4) IV 32'-34' (83), as edited
     by L. Jakob-Rost and V. Haas, *AOF* 11 (1984), 31, 76 and
     78-79.

25   The point was made by H.G. Güterbock, *NHF*, 1964, 54 and both
     made and put into practice by O.R. Gurney, *Schweich*, 1977, 4-6;
     see, too, R. Lebrun, *Hymnes*, 38-43. See for the God-lists in
     Ancient Near Eastern Treaties in general V. Korosec, *Or* 45 (1976):
     120-129.

26   The passages quoted are taken from J. Friedrich, *SV* I, 1926, 68-
     69; II, 1930, 110-111 and 82-83 respectively, but also Instructions
     and Akkadian Treaties found in Hattusa and Ugarit show numerous
     comparable examples. See especially the detailed treatment of these
     God-lists by G. Kestemont, *Or* 45 (1976): 147-177 which apparently
     appeared too late for inclusion in Gurney's highly valuable bibli-
     ography.

27   See with respect to Mesopotamia especially Th. Jacobsen, *Treasures
     of Darkness*, 1976, 86-91 and *Wörterbuch der Mythologie* I (note
     21): 60 (Mesopotamia), 185, 192-193, 199 (Anatolia) and 258, 265,
     280-281 (Ugarit). The mythological texts published by E. Laroche in
     the second part of his text-edition, *Mythologie d'origine étrangère*,
     RHA 26, fasc. 82, 1969, 7/[121]-80/[194] offer clear and unmistak-
     able proof that the notion of an 'Assembly of the Gods', in the form
     developed in Mesopotamia, reached Anatolia during the Empire
     Period, presumably in particular through Hurrian mediation:
     Gilgamesh Epic, creation of Enkidu (*o.c.*, 8/[122]), the discussion
     in the 'Assembly of the Gods' about the Flood (*o.c.*, 22/[136]), The
     Myth of Hedammu, *o.c.*, 53/[167] = J. Siegelová, *StBoT* 14, 48-49
     and the large fragment of the Myth which Laroche edited under the
     title "L'assemblée des dieux", *o.c.*, 48/[162]-49/[163] = Siegelová,
     o.c., 50-53; the 'Song of Ullikummi', 3rd Tablet, A III 6' = H.G.
     Güterbock, *JCS* 6 (1952): 24-25; CTH 351.1 = KUB 36.32: 12' =
     o.c., 78/[192]. It is, I think, indicative that the epithet of the Sun
     God in the Appu Myth II 15 = Siegelová, *o.c.*, 8-9, 'Shepherd of
     the population', which ultimately goes back to an Akkadian proto-
     type (cf. Siegelová, *o.c.*, 22-23, as far as Shamash is concerned),
     but which, significantly, is also used with respect to the
     Mesopotamian Kings (cf. J.M. Seux, *Épithètes Royales Akkadiennes
     et Sumériennes*, 1967, 248-250 and 444 not only returns in the
     Prayer of the Ritual KUB 36.83 I 13' (CTH 433.2) in the close
     parallel 'Shepherd of mankind', but also in the God-list of the
     Alaksandus Treaty IV 1 = J. Friedrich, *SV* II, 78-79 and in the
     'Prayer to be Spoken in Emergency' KUB 6.45 + III 13 (see below
     sub 4), two official texts of Muwattallis. In all three texts the
     epithet is used with respect to the Sun God of Heaven, while the
     1st and the 3rd example emphasize his judicial functions in the

direct context. The point as such, usage of the title 'Hirte der
Menschen' for both Mesopotamian Gods (among them Shamash) and
Kings (actually among them Hammurapi of Babylon), was already
made by Tenner 1930 (see 1 note 13, 390-391), while Güterbock
1978 (4 note 45), 132 specified that the usage for Shamash is in
fact attested in ‚a small fragment of a bilingual found in Hattusa
(KUB 4.11 obv.˙ 3'). The image is of importance since both the
Hittite King and the Sun God of Heaven are depicted carrying the
lituus, in fact the shepherd's crook (see 1 and 4). The data collected throughout this study may serve, I hope, as an adstruction
of the very fortunate and highly concise description of the character of the Sun God of Heaven given by E. von Schuler in
Wörterbuch der Mythologie I, 199, 201 and 188-189 ('Notzeit').

28   Cf. O.R. Gurney, *Schweich*, 1977, 7 and 14-15. Gurney remarks
about CTH 139: "Here we find only the Sun-god of Heaven, the
Weather-god, the gods KAL and ZABABA' (*i.e.* the Tutelary Deity
and the War God), the Moon God (omitted by Gurney) and 'the
goddesses whose names appear in the guise of Ishtar and Ishhara
and the group of Primeval gods. Here all local deities are omitted,
even the Sun-goddess of Arinna. They are simply the great types,
...". See, too, G. Kestemont, *l.c.* (note 26), 148.

29   The listing of CTH 133 shows a similar character; it starts out with
the Sun God (of Heaven), the Storm God (of Heaven) (and) the
Sun Goddess of (the to[wn of) Arinna].

30   Cf. G. Beckman, *JAOS* 102 (1982), 436 and 441-442 in his excellent
treatment of the *pangus*, *ibidem*, 435-442. See, too, below note 43.

31   Cf. R. Werner, StBoT 4, 1967, *Introduction*, VII. The Ritual has
been edited by E. von Schuler,*Die Kaskäer*, 1965, 168-173. The
fact that it originates from the Early Empire Period was recognized
by H.A. Hoffner, *JNES* 31 (1972): 34 and has been confirmed by
Cr. Melchert, *Ablative and Instrumental*, 1977, 96 and N.
Oettinger, *Stammbildung*, 1979, 580. In I 5-6 the Ritual mentions
"the male Gods, the female Gods, all the Gods of the Assembly",
cf. the CHD 3.3, 1986, 328 a.

32   The passages more specifically quoted and referred to are: I 10-22
and II 1-18. See, too, KUB 17.30 III 3'-5', as quoted by Beckman,
l.c., 438.

33   See for the order of the Plague Prayers of Mursilis II, H.G.
Güterbock, *RHA* 18, fasc. 66-67, 1960, 57-63; see with respect to
this text Güterbock, *l.c.*, 59-61. In a characteristic manner also
attested in other texts (cf. A. Goetze, *Kleinasien*[2], 132 together
with notes 4-6), the Prayer refers to "all of the Storm Gods" (I˙
6'), "all of the Hebat-sarruma's" (I 10'), "all of the Ishtar's" (I
13'), "all of the Telebinu's" (I 14') and "all of the ZABABA's" (I
15'). Before the Prayer mentions the meeting-place itself, it mentions "all the male Gods of the Assembly, all the female Gods of the
Assembly", cf., although still somewhat hesitantly, the CHD 3.1, 60
b and note 31.

34   *Ibidem* I 21'-22'.

35   See now for this Prayer R. Lebrun, *Hymnes*, 1980, 256-293, a
text-edition in which the author did not make full use of, in particular, A. Goetze's translation in *ANET*[1], 1950, 397-399. Already the
introduction paralleled by the replica of CTH 375, 'Prayer of
Arnuwandas and Asmunikkal concerning the Ravages inflicted on
Hittite Cult Centres', starting out as if the Prayer constitutes, if
not an Edict at least an official declaration of the King, is rather
peculiar and different from the other Royal Prayers. See with
respect to the earlier example, the remarks made by E. von
Schuler, *Die Kaskäer*, 1965, 164 which are fully confirmed by the

more recently published duplicate KUB 48.107 (Tablet II), more strongly evidencing the presence of a list of witnesses from the Gasgaean side. The offering preparations in this Prayer show that Muwattallis made a distinction between, on the one hand, 'the Sun Goddess of Arinna' and, on the other, '[all the (other)] Gods' (A I 4-6; cf., too, A III 18-19 below sub 4). Two offering-tables (made) of wickerwork are placed on the roof so that they may be seen by the Sun God (of Heaven).

36 Also in the list of the offerings the Sun God of Heaven receives his share first, cf. KUB 6.45 + IV 2, as to be restored in accordance with KUB 6.46 I 39 where copy B, in a different phrasing, seems to add that the Sun God of Heaven "must listen".

37 The fragment of what is presumed to be the Egyptian 'original' letter belonging to the correspondence of the period itself, twice mentioned in the literature on the subject, cf. E. Edel, IF 60 (1949), 75[1] and H.G. Güterbock in the article mentioned in note 33, 57[1] on 62 has been published in text-copy in KBo XXVIII (1985) under no 51, after it had already been edited by Professor Edel in 1978 (see Inhaltsüb., V).

38 See for this passage, KUB 6.45 + I 16-24 (in my personal opinion a short intermittent Prayer, but note the differing opinion of H.G. Güterbock, JAOS 78 (1958), 245) = A. Goetze, o.c., 398 a and Lebrun, o.c., 257-258 and 274. The proposal formulated here actually constitutes a 'formalization' of the viewpoint expressed by H. Otten, HbOr 1-VIII-1-I, Religionsgeschichte des Alten Orients, 1964, 106, "Eine ähnliche ordnung liegt auch in der Götterliste des Muwatalli vor.", and of the more precise formulation of O.R. Gurney, Schweich, 1977, 6, "These lists are supplemented by the prayer of Muwatalli, which enumerates the pantheon in the order of cult centres". See for I 21-24 the CHD 3.2, 105 b.

39 D. Sürenhagen, AOF 8 (1981), 84-168.

40 Sürenhagen, l.c., 98-99 and 108-109 (cf, too, KUB 21.27 + III 17'-22' = l.c., 114-115).

41 Sürenhagen, ibidem.

42 Cf. A. Götze, KIF 1 (1927-1930): 164-165, Par. 1: 1-5.

43 See note 8 sub 1. It follows, I think, from the five studies in more recent years devoted to the pangus, originally assumed to have been a class-designation, 'the totality' or 'the whole (of the nobles who were obliged to assist the King in warfare)', and its tuliya-, 'meeting, assembly', that the pangus met in ad hoc sessions and was - as general rule - convoked by the King: G. Beckman, JAOS 102 (1982), 435-442; M. Marazzi, WdO 15 (1984), 96-102 (pangus) and Fs Neumann, 1982, 151-153 (tuliya-); Cl. Mora, GsPintore, 1983, 159-184; cf., too, I. Hoffmann, THeth 11, 1984, 76-80 and 123-128. G. Beckman, l.c., 440[63] made the points in unmistakable terms: cf. KBo 3.1 II 34 = 'Proclamation of Telebinus' Par. 27 = THeth 12, 30-31 (Mora, 160); KBo 22.1, left edge: 16' = A. Archi, FsLaroche, 1979, 46-47 (Beckman, 441; Mora, 178); KUB 26.12 + VBoT 82 III 29 = E. von Schuler, Dienstanw., 27 (showing Akkadographic puhru; Beckman, 438 and 441). Cl. Mora, 178 rightly assumes that the expression should be restored for the First Series of the Laws, Par. 55: B III 21 = J. Friedrich, HG, 1959, 34-35. Presumably Goetze had in mind the passage in the 'Deeds' which describes Suppiluliumas I's reaction when the first letter of the Egyptian Queen-widow arrived, a passage, admittedly without the key-word tuliya- "When my father heard this, he called forth the Great Ones for council (saying): "Such a thing has never happened to me in my whole life!"" (fr. 28 A iii 16-19, in Güterbock's translation, cf. JCS 10 (1956): 94-95).

44 See above sub 3. note 27.
45 KUB 6.45 + III 13-24 = KUB 6.46 III 52-64 = Goetze, ANET[1], 398
    a-b = Lebrun, *Hymnes*, 266, 280; see, too, E. Tenner, *KIF* 1,
    1930, 390-392 (A III 13-17). In my rendering of *arkuwai-* and its
    derivations I follow the ÇHD, referred to in 3. note 38 and, to a
    certain extent, also HW[2], 309-313. A. Kammenhuber, HW[2], 247
    b-248 a prefers 'bring to a standstill' (German: 'anhalten') instead
    of 'arouse' for III 20-21. It is well-established, especially after the
    exemplary treatments of the evidence by H.G. Güterbock, *JAOS* 78
    (1958): 237-245, *NHF* (1964): 57-58, *JNES* 33 (1974): 323-327, *The
    Frontiers of Human Knowledge* (Acta Universitatis Upsaliensis,
    1978): 128-129 and 130-139, *AnSt* 30 (1980): 41-50, that the Hittite
    Prayers to the Sun God, CTH 373-5 show many signs of cultural
    influence of ultimately Mesopotamian origin. Güterbock chose for and
    convincingly defended a direct transmission, at least as early as the
    late part of the Old Babylonian Period. As one of the points which
    Güterbock felt to be typically Anatolian he defined the following:
    'But the idea that Shamash should find the god and transmit man's
    prayer to him is not known from Babylonian texts and thus seems
    to be a Hittite innovation.', cf. Güterbock 1958, 242 and 245. It
    follows, I trust, from this treatment that Güterbock was completely
    right and that this role of the Hittite Sun God of Heaven fits in a
    wider perspective and found a concrete application in the Hittite
    variant of the 'Assembly of the Gods'. I misinterpreted Güterbock's
    remark in my general article, "Hittite Royal Prayers", *Numen* 16
    (1969), 88-89 together with note 49. This may serve as a retrac-
    tion.
46 It is unnecessary, I think, to speak about a priestly dress, since
    the lituus is also referred to in the 'Instruction for the (Royal)
    Bodyguard', IBoT 1.36 II 34 and III 43 = L. Jakob-Rost, MIO 11
    (1966), 184-185 and 194-195 in a description of a hearing granted to
    various emissaries outside the Palace grounds. It is merely acciden-
    tal that the descriptions of the manner in which the King dresses
    himself stem from the highly detailed Festival texts.
47 The usage of this title followed by the name of a King ascertains
    that the text was originally written during his lifetime, while in
    what was for the Hittite ideology of Kingship a highly significant
    manner Mursilis II identifies himself in his 'Annals' with his father
    Suppiluliumas I as the one but last earlier 'My Sun', 'Before I had
    seated myself on the throne of My Father, all the neighbouring
    countries made war against me', cf. KBo 3, 4 I, 3-4 = A. Götze,
    AM, 14-15, as communicated to me by Güterbock on an earlier
    occasion, cf. *Anatolica* 1 (1967), 58-59. Apparently the addition of
    the personal name specifies the 'My Sun' in question.
48 Cf. H.M. Kümmel, TUAT I 5, Hist.-Chron. Texte II, 1985, 459 and
    this author, *Anatolica* 11 (1984), 53-54.
49 H. Otten and V. Soucek, StBoT 8, 1969, 40-41 = E. Neu, StBoT
    25, 22 (no 7 IV' 5'-10'). See, too, the possibly in origin Old Hittite
    'Prayer of Evocation', preserved in 'Middle Script' KBo 7.28 +, now
    available in R. Lebrun, *Hynmes*, 83-91 (in some points the treat-
    ment has to be adapted in accordance with H.G. Güterbock, *Fron-
    tiers* (cf. note 46), 1978, 127-128). This Prayer is addressed to the
    Sun Goddess of the Earth and her circle.
50 This is the characterization in the colophon of the text in question,
    a long Ritual which was edited, translated and commented upon by
    H.M. Kümmel in *StBoT* 3, 1967, 50-110, cf. for the colophon,
    70-71. The list of Deities (*ibidem*: 58-61) starts out in the charac-
    teristic manner with the Sun God of Heaven. It is likely that the
    final clause of the colophon refers to a sun eclipse. An example of

such an event, now identified with a sun eclipse of the spring of 1312 B.C., is referred to in KUB 14.4 IV 24-28, a broken passage in which someone is quoted a having said "With respect to the fact that the Sun showed that (evil) sign [...]" (1.25). H.A. Hoffner, *FsGüterbock* 2, 1986, 90 takes the following preserved clause, after the break, to mean "Did it not signify the Death of the King?" (1.26).

51 *StBoT* 3, 1967, 62-63: B Rev. 14'-19'; see, too, Gurney,*Schweich*, 1977, 57-58 whose translations of both the colophon and this passage have influenced mine. See, too, *StBoT* 3, 91-92.

52 Gurney in S.H. Hooke (ed.), *Myth, Ritual and Kingship*, 1958, 105- 121, 117-118 and 121 with regard to Bo 2544 (now = KUB 41.23) II 18'- 21'. The copy is young and shows mistakes, while the text may be considerably older, cf. E. Neu-H. Otten, *IF* 77 (1972): 185[8] and the CHD 3.1 30 b (with the proposal to read *anda kulam-* instead of *lam-* in I. 19'). Later treatments of the passage are A. Kammenhuber, *ZA* 56 (1964): 166[44] and 208; E. Neu, *StBoT* 5, 1968, 106 (referring in note 1 to the discussions preceding the usage made by Gurney); H. Otten, *StBoT* 17, 1979[90], 27-28 together with note 46; F. Starke, *ZA* 69 (1979), 89[90] continued on 91. Specific application to the Sun God of Heaven is precluded by the fact that another, unpublished text, Bo 5757: 4 ff. (a duplicate?) uses practically the same simile (and the same rather straightforward magical procedure) to achieve 'unity' between[46] the Labarnas and the Storm God of Heaven, cf. Otten, *o.c.*, 28[46]. I have adapted Gurney's translation to the later treatments.

53 Cf. the article quoted above sub 1. note 16: 207. The very difficult, presumably in origin Old Hittite Ritual KBo 21.22 dealt with by G. Kellerman also refers to the Storm God (II. 41-45), while she does not deal with KUB 41.23 and the parallel passage from Bo 5757. In last instance the usage of the term 'mystical' would seem to be provoked by the similarity in iconographical representation to which both Gurney and Kellerman refer.

54 In all likelihood the expression 'The Sun God of the Gods' was already in use during the Old Hittite period, cf. E. Neu, *StBoT* 25, 24: no 9 IV' 6', as supplemented after KUB 43.53 I 16', a duplicate in New Hittite script; see, too, above sub 1. note 13. In addition to KUB 41.23 II 18', 20' (and 23') the expression also occurs in KUB 36.89 + Rev. 13, cf. V. Haas, KN, 152-153 and 170.

55 *FsBittel* 2, 1983, 309-312 and especially 310-311. Laroche uses the passage as an adstruction of the late 13th century form of the sign HH no 191 which is maintained in the subsequent period of the Syro- Hittite States[7]A. Goetze, *Kleinasien*[1], 1933, 129 and *Kleinasien*[2], 1957, 137[(7)]-138 made use of the passage in his treatment of the Sun God of Heaven. See, too, the remark made by J.D. Hawkins, *Kadmos* 19 (1980): 141 regarding the logographic values of the signs HH nos 378 ('lituus' as divine emblem) and 360 ('Deity'), according to him possibly sharing a common conceptual content of 'divine seeing', in the case of the former latent, but in the case of the latter, possibly expressed in the visual form of the sign, if it had developed from a pictogram 'eye', as Hawkins cautiously suggests. The hypotheses of Hawkins and Laroche mutually support one another, while Hawkins's suggestion may entail that the nos 6 and 7 of Laroche's listing of forms of HH no 191 already show the three pairs of eyes.

56 Cf. CTH 381 A III 18-19 quoted above; *ibidem* III 26-27 (with regard to Mursilis II), III 29-31 (again with respect to Muwattallis and used in a manner which practically entails equivalence with Kingship). In all of his Plague Prayers but one stemming from the

2nd decade of his reign, Mursilis II stresses his Priesthood of the Gods in general, for all purposes referring to it as equivalent to his Kingship. A choice of two passages, one in Akkadian, the other in Hittite, may suffice as confirmationn of her role with respect to 'Kingship' and 'Queenship': [1] the introductory trias of the God-list belonging to the Treaty between Suppiluliumas I and Sattiwaza (version of Suppiluliumas I), CTH 51 I, "The Sun Goddess of Arinna, who directs Kingship and Queenship in Hatti-land, the Sun God (Simegi), Lord of Heaven, the Storm God (Tessub) [2] Lord of Hatti," (KBo 1.1 Rev. 40= E.F. Weidner, *PD* I, 28-29); [2] a passage from the introductory hymn of praise for the Sun Goddess of Arinna in the Prayer of Hattusilis III and Puduhepa, CTH 383, "Those wh[o] are Kings (and) Queens of *HATTI*-land - the King (and) the Queen of *HATTI*-land who is loo[ked] at by you, Oh Sun Goddess of Arinna, my Mistress, fares well through the intentions of you, Sun Goddess of Arinna. (You are the one) who chooses, (the one) who abandons!" (KUB 21.19 + I 5-10 = D. Sürenhagen, *l.c.* (note 39), 88-89).

57   Cf. IBoT 1.30 Obv. 2-8, a passage traditionally quoted in descriptions of Hittite Kingship; cf., in addition to the references given in *Numen* 16 (1969): 91[61], H. Otten, HbOr 1-VIII-1-I (note 38): 109; F. Starke, ZA 69 (1979): 81[67] This relationship is likely to have been bound up with the King's military duties. This role of the Storm God (of Heaven) is already obvious in 'The text of Anitta', cf. Obv. 2-4, 20-21, 28; Rev. 48-51, 55-58 (see for the reconstruction of the text F. Starke, StBoT 23, 1977, 169 ex. 269 and ZA 69 (1979): 60-62); see, too, above sub 1 note 15 and below, Karatepe LXXIII.

58   Cf. G. Kestemont, *Or* 45 (1976), 148 (Section I, Group A) and the Chart belonging to it on 156.

59   See for the likelihood or the possibility of this late date I.J. Winter, *AnSt* 29 (1979), 115-151 and the reaction formulated by J.D. Hawkins, *ibidem*, 155-157.

60   Cf. J.D. Hawkins and A. Morpurgo-Davies, *JRAS* 1975: 125-126 and 129 as well as *AnSt* 28 (1978), 118. See M. Weippert, *ZDMG* Suppl. I, 1969, 197-198, 202-203, 203-204, 204-205 for the Semitic evidence with respect to the equations following from a comparison between the two versions. His prime hypothesis, priority of the Phoenician copy, fully legitimate at the time of writing, is now contested, cf. M.G. Amadasi Guzzo and A. Archi in *VO* 3 (1980), 85-102.

'EFFIGIES DEI' IN ANCIENT GREECE: POSEIDON
Jan N. Bremmer

For reasons still unexplained, the Greeks dropped the Indo-European word for 'god', *deiwos (Latin Deus) at an early stage of their history and replaced it with theos. This innovation introduced a term which was not used to invoke a god but which helped to formulate an overwhelming experience. The ancient Greeks never prayed 'o theos', but when Telemachos saw a mysterious light in the room, he realised 'Surely, there is a theos inside' (Odyssey 19.40). Unfortunately, etymology does not help us much further. It has recently been demonstrated that theos is related to Armenian di-k 'gods' and Latin feriae 'festival' and fanum 'sanctuary'[1], but these words do not enable us to advance beyond a general meaning of 'holy'; the precise meaning of theos is still obscure. Recent investigations into Greek religion have concentrated on the problems of myth and ritual rather than on the representation of the Greek gods in general or the nature of individual theoi, and, although studies by Walter Burkert and Fritz Graf have greatly advanced our knowledge of many aspects of the Greek deities, there is still much to do in this field[2]. In this contribution we will present a short sketch of a Greek god, Poseidon, who may serve as an example as of how to construct a modern image of an ancient Greek god by paying equal attention to his cults, myths and rituals.

Older studies of Poseidon automatically started with our earliest piece of Greek literature, Homer's Iliad, which is most commonly dated from the eigth century B.C. In 1952, however, the decipherment of the Linear B clay tablets suddenly revealed that the pantheon of Mycenaean Greece (1400-1200 B.C.) closely resembled that of classical Greece. Zeus, Hera and Poseidon are certainly attested and so, though with varying degrees of probability, are Artemis, Hermes, Ares and Dionysos. These mainly administrative tablets do not allow us much insight into Poseidon's nature but they seem to show that he was the most important god of Pylos. The tablets also mention the Posidaion (a sanctuary most probably located within the city of Pylos) and a goddess Posidaeja (possibly his wife, though she is not heard of in later times). These tantalising data, then, only open up a rather blurred window on Poseidon's early history. When we meet Poseidon again in the Homeric Iliad, the god's position has radically changed. Zeus had become the

supreme god of the Greeks and Poseidon evidently now occupied a much
more marginal position. In the historical period, the god was mainly
connected with the sea, earthquakes, the horse and men's associations.
Is there an underlying unity in these seemingly so disparate aspects?
Somewhat arbitrarily we will start our investigation by looking at
Poseidon's connection with the horse[3].

In Arcadia, Attica and Central Greece, Poseidon was widely associated with horse racing and breeding as is illustrated by his epithet
Hippios, or 'of the horse'. Thessalian myth even spoke of the god as
the father of Sisyphus, the very first horse. As the stories of the
man-eating horses of Diomedes exemplify, the Greeks were particularly
struck by the wild, nervous and powerful nature of the horse. Poseidon
was especially connected with this aspect of the horse, and in Olympia
he was worshipped with the epithet Taraxippos, or 'the frightener of
horses'. At various places, Poseidon Hippios was associated with an
Athena Hippia, yet the two gods did not perform the same function for
their worshippers as their relation to the Corinthian horse Pegasus may
illustrate. Poseidon was the father of the horse but Athena was credited
with its bridling. In other words, Poseidon was connected with the
power of the horse in general, but Athena was considered to be re-
sponsible for the proper handling of the horse. Consequently, Athena
was invoked during races but Poseidon before or after[4].

Besides horses, Poseidon was also connected with the power of the
earth. His anger was considered the cause of the earthquakes that
(still!) hit Greece regularly and Homer already calls him the
'Earth-shaker' (Ennosigaios, Enosichthon). When in *Iliad* XX the battle
of the gods is described, Zeus naturally threw his lightning, but
Poseidon 'from below shook the boundless earth and the lofty tops of
mountains' (57f.). The god was also invoked to end earthquakes.
Xenophon (*Hellenica* 4.7.4) tells that when the Spartans invaded Argos
in 388 B.C., on their very first evening there, 'the *theos* (!) shook
the earth'. Immediately, in the king's tent a hymn was started, in
which all the Spartans joined - a hymn to Poseidon. In many cities,
especially on the western coast of Asia Minor, Poseidon was worshipped
with the epithet Asphaleios, or 'the immovable one'. When volcanic
activity in 198 B.C. caused the emergence of a new, small island, the
inhabitants of Thera (modern Santorini), as was typical, dedicated a
temple to Poseidon Asphaleios on it. In Kolophon and Sparta, the god,
exceptionally (see below), was even worshipped in the city centre - a
sign of his great importance[5].

Poseidon was also connected with men's associations. His temples in Helike and at Kalaureia were the meeting places of the Pan-Ionic league and of the early amphictyony that comprised Athens and its neighbours, and in Delphi, the clan of the Labyadai took the oath of membership in the name of Tribal (Phratrios) Poseidon. Other groups considered him to be their ancestor. The eponymous heroes of the Aeolians and Boeotians, Aeolos and Boeotos, were his sons and the descendants of Hellen sacrificed to Ancestral (Patrigeneios) Poseidon. This connection with men's associations cannot be separated from Poseidon's involvement in initiation. In many places, Poseidon was worshipped with the epithet *Phytalmios*, or 'the fostering one', which points to a concern for education. We find a more explicit indication in Ephesus where boys acting as wine pourers at a festival for Poseidon were called 'bulls', just as the god himself was sometimes called 'bull' and received sacrifices of bulls. In Greece, the office of pouring wine was typical for youths on the brink of adulthood. In this way, the distinction between adults who were allowed to drink and youths who were not was sharply marked. If we combine the function of Poseidon as god of men's associations with that of his youths as 'bull', it is suggestive to see in these 'bulls' the civilised descendants of ecstatic bull-warriors, who could also be found among early Celtic and Germanic *Männerbünde*[6].

The connection between Poseidon, initiation and ecstatic warriors is well illuminated by an archaic Greek myth which is already mentioned by Hesiod. The Thessalian princess Kainis agreed to make love to Poseidon on the condition that he gave her whatever she would ask for. After his consent, she requested to be changed into an invulnerable man. Now known as Kaineus, he became king of the Lapiths, but drew the wrath of Zeus upon him because he ordered his people to worship his spear. In the end, the Centaurs managed to bury him in the earth. The initiatory content of this myth seems evident, since the sex-change connected with adulthood is a clear reflection of the wide-spread custom to dress up male initiands as girls, a custom which is also in the background of Achilles' stay in the women's quarters of king Lykomedes of Scyros before he went to Troy: as so often, Greek mythology tends to make absolute what is only symbolic in ritual; similarly, the ecstasy of the archaic warriors which made them insensitive to their wounds is represented as invulnerability. In this myth, then, Poseidon is not only associated with initiation, but he is also closely connected with the brute force of the archaic warriors which apparently tended to hybris and was perceived as a danger for the correct relationship between men and gods[7].

Finally, Poseidon was worshipped as the ruler of the sea. Homer charmingly pictures him in action when he drives over the waves. His chariot remains dry and the monsters of the deep play beneath him: 'they know their lord' (*Iliad* XII.28). However, Poseidon only arouses or calms the brute force of the sea: he does not help the pilot to guide a ship through the storms; technical assistance is once again the domain of Athena. In the post-Homeric period, Poseidon was not so much the god of the sailors as of the fishermen, whose tool, the trident, became his symbol. The difference between Homer and subsequent periods strongly suggests that Homer innovated by making Poseidon the ruler of the sea, since the Greeks had many, evidently older, gods of the sea, such as Phorkys, Proteus and Nereus. Moreover, fishing is a typically male activity and Poseidon's connection with the fishermen may well derive from his association with *Männerbünde* rather than from his rule over the sea. In fact, we now know that the myth which explains Poseidon's rule of the sea was inspired by the Orient. In the *Iliad* (XV.187-193), the god himself relates that the sons of Kronos divided the kosmos between them by drawing lots: Zeus received the sky, Poseidon the sea and Hades the Underworld; the earth and the Olympus remained common property. A similar lottery occurred in the Akkadian epic *Atrahasis* (published only in 1969), and it seems certain that this poem is the ultimate source of the Homeric passage. The sea had strongly negative connotations for the Greeks and the allotment of the sea to Poseidon is therefore a sign of his negative standing. The god, although not to be neglected, was literally located in the margin of the civilised world[8].

This marginality is also expressed by a number of myths in which Poseidon through a contest or a gift-exchange loses to another god a part of Greece which he previously owned. Two examples may suffice. In Athens, myth related (and the Parthenon showed) a contest between Poseidon and Athena for Attica. Poseidon asserted his claim by bringing forth a salt sea, Athena by planting the very first of the famous olive-trees of Attica. In the ensuing trial, Athena prevailed, and Poseidon began to flood the plain of Eleusis until halted by Zeus. In Delphi, it was related that Apollo had obtained Delphi from Poseidon in exchange for the oracle of Taenarum; according to another version, Poseidon had ceded Delphi to Apollo in return for Kalaureia.

Earlier generations of scholars, such as Rohde and Nilsson, explained these myths as the historical reflection of the replacement of Poseidon by Athena and Apollo, but this view is not supported by any historical or archaeological evidence. Modern students of Greek religion prefer a more structuralist point of view. As Plotinus (*Enn.* 3.5.9) observed: 'myths have to separate in time things which are really simultaneous'. In other words, these myths describe a relationship between gods in which their position within the city is articulated: even though he occupied a place in Athenian and Delphic cult, Poseidon's position was subordinated to Athena and Apollo[9].

Poseidon's position at the fringe of the Greek polis was also stressed by the location of his sanctuaries. The Greeks did not always employ the same spatial arrangement for the temples of their gods, but certain patterns are observable. Zeus and Apollo, the gods connected with the maintenance of the social order, are often situated in the center of the polis, Eileithuia, the goddess of polluting birth, near the walls, and Demeter and Artemis outside the city. As we already saw, Poseidon Asphaleios had a temple in the centre of Sparta and Kolophon, but in most cities Poseidon's sanctuaries were located outside the walls. Many temples were situated near the sea, such as those at Taenarum, Sounion, and Hermione, others were near the mountains as in Mantinea, on a river as in Methydrion, or in a sacred wood as in Trikolonoi. The message seems clear. While his power was inescapable, Poseidon was not given a place within the ordered society of the Greek city-state[10].

It is time to come to a conclusion. Poseidon's connection with the nervous energy of the horse, the unpredictable strength of sea and earth, and the brute force of ecstatic warriors show that he was closely associated with the terrifying powers in man and nature[11]. By allotting specific areas of their experience to specific gods, the Greeks had constructed a framework of explanation which helped to make their world easier to understand and live with: once an earthquake or a storm had been identified as the work of Poseidon, the god could be invoked by songs (above), prayer or sacrifice. At the same time, by situating Poseidon's sanctuaries outside the *polis*, the Greeks pronounced a value judgment on the acceptability of brute force in human society, a judgment reinforced by the marked opposition in Greek myth (above) between Poseidon and his fellow gods Athena and Apollo: the god of brute force and chaos is always subordinated to the gods of intelligence and order.

Finally, in the Mycenaean period, Poseidon was apparently more important than Zeus (above), but in the classical period his position was at the margin of the Greek pantheon. Classical Greek society stressed the importance of beauty, charm and *sophrosyne*, or 'the control of emotions'[12]; only myth preserved memories of the one-time existence of ecstatic warriors. The changing fate of Poseidon, then, cannot be separated from the changing ideals of Greek society: the Greeks had realised that the growth of civilisation entails the marginalisation of brute force. They certainly did not always practice this ideal, but the insight remains no less valid for us today[13].

NOTES

1   H. Rix, *Kratylos* 14 (1969 (1972)) 179f (I owe this reference to R.S.P. Beekes); see also W. Burkert, *Greek Religion* (Oxford 1985) 271f; on *daimon* see most recently I. de Jong and N. v.d. Ben, 'Daimon in Ilias en Odyssee', *Lampas* 17 (1984) 302-316.

2   Cf. Burkert, *Greek Religion*, Ch. 3; F. Graf, *Nordionische Kulte* (Rome 1985); note also the study of Dionysos by A. Henrichs, in B.F. Meyer and E.P. Sanders (eds), *Jewish and Christian Self-Definition* III (London 1982) 137-160, 213-266. For a panoramic overview of scholarly opinions of the last hundred and fifty year, see A. Henrichs, *Die Götter Griechenlands. Ihr Bild im Wandel der Religionswissenschaft* (= Thyssen-Vorträge, Auseinandersetzungen mit der Antike, Heft 5 (Bamberg 1987).

3   The fullest collection of sources for the cult of Poseidon is still the reliable discussion in L.R. Farnell, *The Cults of the Greek States* IV (Oxford 1907) 1-97. F. Schachermeyr, *Poseidon und die Entstehung des griechischen Götterglaubens* (Bern 1950), the only book-length study of Poseidon, is too speculative. The best modern introduction to the god is Burkert (n. 1), 43f (Mycenaean evidence), 136-9.

4   On Poseidon Hippios and Athena Hippia, see J.-P. Vernant and M. Detienne, *Les ruses de l'intelligence*, 2nd ed (Paris 1978) 178-202; see also Graf (n. 2), 171f; M. Jost, *Sanctuaires et cultes d'Arcadie* (Paris 1985) 284-290.

5   Poseidon Asphaleios: Graf (n. 2), 175.

6   Men's associations: Burkert (n. 1), 136; add the central role of the sanctuary of Poseidon Samios in Triphylia (Strabo 8.3.13; E. Meyer, *Neue Peloponnesische Wanderungen* (Bern 1957) 74-9), the amphictyony at Onchestos (P. Roesch, *Études Béotiennes* (Paris 1982) 266-282; C. Habicht, *Pausanias* (Munich 1985) 46f.), and Poseidon's position at Mantinea (Jost (n. 4), 290f). Poseidon Phytalmios and bull-warriors: Graf (n. 2), 207f, 415f. Winepourers: Bremmer, 'Adolescents, Symposium and Pederasty', in O Murray (ed.), *Sympotica* (Oxford 1987).

7   Hesiod fr. 87; Akusilaos *Fragm. Gr. Hist.* 2 F 22 (cf. P. Maas, *Kleine Schriften*, Munich 1973, 63-6, 173); Frazer on Apollodorus *Ep.* 1.22; F. Sommer, *Schriften aus dem Nachlass*, ed. B.

Forssman (Munich 1977) 307-9 ('Kaineus und andere Lapithennahmen'); Burkert (n. 1), 449 n. 4; B. Schmidt-Dounas, 'Bemerkungen zu Kaineus', *Istanbuler Mitt.* 35 (1985) 5-12. The existence of a virgin priestess in Poseidon's sanctuary at Kalaureia also suggests a connection with girls' initiation, cf. P. Schmitt, 'Athéna Apatouria et la ceinture', *Annales* 32 (1977) 1059-73; Bremmer, 'The role of the temple in Greek initiatory ritual', in *Actes du VII Congrès de la F.I.E.C.* I (Budapest 1983) 121-4.

8   Poseidon and Athena: Detienne and Vernant (n. 4), 223-6. Trident: C. Bérard, *Études de lettres 1983*, 15-20, 35. *Iliad* and *Atrahasis*: W. Burkert, *Die orientalisierende Epoche in der griechischen Religion und Literatur*, SB Heidelberg, Philos.-hist. Kl. 1984, no. 1, 85-88.

9   Cf. R. Parker and C. Sourvinou-Inwood, in Bremmer (ed.), *Interpretations of Greek Mythology* (London 1987) 198-9 (Athens) and 231-3 (Delphi), respectively.

10 For these and other examples, see Pausanias and Strabo, passim.

11 This connection with brute force reflected itself also in a different way. In Greek mythology, Poseidon is the father of wild or cruel men such as the Cyclopes, Aloades, Busiris and Prokrustes, cf. O. Gruppe, *Griechische Mythologie und Religionsgeschichte* II (Munich 1906) 1154f.

12 For the development of Greek civilisation and the control of emotions, see Christian Meier, *Politik und Anmut* (Berlin 1985); Bremmer (n. 6).

13 The notes have been kept down to the most recent literature. I thank André Lardinois for his comments and Ken Dowden for the correction of my English.

WHAT DID ANCIENT MAN SEE WHEN HE SAW A GOD?
SOME REFLECTIONS ON GRECO-ROMAN EPIPHANY
H.S. Versnel

1. The account of St Paul's vision near Damascus has been handed down in three divergent versions: *Acts* 9.3-9, 22.6-11 and 26.12-16. They do share a number of elements: the light shining round the apostle, his falling to the ground, the voice saying: 'Saul, Saul why do you persecute me?' and the apostle's question: 'Who are you, Lord?' with the reply: 'I am Jesus, whom you persecute'. Then the command: 'Arise'. But there are differences as well, to the distress of many a theologian. In the first report 'the men with him stood speechless, hearing a voice, but seeing no man', in the second 'they saw the light (...) but did not hear the voice' and in the third the companions did not stand, but fell to the ground together with St Paul.

Miracles of ingenuity have been produced in attempts to reconcile these versions, not only by scholars of a conservative breed, whose efforts need not surprise us, but also by adherents of the 'form-geschichtliche' school. It appears that Greek *heistèkesan* besides 'they stood' can also mean 'they were', which, of course, is practically identical with 'they were lying'. Understandably the discussion concentrates on the question of exactly what the apostle may have seen. Some scholars argue that his enquiry, 'who are you, Lord?' proves that he saw no one at all (why the question, if he did?), while others hold that he must have seen some one, though an unidentifiable person (why the question if he did not?) and so on and so forth.

2. In his fundamental article on epiphany in antiquity F.Pfister defines epiphany: 'dem bei uns wohl meist üblichen Sprachgebrauch folgend, in etwas engeren Sinne als die Griechen das Wort *epiphaneia* nämlich für diejenige Form der göttlichen Offenbarung, bei der das übermenschliche Wesen, ein Gott, ein Heros, ein Totengeist persönlich sichtbar unter den Menschen erscheint'. The difference to which he refers between our concept of epiphany and Greek *epiphaneia* is that the latter term can also indicate a display of divine power manifesting itself in a miracle, for instance a miraculous rescue or healing, but without the personal appearance of the god. W.Pax, author of the only monograph on epiphany appreciates this broader meaning in his definition: "Unter

'Epiphanie' verstehen wir das plötzlich eintretende und ebenso rasch weichende Sichtbarwerden der Gottheit vor den Augen der Menschen unter *gestalteten* und *ungestalteten* Anschauungsformen' and he calls them - after Weinreich - 'totale' and 'partielle Epiphanie' respectively.

However, in 1971 D.Lührmann launched a forceful attack on this *communis opinio*. He contended that our concept of epiphany has little or no relationship at all with ancient Greek *epiphaneia*. In his view the latter term *never* occurs in the sense of the personal appearance of a god but only in the sense of a divine manifestation, a miracle or aid, comparable to the Hellenistic meaning of Greek *aretè*. The few exceptions are the result of later development.

3. These two observations form an excellent introduction to the question which I would like to discuss: what did ancient man see when he saw a god? They offer an exemplary illustration of some fundamental misunderstandings concerning such themes as: the nature of visionary perception, the potential (and limitations) of language to provide an adequate verbal reproduction of this type of experience, and, last but not least, the variety and multiformity of the means of communication with the 'other reality'. Although the position taken by Lührmann can certainly not stand up to being confronted by the total material, as I shall demonstrate on another occasion, I shall not go into this matter now. For the moment it is important that his thesis draws our attention to the essentially ambiguous nature of ancient - if not all - epiphany-phenomena. In order to illustrate my point I shall give a very selective survey of the ways in which divine intervention in human affairs could take shape: a graph in visibility. Most of the data are generally known so that I feel excused from amply citing sources and literature. It is not the novelty but the arrangement of the facts which will, I hope, demonstrate that the questions broached in the first two sections are at least misleading and that particularly in this matter adopting dogmatic positions can never do justice to the kaleidoscopic reality.

4.1. Greeks, including Greeks in Hellenistic times, and Romans after their first contacts with the Greek world imagined their gods as beings distinct from mortals in power, size, beauty, eternal health and vigour, but not in appearance. With a few minor exceptions gods look like human beings even to having their own specific features: walking through a museum of antiquities one learns to recognize Demeter,

Dionysus, Apollo, Hermes and Aphrodite even when they happen to be devoid of their specific paraphernalia. Confusion, however, cannot always be avoided since artistic standards tend to change and Zeus, *pater andrôn te theônte*, has lent his features to a considerable number of other gods.

In the epics of Homer, the creator of anthropomorphic gods according to Xenophanes, mortals see and meet with gods, albeit infrequently; they converse with them and sometimes even touch them. These 'epic' epiphanies, to be true, are sometimes markedly vague. The god may be veiled in a haze or he is not quite identifiable or is seen by only one person: *ou gar pôs pantessi theoi phainontai enargeis* ('it is by no means to everyone that the gods grant a clear sight of themselves', *Od.*16, 161). In the 'mythical' epiphanies related in the Homeric Hymns we observe the same picture: Apollo appears as a 'vigorous youth on the brink of manhood' (*H.Ap.* 449) and so does Dionysus (*H.Dion.* I,3). In the same way Demeter reveals herself in full divine bliss: tall, handsome, brilliant, sweet-smelling and awe-inspiring. Without exception these are stereotyped elements in epiphany-reports (*H.Dem.* 275ff.).

In 'historical' or legendary reports heroes easily outnumber gods but both categories are reported to have appeared in what people imagined to be their personal aspects. In 480 B.C. Delphi was defended by two heroes, Phylakos and Autonoos, just as Theseus was seen fighting for the Athenians in the battle of Marathon in 490 and the Aiacides at Salamis in 480. In 279 B.C. Delphi was again assaulted and this time Apollo himself, accompanied by a host of heroes and unidentified divine persons called the *leukai korai* (Athena and Artemis?) came to its rescue. The Dioscures are unmatched in the art of appearing; many reports relate their sudden appearance as horsemen in the sky coming to the rescue of armies in peril or survivors of shipwrecks. Heracles was seen during the battle at Leuctra in 371 B.C. and Asclepius, who usually appeared in dreams to heal sick people, was also observed in reality: 'I saw Asclepius, but *not* in a dream' writes Maximus of Tyrus, *Or.*9,7, in the second century A.D.

Although there is room for doubt in some instances (see below 4.2) we may assume that generally the gods and heroes were considered to have appeared in what people believed to be their normal shapes. This conviction gave rise to attempts at imitating gods in order to suggest their personal presence. The best-known instance is the one of a tall lady, Phue, who was provided with the attire of the goddess Athena in order to guide the tyrant Pisistratus safely back to Athens. And many witnesses swallowed this, much to the scorn of Herodotus, who relates the story (1, 60). Further, there are references to war-tricks based on this principle, including two men imitating the Dioscures in the dark of the night and indeed managing to frighten the enemy by their 'epiphany'. The same principle underlies the Roman triumphal ideology: on the day of his glorious entry the triumphator impersonated the god Iupiter, wearing his insignia and with his face painted red, the colour of the gods.

4.2 However, we are immediately confronted with an ambiguity. Apollo and Dionysus appeared *aneri eidomenos aizèiôi* (above 4.1). It is difficult to decide whether this means 'having assumed the appearance of a young man' or 'in *his* (own) appearance of a young man'. For gods could adopt human features. In Hom. *Od*.16,157ff. and 20,30ff. Athena manifests herself in the shape of a 'tall, handsome and accomplished woman'. The text has *eïkto*: 'had the appearance of, looked like'. In *Od*.2,268 the goddess even appears in the shape of the old lord Mentor. In the Homeric Hymn Demeter, before revealing her divine nature, has the shape of a humble old woman. Indeed, gods used to wander on earth in human shapes, especially, but not solely in primordial times when harmony, justice and peace prevailed. The tale of Philemon and Baucis is there to illustrate this, but even in historical times gods might sometimes descend to earth in a human form. Herodotus 6,61 tells us that at Sparta the nurse of an ill-favoured infant-girl daily visited the temple of Helen to beseech the goddess to grant beauty to the poor girl. One day a woman appeared (*epiphanènai*),inspected the girl and disappeared again after having blessed her with charm. This woman must surely have been the goddess Helen in human guise, just as the giant peasant who was seen killing many enemies with his plough during the battle of Marathon must have been the hero Echetlaios, and doubtless the woman who killed king Pyrrhus of Epiros with a tile was Demeter in human shape. In the battle at Thurii in 282 B.C. the Romans noticed a youth of extraordinary height marching in front of them and performing miracles of bravery. It was only afterwards, when no candidate for the crown of honour turned up, that they 'realized and believed' (*cognitum pariter atque creditum*, Val.Max. I,8,1,6) that it was the god Mars who had come to the rescue of his people. In the second century A.D. a priestess of Demeter Thesmophoros in Asia Minor asked an oracle why 'since first I assumed the priesthood, the gods as never before have been visible through their attentions and this sometimes through the virgins and matrons, sometimes through men and boys'.

The result was that ancient man could never be sure whether the person he was talking with was not actually a god in disguise. St Paul and Barnabas discovered at Lystra that they were really Hermes and Zeus and this was, we may assume, not because of their tallness, beauty or sweet odour, but because of the miracles they had performed and the mighty words they had spoken.

4.3. Gods appeared not only as men imagined them in their minds or in plastic arts: *agalmasin homoioi* ('just like their images',Longus, *Daphnis and Chloe* 2,23), but sometimes they were represented by their very images or statues during a vision. In the so-called Marmor Parium it is reported that 'the statue of the Mother of the gods appeared', just as the poet Pindarus in a vision saw 'the stone statue of the Mother of the Gods nearing on foot', literally: 'with her feet'. In his *Dreambook*, 2,35 Artemidorus (2nd century A.D.) explains that' it makes no difference whether we see the goddess herself as we have imagined her to be or a statue of her. For whether gods appear in the flesh or as statues (...) they have the same meaning'.

On the other hand, in certain cases real statues or images could be regarded as epiphanies of the god. For instance when Camillus had captured the city of Vei and asked the statue of the city-goddess Iuno whether she was willing to follow him to Rome, it was said that the statue answered him in a low voice. Arguing against sceptics who suggested that it was the bystanders who had spoken, Plutarch (*Cam.* 6) refers to many similar *epiphaneiai* besides sweating, moving, wailing or turning statues. And indeed, there are many stories like this. The statue of the Dea Syria looks back when you stare at her face and her eyes follow you when you move away. Small wonder, then, that Sapor I, while planning to attack the temple of Apollo Bryaxis at Daphni near Antiochia, was 'converted' by the mere look of the statue of the god and withdraw his troops. Staring intensely at the face of a statue of a god was one way to experience the divine presence as besides Apuleius and others especially the theurgists of late antiquity taught.

Images and statues were regarded as the vehicle of the divine *parousia* far more directly and concretely than we usually realize: the

emperor's statue was the concrete sign of his personal attendance and
as such functioned as an asylum. This means that statues could be used
and activated in order to ensure the presence and aid of the god. One
widespread custom in oracular practice was to carry around the statue
of the god and to read from its (= his) movements the divine answers
to oracular questions. Macrobius (5th century A.D.) still witnessed this
practice at Antium in Italy (*Sat*.I,23,13). In wartime particularly gods
used to be summoned (*parakalein*) by fetching their statues. Among
several reports one by Herodotus (8,64) is revealing: 'they summoned
(*epekaleonto*) Aias and Telamon from Salamis and sent a ship to Aegina
to fetch Aiakos and the other Aeacids'. Obviously the fetching of the
statues is identical to the summoning of the gods.

4.4. Nor is this. In the Homeric Hymn cited above Apollo appears not
only as a youth but also as a dolphin and as a star shining in the
middle of the day. In the same way Dionysus takes the shape of a
roaring lion, as he likes to do in other stories. When Asclepius appears
in dreams, it is usually in his 'normal' shape, but 'in reality' he was
seen once as 'a handsome man' (*IG* IV, 952, 26ff.) and he often appears
in the form of a snake. It was in this shape that he was transported to
Rome in 293 B.C. With snakes, for that matter, you can never be sure:
they may be the incarnation of Zeus Meilichios. Moreover, once a snake
turned out to be the hero Sosipolis and another time the hero
Kychreus. In Italy the god Mars used to lead colonization-expeditions in
the shape of an animal: wolf, bull or woodpecker.

5.1 The types of manifestation mentioned so far, different as they may
be, share one characteristic: they seem to be clear, unmistakable and
distinct phenomena, concrete and sometimes even tangible. Yet, our
reports are by no means always as unequivocal as the ones I have
cited. In a passage of Dionysios Hal. (6,13) where he describes the
bodily appearance of the two Dioscures at the battle of the Lacus
Regillus (494 B.C.), he refers twice to their appearance with the term
Dioskourôn ta eidôla, and once *astôn theôn ta phasmata*. Now, *eidôlon* is
any unsubstantial form, a phantom, and also an image in the mind,
fancy. *Phasma* comes very close to this: in the mysteries *phasmata* of
the gods are shown in order to impress the awe-struck audience who
think they are real gods. During the battle of Marathon according to
one report it was not Theseus himself but the *phasma* of Theseus that
was observed (Plut. *Thes.* 35,7). No wonder that these terms function

especially in the atmosphere of death and the uncanny. Periander's dead wife, for instance, appeared as an *eidôlon*, which does not prevent Herodotus (5,92) from using the participle *epiphaneisa* of the verb which is usually used for epiphany proper. Neither does the term *phasma* necessarily or exclusively imply the notion of ghostly shapes belonging to the realm of death or non-existence. Herodotus 6,69 relates how the same Spartan girl that we have mentioned before (4.2), once she was grown up and married, one night thought she lay with her husband Ariston. The next day, however, it turned out that the husband had not been home the previous night, and the only solution to the riddle was that it had been a *phasma eidomenon Aristôni*, while, moreover, material evidence proved that in reality it was a divine affair: *theion eiè to pragma*.

This brings us very close to the concepts of hallucination, vision and dream (*phasmataô* means 'to see hallucinations') and it is essential to note that our material does not allow us to draw a clear distinction between epiphany 'proper' and dream-vision. I do not deny that at times people assert that they have seen a god '*not* during their sleep', as an inscription has it (Kaibel, *Epigr.* 8O2 = *IG* XIV 1014, and cf. above 4.1) that Pan appeared 'overtly, not in a dream but in the middle of the day'. In these cases the term *enargès* ('clear', 'distinct') is often used to indicate the reality of the vision. But the same term also turns up in reports of dream-visions, and so does the word *epiphaneia*. In Plut. *Them.* 30 and in the famous *epiphaneiai*-inscriptions from Lindos *epiphaneia* refers to an apparition in a dream. The distinctions between dream-vision and 'real' epiphany are so vague that it is hardly ever possible to decide whether a divine order to publish a votive inscription (marked by terms like *kat'epitagèn, kata keleusin, iussu, monitu, visu, etc.) has been given in a dream, in an apparition while awake, or by other means of communication. Only if the indication kat'onar vel similia* is added we can be sure. An illustration of the complexity of the problem is provided by *POxy* 1381. It describes how a sick person falls asleep with his mother awake at his side. This mother 'suddenly saw, not in a dream and not in her sleep, (...) although she did not see clearly, for a divine and terrifying *phantasia* came to her preventing her from observing the god himself or his servants'. This apparition is then described and it is related how the sick man awakes, finds that he is healed and reveals that he has seen exactly the same apparition in his dream (not a unique phenomenon as some miracles from Epidaurus testify). The total event is referred to as an *epiphaneia*. Quite frequently people confess that they do not know whether they have seen the god while being awake or asleep and this very condition 'in between' (*metaxu hupnou kai egrègorseôs*, Iambl. *De myst*. III,2) is lauded as ideal for receiving divine visions. Aelius Aristides, *Or*. 48,31 ff. is most revealing both on acount of what he saw and how he phrased his experience. He saw Serapis between sleep and waking: 'It was like seeming to touch him, a kind of *awareness* (my italics V.) that he was there in person (...). One listened and heard things, sometimes as in a dream, sometimes as in waking life (...). What human being *could put that experience into words?*' (my italics V.; the translation is by Dodds, 113, where see his discussion).

5.2. So we observe that in a special state of mind, often labelled as half-sleep, but at other times as ecstasy or theolepsy, humans could experience the presence of a god with an extreme directness, nearness and reality without, however, 'seeing' him in the usual sense of that word. The god is present - no doubt about that - he may even be close enough to be touched and yet the terms in which his presence is described do not refer to the visual senses. Artemidorus in his *Dreambook* 2,34 even draws a distinction between gods who can be perceived by the senses (he mentions Hecate, Pan, Ephialtes and Asclepius) and gods who can only be apprehended by the intellect: the Dioscures, Heracles, Dionysus, Hermes, etc. Although it is not quite clear what he means by this distinction and the passage savours of an autoschediasma, the perception 'by the sense' may very well refer to such bodily experiences as the one related by Aelius Aristides above. This is indeed typical of gods like Pan or his counterpart Ephialtes, one of the many incarnations of the midday-demon.

While he was on his way from Athens to Sparta the runner Pheidippides passed through Arcadia, where 'Pan fell in with him (*peripiptei*, Herodot.6,105, stressing with this verb the suddenness of the experience) and spoke to him'. There is no reference to optical observation (*phanènai* in ch.106 does *not prove* visual appearance), and the fact that Pan 'shouted' to him seems to point to a different kind of contact. Reports exist of people who were suddenly 'taken', 'seized', 'touched' or 'striken' by the god (mostly Pan or the Nymphs, also Apollo and Hecate). This so-called theolepsy may express itself in the form of an epileptic or kataleptic fit. The Bacchic frenzy ,too, was

explained as caused by the god (in this case Dionysus) taking possession of the human being. Both Dionysos and Pan are 'appearing gods'
par excellence. Dictionaries from late antiquity even explain the name
Pan: *apo phainein dia to epiphainein*. Yet their epiphany is often not of
the usual visual type. There is a splendid illustration of the way people
experienced the presence of the gods in such 'theoleptic' fits in
Plutarch (*Marc.* 20). He tells us that the small Sicilian town of Enguion
is famous for the *epiphaneiai* of the local goddesses, whom they call 'the
Mothers'. One of the inhabitants, a certain Nicias, in order to escape
the aggression of his fellow-citizens, wilfully derided the *epiphaneia* of
the goddesses and feigned that he was seized by them in punishment.
He simulated an epileptic fit shouting that he 'was being ridden by the
Mothers'.

So it appears that the immediate presence of gods could be perceived
and experienced without their personal appearance in visual form. Such
manifestations could nonetheless be referred to as *epiphaneiai*. Moreover, it should be noticed that even when dream-visions are only
auditory, visual terminology prevails in their descriptions. In Plutarch,
Agesil. 6,5, for instance, Agesilaos tells his friends *ta phanenta* (the
things which appeared in his dream), whereas the dream-vision itself
gives no evidence that anything was seen at all (cf. also *Acts* 18,9;
Dion. Hal. 8,89,3).

6. Still, we have not reached the ultimate degree of (in)visibility. The
final step is that the god manifests his presence not by his personal
perceptibility whatever its nature, but by the signs or miracles he
performs. The stories about the rescue of Delphi in 480 make mention of
flashes of lightning, two huge rocks tumbling down on the enemies and
voices coming from the temple of Athena Pronoia, but not of an
epiphany proper. In the *epiphaneia* of 279, on the other hand, besides
the appearance of many heroes, there are falling rocks again, an earthquake, a thunderstorm, snow etc. which cause panic among the
enemy-troops, but this time one version explicitly mentions the personal appearance of Apollo himself. In the mean time Pausanias'(8,10,9)
careful phrasing is revealing about the hesitation of later commentators:
'Delphi is saved by the god and *in distinct appearance (enargòs)* by
the *daimones*'. The Phrygians told that they had once repelled an
attack with the support of Marsyas, who helped them 'with the water of
a river and with the sound of flutes' (Pausan. 10,30,9). During the

battle of Mantinea (249 B.C.) Poseidon appeared personally (*phanènai*), but in another battle the enemies were drowned in a flood of water, which was also a sign of his presence (Pausan. 8,10,8; Posidonius, *FGrHist* 87, F 29). It was Isis herself who, albeit invisible, launched fire at the siege-works of Mithridates VI at Rhodes in 88 B.C. (Appian. *Mithrid*. 105), just as Athena in her own person had crushed the siege-works of the same prince through a sudden storm at Cyzicus (Plutarch. *Lucull*. 10). Zeus defended his own temple at Stratonikeia several times by striking the enemies with panic through flames coming out of his temple, mist, lightning etc., as an inscription published and discussed by P.Roussel informs us. In 340 B.C. Hecate 'appeared' to the inhabitants of Byzantium in so far as her presence was proved by a blaze of fire all over the city and the barking of dogs (Pausan. 6,20). The presence of Dionysus is betokened by light (Aristot. *Mir.ausc*. 122), or by a flash of fire (Eurip. *Bacch*. 1077 ff.) or by the sudden effusion of springs of milk or wine. In late antiquity Hecate is asked to appear in a variety of luminous shapes, as a 'fiery child', a 'sumptuous light', a 'dazzling horse' or a 'formless fire' (*Oracl. Chald*. 146). Many are the reports of voices or sounds coming from the temples of the gods or from heaven. All these *parousia*- miracles could be, and many (many more than I have cited) were indeed called *epiphaneiai*. The gods were neither seen nor perceived by any other senses, but their presence was proven by their performance. Wodan is there when he hurls the light-ning, Jahweh is there when he 'appears' in the theophany of the thun-derstorm and so are Greek - and occasionally Roman - gods in their miraculous manifestations, natural or supernatural.

7. Let us reserve theory for another occasion and just note what we have seen:

1) Gods manifested themselves in a great variety of forms and shapes: 'their own', human shapes, as statues or in animal forms. Sometimes their manifestation was perceived as different from normal bodily existence. Then they are described as *phasmata*, or *eidòla* or *phantasiai*, similar to images seen in dreams. And dreams were favourite occasions for appearing.

2) The presence of a god could be perceived by other means than the visual or visionary illusions. Sometimes it is a mere awareness that the god is close by. One simply *knows* that he is there but language falls short in its task of providing an adequate description (cf.

Aristides and *e.g.* Thessalos 24, who did see the god Asclepius, but had to give up when it came to articulating what he had seen 'for no human speech could adequately describe the features of the [god's] face ...'). Sometimes it is only flashes of light, sounds or odours which testify to the divine presence.

3) Finally, the presence of the god could find expression in other forms than personal manifestations. Miracles - often of a kind that betrays the specific nature of the god involved - prove his presence. It may be true, as A.D. Nock once wrote, that 'miracle proves deity', but it is equally true that specific - if not all- miracles prove the actual *parousia* of the god. It was also Nock who suggested the only correct translation of a passage in Strabo 8,6,15 on the little city of Epidaurus, which was famous for the *epiphaneian tou Asklèpiou*, namely: 'the constant visitation to do miracles'. To put it another way, we may infer that Greeks had considerable difficulty in imagining a miracle happening without the god who was responsable for it being in the immediate proximity. Asclepius used to appear at Epidauros and that is why miracles happened there, but this implies, on the other hand, that the miracles of Epidaurus are warrants of the immediate presence of the god.

For this reason, and no other, the term *epiphaneia* denotes two things: the personal appearance of a god and his miraculous deeds. For the same reason the position defended by Luhrmann is to be condemned, even irrespective of the fact that a number of textual testimonies unequivocally refute it. To the Greek mind both constituents are merely the two aspects of one indissoluble unity, of which now the one, then the other may dominate the description. That Greeks and Romans simply did not differentiate sharply between these concepts is well illustrated by the lists of miracles handed down by a few Roman authors. One is Cicero, who writes (*Nat.Deor.* 2,6, cf. 2,166) that the gods often demonstrate their presence (*praesentiam saepe suam divi declarant*, in which Casaubonus already recognized a translation of Greek *epiphaneian*). In order to illustrate what he means Cicero first gives some instances of epiphany proper and he ends with what we would call miracles. The very same procedure can be found in a list of Valerius Maximus 1,8, probably stemming from the same source but this time labelled *miracula*. This is what the Greek would have called *epiphaneiai*.

All over the Mediterranean world the museum visitor will find pictures or reliefs of two feet or rather of two footprints. They are practically always (part of) a votive gift, although the motives for the gratitude they intend to express may differ: a few times the feet may indicate the healing of an ailment of that part of the body. More often they bear witness to the visit of an ancient 'pilgrim' to a sanctuary. But there are plenty of instances in which the accompanying text proves that they are meant to give evidence of a miracle. This is perhaps the most significant illustration of the solid connection between miracle and the coming of the god ('with his feet', cf. above 4.3).

8. To conclude: what did St Paul see? Our answer is the same as to the question that formed the subject of this essay: what did ancient man see when he saw a god? Sometimes he saw a god, sometimes a human shape, sometimes a phantom, sometimes an animal form, sometimes he had an hallucination of light or a vision of bliss and sometimes he did not see anything at all but was none the less aware of the divine presence which is too overwhelming to be described. And this is one of the reasons why we have three different versions of that portentous event near Damascus.

BIBLIOGRAPHICAL NOTE

I have refrained from adding notes for two reasons: first, they would have consumed too large a part of the available space and, secondly, what I have to say is only a preliminary and rapid sketch of what I intend to explore more thoroughly on another occasion, namely the precise meaning and implications of the term *epiphaneia* and the various functions epiphany could have. Instead I give a short list of the most relevant studies, to some of which I have referred in the text. The most important studies on ancient epiphany are: F. Pfister, Art. 'Epiphanie' in: Pauly-Wissowa, *Realencyclopädie der classischen Altertumswissen- schaft*, Suppl. 4 (1924) 277-323; E. Pax, Art. 'Epiphanie' in: *Reallexikon für Antike und Christentum* 5 (1962) 832-909; idem, *EPIPHANEIA. Eine religionsgeschichtliche Beitrag zur biblischen Theologie* (München 1955); D. Wachsmuth, Art. 'Epiphanie' in: *Der kleine Pauly* 5 (1975) 1598-601; W. Speyer, 'Die Hilfe und Epiphanie einer Gottheit, eines Heroen und eines Heiligen in der Schlacht' in: *Pietas. Festschrift B. Kötting = Jahrbuch für Antike und Christentum. Ergänzungsband* 6 (1980) 55-7. On the meaning of the Greek term *epiphaneia* two older studies have much to say: M. Rostovtzeff, 'Epiphaneiai' in: *Klio* 16 (1919) 203-206, and P. Roussel, 'Le miracle de Zeus Panamaros', in: *Bulletin de Correspond- ance Hellénique* 55 (1931) 70-116. The more recent study by D. Lührmann, 'Epiphaneia. Zur Bedeutungsgeschichte eines griechischen Wortes' in: G. Jeremias, H.-W. Kuhn, H. Stegemann (edd), *Tradition und Glaube. Das frühe Christen- tum in seiner Umwelt* (Göttingen 1971) 185-199, should be used with prudence. Works by A.D.Nock which should be consulted with regard to this subject are: *Conversion. The Old and the New in Religion from Alexander the Great to Augustine of Hippo* (Oxford 1933=1961); *Essays on Religion and the Ancient World* I,II (Oxford 1972). The quotation in ch.7, 3) can be found in *Gnomon* 29 (1957) 229.

A good survey of the *status quaestionis* on dream-visions and visions in general: J.S.Hanson, 'Dreams and Visions in the Graeco-Roman World and Early Christianity', in: *Aufstieg und Niedergang der römischen Welt*, II, 23, 1, 1395-1427, and on miracles (including epiphany): K.Berger, 'Hellenistisch-heidnische Prodigien und die Vorzeichen in der jüdischen und christlichen Apokalyptik', *ibidem*, 1428-1469. Cf. also E.R.Dodds, *The Greeks and the Irrational* (Berkeley 1951). On representations of (dream-)visions in plastic art: F.T. van Straten, 'Daikrates' Dream: a Votive Relief from Kos and some other *kat'onar* Dedications'in: *Bulletin Antieke Beschaving* 51 (1976) 1-38.

For general information on the belief-system which fostered - though sometimes reluctantly - belief in epiphany, one may consult: R.MacMullen, *Paganism in the Roman Empire* (New Haven and London 1981); H.S.Versnel (ed), *Faith, Hope and Worship. Aspects of Religious Mentality in the Ancient World* (Leiden 1981). P.Veyne, *Les Grecs ont-ils cru à leur mythes?* (Paris 1983), deals with ambiguities in ancient belief, some of which are very similar to the one discussed by me. As to the separate sections the following studies may be helpful. Ch.1. The amount of literature on St Paul's vision is overwhelming. See *e.g.* E.Pfaff, *Die Bekehrung des H.Paulus in der Exegese des 20 Jhdts* (Rome 1942). There is a reasonable, though by no means unbiased survey in G.Lohfink, *Paulus vor Damaskus. Arbeitsweisen der neueren Bibelwissenschaft dargestellt an den Texten Apg. 9,1-19; 22,3-21, 26,9-18* (Stuttgart 1966). Ch.3. On vision and epiphany in general I found useful the studies of E.Benz, *Die Vision. Erfahrungsformen und Bilderwelt* (Stuttgart 1969) and J.Runzo, 'Visions, Pictures and Rules' in: *Religious Studies* 13 (1977) 303-318. Ch.4.1. On epiphanies in Homer and lyric poetry the most recent publication is B.C.Dietrich,'Divine Epiphanies in Homer' in: *Numen* 30 (1983) 53-79. On mortals imitating gods in the Roman triumph and elsewhere: H.S.Versnel, *Triumphus. An Inquiry into the Origin, Development and Meaning of the Roman Triumph* (Leiden 1970). Ch. 4.2. On the visionary priestess see L.Robert, *Hellenica* XI-XII (1960) 544 ff., with a correction by F.T. van Straten *o.c.* Ch. 4.3. On statues as present gods: R.Gordon, 'The Real and the Imaginary. Production and Reproduction in the Graeco-Roman World' in: *Art History* 2(1979) 6-34; B.Gladigow, 'Präsenz der Bilder - Präsenz der Götter' in: *Visible Religion* 4 (1986) 114-133. On the case of Sapor: A.D. Nock, 'Sapor I and the Apollo of Bryaxis' in: *American Journal of Archaeology* 66 (1962) 307-310. On the summoning of gods through their statues in war-time: W.K.Pritchett, *The Greek State at War* III (Berkeley 1979) 11-46; R.van Compernolle, 'Aiax et les Dioscures au secours des Locriens' in: *Hommages à M.Renard* (Bruxelles 1969) 733-766. Ch. 5.1. On various aspects see the works of Dodds and Hanson cited above. On double dreams see also: A.Wikenhauser, 'Doppelträume' in: *Biblica*, 29 (1948) 100-111. Ch. 5.2. On theolepsy and related phenomens see besides Dodds: N.Himmelmann-Wildschütz, *Theoleptos* (Marburg 1957); W.D. Smith, 'So-called Possession in Pre-Christian Greece' in: *Transactions and Proceedings of the American Philological Society*, 96 (1965) 403-426; F.Pfister, Art. 'Ekstase', in: *Reallexikon für Antike und Christentum* 4 (1959) 944-987; M.Detienne, 'De la catalepsie à l'immortalite' de l'âme. Quelques phénomènes psychiques dans la pense d'Aristote, de Cléarque et d'Héraclide' in: *La nouvelle Clio* 10 (1958) 123-135. Ch.6. On the two *epiphaneiai* of Delphi see: R.Flacelière, *Les*

Aitoliens à Delphes. Contribution à l'histoire de la Grèce centrale au IIIe siècle av. J.-C. (Paris 1937); G.Nachtergael, *Les Galates en Grèce et les Sotèria de Delphes* (Bruxelles 1978). Ch.7,2). On the vision of Thessalos: J.Z.Smith, 'The Temple and the Magician' in: *idem, Map is not Territory. Studies in the History of Religions* (Leiden 1978) 172-189. Ch. 7,3). On the footprints there is an extensive literature. L.Castiglione's announced study *Vestigia. Foot and Footprint in the Symbolism of the Oriental Religions in the Graeco-Roman World (EPRO)* has not yet appeared. The most extensive study is M.Guarducci, 'Le impronti del "Quo vadis" e monumenti affini figurati ed epigrafi' in: *Rend. Pont.Ac* 19 (1942-43) 305-344. Cf. B.Kötting, Art. 'Fuss' in: *Reallexikon für Antike und Christentum* 8 (1972) 722-743. Recently also: P.Herrmann, 'Das Testament des Epikrates' in: *Sitz. Ber. Ak. Wien* 265,1 (1969); P.Veyne, *'Titulus praelatus: offrande, solennisation et publicité dans les ex-voto Grèco-romains'* in: *Revue d'Archéologie* (1983) 281-300. On the feet of statues of the gods see: W.Speyer, 'Die Segens- kraft des göttlichen Fusses' in: *Romanitas et Christianitas. Studia Waszink* (Amsterdam-London1973) 293-309.

THE MEASUREMENT OF THE BODY
A CHAPTER IN THE HISTORY OF ANCIENT JEWISH MYSTICISM

Pieter W. van der Horst

INTRODUCTION

One of the most conspicuous features of Judaism in its setting in the ancient world was undoubtedly that it was a religion without images. That there was no image worship among the Jews struck many outsiders (see *e.g.* Strabo, *Geographica* XVI 2, 35)[1]. This deviance of normal ancient practice had, of course, its basis in the unequivocal Biblical injunctions in the Decalogue (Exodus 20:4-5; Deuteronomy 5:8-9). Nonetheless, in the Bible itself we see already traces of a debate over the question of whether or not this God, who can and may only be worshipped without an image, does have a shape and can be seen. When we compare Deuteronomy 4:12-15 ('the Lord spoke to you out of the midst of the fire; you heard the sound of words, but saw no form; there was only a voice .... You saw no form on the day that the Lord spoke to you at Horeb') to Exodus 24:10-11 (referring to the same scene: 'they saw the God of Israel, ... they beheld God, and ate and drank'), or Exodus 33:20 (God says to Moses: 'You cannot see my face, for man shall not see me and live') to Numbers 12:8 (God says to Moses: 'With him I speak mouth to mouth, ... he beholds the form of the Lord'), it is clear that on the issue of the possibility of seeing (a form of) God there was no unanimity in ancient Israel. Moreover, some of the prophets had actual visions of the deity (whilst other prophets were more of an exclusively auditive type), e.g. Isaiah, who says in 6:1 'I saw the Lord sitting upon a throne, high and exalted', and Ezekiel, who describes a similar vision in which he saw 'a likeness as it were of a human form', which was 'the appearance of the likeness of the glory of the Lord', sitting on a throne (Ezekiel 1:26-28). Especially these two last-mentioned passages formed the starting point of a long tradition of visionary mystical literature in post-biblical Judaism[2]. Beside a current of increasing spiritualization and abstraction in the concept of deity there grew this mystical trend, or rather trends. For within the mystical movement there was much variety. There were those who experienced visions of the heavenly dwellings, the hosts of angels, the throne of God[2a], but who stopped short of visualizing the deity itself (e.g. Apocalypse of Abraham 18:12 - 19:4: the visionary sees the throne, fire around the throne, and angels, but 'I saw no one else there'). There were others who did see the deity and concentrated on its beauty, on the basis of passages like Isaiah 33:17, Zachariah 9:17, Song of Songs 1:16 (e.g. Hekhaloth Rabbati par. 253f.). Finally, there were those who focused on the magnitude of the deity, especially on the basis of Psalm 147:5, 'Our Lord is great, and abundant in power', which was taken to mean that God was very big, even gigantic. This type of mysticism is called Shiur Qomah (SQ).

The SQ literature, the investigation of which is still in its infancy[3], is characterized by an excessive indulgence in an almost provocative anthropomorphism, which is the reason why there has always been bitter antagonism against it in more rationalistic Jewish circles. The name Shiur Qomah itself, meaning 'the measurement of the body' (sc. of God)[4], indicates that it is really God's body, in all its parts and members, that the mystic wanted to become familiar with. In SQ literature the members of God's body are enumerated with their sizes, always astronomical, and their names, always magical or at least mesmerizing, like mantras. The function of this kind of treatises probably was that their repeated recitation induced a hallucinogenic state in the mystic (furthered also by fasting and by putting the head between the knees), so that in the end he attained the desired vision of God's body[5].

When and where did SQ originate?[6]. We don't exactly know. Since the middle of the nineteenth century scholars have advanced theories concerning the time of origin of SQ varying from the second or first century B.C.E. to the eighth century C.E. One of the problems is that all the manuscripts are late, (almost) all of them dating after 1000 C.E., and that there are no unambiguous references to or quotations from SQ before the post-talmudic period, i.e. before the sixth century C.E. The strongest argument in favour of a much earlier dating seems to be the supposed influence of SQ on Elchasai, a Jewish-Christian prophet from about 100 C.E., who describes an angel, most probably Christ, of enormous dimensions, 96 miles long, 24 miles wide, etc. (see Hippolytus, Refutatio IX, 13, 2; Epiphanius, Panarion XIX 4, 1). But quite apart from the fact that the 96 miles of Elchasai and the 100.000.000.000 parasangs of SQ are really incomparable quantities, the other essential SQ element, the names of God's limbs, is wholly lacking in Elchasai[7]. Another passage often adduced to prove the antiquity of SQ is 2 Enoch 39:6: 'You, you see the extent of my body, the same as your own; but I, I have seen the extent of the Lord, without measure and without analogy, who has no end'. Admittedly, this parallel is closer than Elchasai's passage, but apart from the fact that the dating of the Slavonic *Enoch* is itself notoriously problematic and highly uncertain, the names are lacking again[8]. Moreover, as the most recent authority on *SQ* remarks: 'The complete absence of any citations from the *Shiur Qomah* in the collection of mystic data in the second chapter of Tractate Hagigah in both the Palestinian and the Babylonian Talmuds suggests, at least *ex silentio*, that those traditions were unknown to the redactor of those sections of the Talmuds'[9]. It is not of much help to argue that *Hekhalot*-mysticism is demonstrably early, possibly even pre-Christian, for it can be shown that there have been, probably for a long time, *Hekhalot*-traditions without any *SQ* elements. Several *Hekhalot*-recensions do not have any *SQ* passages[10]. Although certainty is impossible in this matter, it is safe, for the time being, to date *SQ* to the early post-Talmudic or gaonic period[11]. That the attribution of the *SQ* revelations to some famous second century C.E. rabbis (Aqiva, Ishmael, Nathan) is pseudepigraphic has never been contested.

SQ texts are extant in 34 manuscripts of various dates and provenances, representing 7 recensions, all of which go back to a now lost 'Urtext'[12]. Although lost, we may come very close to it in one particular manuscript which was very recently published, British Library ms. 10675. It is not only the oldest *SQ* manuscript (possibly 10th cent.); contrary to other mss. or recensions, it is titled *Shiur Qomah*; it is the only ms. to present *SQ* alone; it contains the sections that are common to all the recensions. All this adds up to the not improbable hypothesis that this ms. is either a copy of the Urtext or at least very close to it[13]. It's Hebrew text is translated here for the first time[14].

TRANSLATION

Shiur Qomah

1. With the help of the Rock and His redemption, with the aid of Heavens,
2. with the help of the Lord, we will begin and finish. My help is from the Lord, the maker of heavens and earth[15].
3. I will begin to write the measure of the body (*shiur qomah*). All Israel has

4. a portion in the world to come, as it is said: 'And your people, all
    of them righteous,

5. will inherit the earth forever; (they are) the shoot that I planted,
    the work of my hands,

6. designed for glory'[16].

7. Rabbi Ishmael said[17]: 'I saw

8. the King of the kings of kings, the Holy One,

9. blessed be He, sitting on a high and exalted throne, and His
    soldiers

10. were standing before Him on His right and on His left side[18].
    Then spoke to me the Prince

11. of the presence, whose name is Metatron[19], Ruah, Pisoqonyah[20],
    Pasqon,

12. Itimon, Hagaon, Igron, Sigron, Danigron, Meton,

13. Mekon, Hastas, Hasqas, Sartam, Haskam, Hiqron,

14. (...)na, Rabba, Bantasazantaf.'[21].

    Rabbi Ishmael says:

15. 'What is the measure of the body of the Holy One, blessed be He,

16. who is hidden from all mankind (litt. creatures)?' The soles of His
    feet[22]

17. fill the entire universe, as it is said: 'The heavens

18. are my throne and the earth is my footstool'[23]. The length of His
    soles is

19. 30.000.000 parasangs[24]. The name

20. of His right foot is[25] Parsamyah, Atraqat, Shamah, and

21. the name of His left foot is Agometz. From His foot till

22. His ankle (the distance is) 10.000.500 parasangs

23. in its height (on the right side) and thus also on the left side.
    The name of His right ankle

24. is Tsagmiyah Tasasqam, the name of the left one

25. is Astamets. From His ankle(s) till His knees

26. (the distance is) 190.005.200

27. parasangs in its height (on the right side) and thus

28. also on the left side. The name of His right calf is Qanagago
    Mahadyah Tasasqam,

29. the name of the left one is Memgehawwaziya

30. (...)zaziyah. From His knees till His thighs

31. (the distance is) 120.000.000 parasangs

32. and 1.200 parasangs in its height (on the right side) and thus

33. also on the left side. The name of His right knee is Stamgagats Yahamay

34. and of the left one Magahanoriya. The name of

35. His right thigh is Shashtesatparnasay and of the left one

36. Tephagnihaziza. From His thighs until His neck (the distance is)

37. 240.000.000 parasangs. And the name of His loins[26] is

38. Astanah (...)dadyah. And on His heart stand seventy names[27]:

39. Tsats, Tsedeq, Tsehiel, Tsur, Tsevi, Tsaddiq, Sa'af, Sahats,

40. Tsevaoth, Shadday, Elohim, Ziv, Yah, Yah, Yahweh, Tsah, Dagol,

41. Adum, Sasas, A'a, Wa'a, Aya, Ah, Hav, Yah, Hu, Wekhu, Tsatsats,

42. (...)faf, Nets, Hah, Hay Hay Hay, Hehavav, Aravoth, Yav, Hah, Wah, Mamam,

43. (...)nan, Hawu, Yah, Yahah, Hafets, Qatsats, Ay, Za, Tsa'a, Za, A'a,

44. (...)hah, Qasher, Buzakh, Nitar, Ya, Ya, Yod, Hon, Paf, Ra'u, Yay,

45. (...)af, Waw, Waru, Bavav, Bavav, Tatat, Baphakh, Palal, Sis, Otiotav[28].

46. Blessed be the name of the glory of His Kingdom forever and ever. Blessed be the name of the glory of His Kingdom forever and ever.

47. Blessed be the name of the glory of His Kingdom forever and ever[29]. His neck is

48. 130.000.800 parasangs

49. in its height. The name of His neck is Sangihu Yavah Tiqats. The circumference of His head is

50. 3.000.000.033

51. and one third (parasangs), something which the mouth cannot express

52. and which the ear cannot hear[30]. Atar Hodriya

53. Astiyah is its name. His beard is 11.500

54. parasangs. Hadaraq Semya is its name. The appearance of the cheeks

55. is like the image of the spirit and like the form of the soul, and no soul

56. is able to recognize (it)[31]. Like *tarshish*[32] is the shining of His splendour, a bright light[33]

57. in the middle of the darkness, and a cloud and mist surround

Him[34]. All the princes

58. of the presence and the seraphs are before Him like a jar. We have in our hands no measure (than?)

59. (...) of[35] the names that are revealed to us. The name of the nose

60. is Lagbagtsiya, indeed Gagtaphiya is its name. His tongue extends

from one end of the world to

61. the other end, as it is said: 'He makes known his words to Jacob, his statutes and decrees

62. to Israel'[36]. Isasgyhu'ya is its name. The width of His forehead [is 130.000.800 parasangs][37] (?)

63. Its name is Mesasgihu Na'aya. On His forehead are written 72

64. letters[38]: yyhw, hyh, ywh, wyh, h', hy, hy, hy, h', hh, wwh, yyhw,

65. wh, wyhw, hh, yh, y', h', yh, yhw', hw, hw, yyhyw, hyh,

66. wyh, yhw, h', h', hyh, wyh. The black of His right eye is

67. 11.500 parasangs, and thus also of His left eye. And the name of

68. His right (eye) is Uriq At Tisum, and the name of its prince is Rahbiel[39].

69. And the name of His left (eye) is Metatgariamtsia. And the sparks that go forth (from them)

70. shine to all creatures. The white which is in His right eye is 20.000 (parasangs)

71. and thus also of His left (eye). The name of[40] the right (white of the eye) is Padarnaphsya and of the left one

72. (...)uqtsatya. From His right shoulder to His left shoulder (the distance is)

73. 160.000.000 parasangs, and the name of the

74. right shoulder is Metatgia'a Anagats and of the left one Tatmahangiya,

75. and that one still has another name, Shalmahingiya. From His right arm till His left

76. arm (the distance is) 120.000.000 parasangs. His arms

77. are folded. The name of His right arm is Gevarhazazyatakhsi[41], and of His left one

78. Metatgahagtsiqu. The fingers of His hands are 100.000.000

79. parasangs, each individual finger, that is, also of the left hand.

80. (The names of the fingers) of the right hand are Tatmah,

Tatsmats, Gagmuh, Gagshemesh, and Gagshash, and of

81. the left one Tatsmats, Tatmah, Agagmats, Ugmah, and Shoshnas.

82. And thus you have to count from the big one onwards[42]. The palms of His hands are

83. 40.000.000 parasangs, also at the left side. The name of

84. the right one is Zazya Etgaray and of the left one Sheqizazya.

85. His toes are 100.000.000 parasangs,

86. 20.000.000 parasangs for each toe, that is[43], also on the

87. left side. (The names) of the right (toes) are Adumats, Asumath, Darmenath, Kevat (...)

88. (...)ramon, and of the left (toes) Yeshnayin, Baznayin, Hatsmat, Ahuz, and Tahamum.

89. (And thus) like with the hands you begin to count[44]. Therefore He is called the great,

90. mighty, and awsome God[45], as it is said: 'For the Lord your God is God

91. and the Lord of Lords, the faithful God, who keeps His covenant and (shows) His loving kindness

92. to those who love Him and keep His commandments for a thousand generations'[46]. But he[47] said to me:

93. 'I will tell (you) the calculation of the parasangs, how much their measure is[48]. Each parasang

94. is three miles, and each mile is 10.000 cubits[49]

95. (and) each cubit is two spans [in His span], and His span fills the whole

96. world, as it is said: 'Who measured the waters with the hollow of his hand and gauged the heavens with

97. His span (etc.)'[50].
Rabbi Nathan[51], a student of Rabbi Ishmael, says:

98. 'Even (of) the nose he gave me the right measures and also (of) the lip and also

99. (of) the cheeks. The appearance of the face and the appearance of the cheeks is like the measure and form

100. of a soul. No creature is able to recognize it even though he gave me

101. the measurement of the forehead. The width of the forehead is like the height of the neck, and also the shoulder like the length

102. of the nose. The length of the nose is like the length of the little finger[52]. The heigth of the cheeks

103. is like half of the circumference of the head. And so is the size of every[53] man. His lip is about

104. 770.000 parasangs. The name of His upper lip is Gevarhatya

105. and the name of His lower lip is Hasharhiya. His mouth is a consuming fire, whatever He says.

106. (...)sadarsa is its name. And whatever He desires, the Spirit in His mouth says it. The crown on His head

107. is 500.000 by 500.000 (parasangs). Its name is Israel. And the precious

108. stone that is between its horns is engraved: 'Israel is my people, Israel is my people'.

109. '(My) beloved[54] is fair and ruddy. His head is gold, fine gold, his locks are palm fronds, his eyes

110. are (like) doves beside brooks of water, his cheeks are like beds of spices, etc.'

111. 20.000.000 parasangs[55]. And everyone who does not conclude with this biblical verse,

112. Lo, he errs[56]. '(Like) banks sweetly scented, his lips are lilies,

113. dropping liquid myrrh. His hands are rods of gold, his legs are pillars

114. of marble, his conversation is sweetness, he is altogether lovable, such is my friend, such is my beloved'.

115. Antaya Tahon Yahon is good and pure. Yod Yod Yod Yah Yah Yah Hasiv

116. (Ya)h YHWH in the place of Yah Yah[57]. 'Holy Holy Holy is the Lord of hosts,

117. the whole earth is full of His glory'[58]. His eyebrows are like the measure of the height of His eyes. The name of

118. His right eye[s][59] is Hadarzulad, and of His left one Ephdah Tsetsihu.

119. The height of His ears is like the heights of His forehead. The name of His right (ear) is

120. Etstahiya and the name of the left (ear) is Metatutstsiya. It turns out that the entire measurement

121. is 100.000.000.000 parasangs in height and

122. 10.000.000.000 parasangs in width[60]. Rabbi Ishmael said: 'When I said

123. this thing[61] before Rabbi Aqiva[62], he said to me: 'Everyone who

124. knows the measurement of the body of his Creator and the glory

of the Holy One,

125. blessed be He, who is hidden from all mankind, it is certain for him

126. that he is a son of the world to come[63] and that they will lengthen his days in this

127. world'[64]. Rabbi Ishmael said: 'I and Aqiva are guarantors

128. in this matter, but only if he recites this as a *mishnah*

129. every day'[65].

Blessed be the Lord forever. Amen and Amen.

NOTES

1   See for further passages M. Stern, *Greek and Latin Authors on Jews and Judaism* I, Jerusalem 1974, 306.

2   On this literature in general see G. Scholem, *Major Trends in Jewish Mysticism*, New York 1941. One of the earliest exemplars of a post-biblical vision of God is discussed in my 'Moses' Throne Vision in Ezekiel the Dramatist', *Journal of Jewish Studies* 34 (1983) 21-29. For visions of god as a literary genre in early Judaism see also C. Rowland, 'The Visions of God in Apocalyptic Literature', *Journal for the Study of Judaism* 10 (1979) 137-154.

2a The heavenly palaces are called *hekhaloth*, the throne *merkavah*, hence in current terminology one often speaks of *merkavah* or *hekhalot* mysticism and literature.

3   The most important studies are M. Gaster, 'Das Schiur Komah' (orig. 1893), in his *Studies and Texts* II, New York 1928 (repr. 1971), 1330-1353. Scholem, *Major Trends* (n.2.) 63-67. Scholem, *Jewish Gnosticism, Merkabah Mysticism, and Talmudic Tradition*, New York 1960, 36-42 (addenda on pp. 129-131 in the 2nd ed. of 1965). Scholem, *Von der mystischen Gestalt der Gottheit*, Zürich 1962, 7-47. Scholem, 'Shiur Qomah', *Encycl. Jud.* 14 (1972) 1417-18. I. Gruenwald, *Apocalyptic and Merkavah Mysticism*, Leiden 1980, 213-217. The best study to date is M.S. Cohen, *The Shi'ur Qomah. Liturgy and Theurgy in Pre-Kabbalistic Jewish Mysticism*, Lanham-London 1983. Cohen also prepared the text-edition: *The Shiur Qomah. Texts and Recensions*, Tübingen 1985. Cohen's first book will be referred to as Cohen (1983), the edition as Cohen (1985).

4   Extensive discussion of this name in Cohen (1983) 77-81.

5   Cohen (1985) 3: 'the authenticity of the original experience allowed the tangible results of that experience - the facts and the figures - to serve as the meditative spring-board for others' mystic jour- neys'.

6   Detailed discussion in Cohen (1983) 51-76. A survey of other scholars' opinions *ibid*. 13-41.

7   This is insufficiently taken into account by J.M. Baumgarten, 'The Book of Elkesai and Merkabah Mysticism', *Journal for the Study of Judaism* 17 (1986) 212-223. The matter is not discussed by G.P. Luttikhuizen, *The Revelation of Elchasai*, Tübingen 1985.

8   Two other frequently referred to passages in this connection, sc. Irenaeus' quotation from Marcus the gnostic in *Adversus Haereses* I 14, 1-3 and Origen's remark in his *Prologus in Canticum (Patrol. Lat.* 13, 63), have still less probative value than the passages

referred to in the text. Cohen's (1983, 23 ff.) criticisms of Scholem on this point are convincing.

9   Cohen (1983) 52.
10   This can now be easily verified by a glance in P. Schäfer's *Synopse zur Hekhalot-Literatur*, Tübingen 1981, esp. pp. 158-162.
11   See J. Maier, *Geschichte der jüdischen Religion*, Berlin-New York 1972, 201. Cohen (1983) 51 ff.
12   Cohen (1983) 43-49; Cohen (1985) 1-26. The idea of a *merkavah*-'Urtext' has rightly been dropped by Schäfer, *op.cit.* (n. 10) V-VII, but for *SQ* the situation is different, as Cohen (1985) has pointed out.
13   On this ms. see Cohen (1985) 5-6; his edition *ibid.* 192-195. That the text of this ms. was regarded as holy writ is indicated by the fact that several letters in it are decorated with coronets, like in ritually proper Torah scrolls.
14   For reasons of space a commentary to this text cannot be given here. We have restricted ourselves here to a very limited number of elucidating notes. Parallels in other *SQ* recensions and in *Hekhalot*-texts can be found in Cohen's apparatus. Brackets (...) indicate either a gap in the ms. or necessary supplements.
15   These two liturgical lines are given in the ms. in abbrevation, *i.e.* of each word only the first letter has been written.
16   Lines 3-6 are a quotation of Mishna, *Sanhedrin* 10:1 (including the scriptural quote Is. 60:21), which constitutes the standard formula used to introduce a liturgical reading of the Mishna treatise *Avoth*. So our writing is clearly presented as a liturgical text.
17   Rabbi Ishmael and still more so his contemporary Rabbi Aqiva (see 123) are mentioned elsewhere as the leading mystic tradents of their generation, *e.g.* Babyl. Talmud, *Hagigah* 14b *et al.*
18   A combination of Isaiah 6:1 and 1 Kings 22:19.
19   On Metatron, the highest angel ('Prince of the presence [lit. "face"]' is the angel who serves in front of God), see the litera-ture mentioned by Cohen (1983) 203 n. 9, esp. H. Odeberg, *3 Enoch or the Hebrew Book of Enoch*, Cambridge 1928 (repr. New York 1973), 79-146. There follow 17 or 18 other names. More often Metatron is said to have 70 names (cf. ll. 38-45). Most of these names, like the names of God's limbs from l. 20 onwards, are incomprehensible. For an extensive list of names of angels (269!) see J. Michl, Engel (V), *Reallexikon für Antike und Christentum* 5 (1962) 200-239.
20   The ms. has *ruhphi soqonyah*. On the basis of parallel versions I have corrected to *ruah pisoqonyah*, which in its turn is probably a paleographical corruption of *ruah pisqonit*, which is how an inter-ceding spirit (*ruah* = spirit) or angel is called in Bab. Talmud, *Sanhedrin* 44b, where it is also said that his names are Pisqon, Itmon, and Sigron; cf. ll. 11-12.
21   One expects a quote of Metatron's words, which is lacking. Either it has dropped out or these lines are displaced and should be read before 93 ff., where the subject of 'he spoke' must be Metatron.
22   This way of describing a body going from the feet upwards was well-known in Graeco-Roman literature, see S.J.D. Cohen, 'The Beauty of Flora and the Beauty of Sarai', *Helios* n.s. 8 (1981) 41-53; but, as Cohen (1983) 109 remarks: 'Such a descriptive technique could reasonably be expected from one who experienced his God while standing at the base of the throne and looking up'.
23   Isaiah 66:1, the first Biblical *locus probans* to support the anthro-pomorphic gigantism.
24   A parasang is roughly 5,5 kilometers, but in 93-5 it will become clear that a divine parasang is infinitely longer than a human one.

Therefore, it is clear, as Scholem, *Major Trends* (n. 2) 64, says, that 'it is not really intended to indicate by these numbers any concrete length measurements'. The numbers are rather meant as an 'essentially inconceivable notion upon which the mystic might focus for the sake of his meditative technique', Cohen (1983) 10.

25 It should be added here that not only the vocalization of these *nomina magica (theurgica)* is very uncertain (hence the many conventional a's), but also the consonantal stock, since the textual corruption of *SQ* manuscripts is at its worst in the names of the limbs, as a comparison of the 34 mss. shows. The names sometimes have clearly recognizable theophoric elements. 'One can never be sure that the name was constructed in the first place for any but its phonological value', Cohen (1983) 103. The names may have originated in glossolalic experiences (See F. Dornseiff, *Das Alphabet in Mystik und Magie*, Leipzig 1925 (repr. 1975), 54-55). That glossolalia was not unknown in early Judaism seems certain, see my 'The Role of Women in the Testament of Job', *Nederlands Theologisch Tijdschrift* 40 (1986) 273-289, esp. 285-287.

26 Understandably the author passes over the size of God's genitalia.

27 The heart is the only inner organ mentioned. The list of names of God that follows contains besides known Hebrew words (for 'righteousness', 'rock', etc.) and Biblical names of God (Shadday, Elohim, Yahweh), especially a whole series of words based on various permutations of the Holy Name (YHWH) and of *'ehyeh* (Exod. 3:14 *'ehyeh 'asher 'ehyeh* = I am who I am). Everyone who has read Greek or Coptic magical papyri recognizes this type of name lists, or rather sound lists. See Dornseiff, *Alphabet* (n. 25) 35-51.

28 The final 'name', Otiotav, means, 'his letters', which refers to the letters of YHWH and 'HYH (see note 27).

29 This *berakhah* (blessing) is repeated thrice, but the second time only in abbreviation, like the liturgical formula in 1-2. This liturgical doxology is part of a daily recited prayer.

30 This is a rabbinic expression (see *e.g. Sifre Numbers* 102, *Shevuoth* 20b, *Rosh ha-Shana* 27a), which is reminiscent of 1 Corinthians 2:9.

31 On these lines see the comments of Scholem, *Von der mystischen Gestalt* (n. 3) 17.

32 The ms. reads *Ktr shysh zwhr*. This, if connected with the preceding words, yields: 'no one is able to gaze upon the crown which is the splendor etc.' (one also has to assume then that, after *shysh*, *nw* has dropped out before *zw*, a common paleographical error). But I feel inclined to correct the ms. according to the other versions which read *ktrshysh*, 'like tarshish', a word of uncertain meaning (here probably a precious stone) that occurs also in Ezechiel 1:16 and Song of Songs 5:14, which are important *Merkavah* and *SQ* chapters (see 109-114).

33 I read *nura* ('fire' or 'light', an Aramaism), not *nora* ('awesome').

34 Contrast the Christian *Visio Dorothei* (Pap. Bodmer 29) 14, where it is said that *no* clouds surround him.

35 The text is in disorder here. Other versions have something like 'we have nothing (or: no measure) in our hands save the names ...'. Gruenwald, *Apocalyptic* (n. 3) 215, suggests that this implies that the names are meant to replace and indicate the measures of the limbs. But I cannot see how the measures can be derived from the names. Moreover, as Cohen (1983) 29 remarks, all the recensions which give the names also give the measurements.

36 Psalm 147:19. It is hard to see how this quotation proves the preceding statement. It may heve been quoted among other reasons

because Ps. 147 was the *SQ* Psalm *par excellence* because of verse 5 'Our Lord is great/big'; see the introduction above; Gruenwald, *Apocalyptic* (n. 3) 216 n. 15 and especially the discussion by Cohen (1983) 114 f.

37 Line 62 is at the end of a leaf, which is why probably the next sentence, indicating the measure, has dropped out. I have supplemented it from other versions.

38 Other versions have '70 letters', another instance of the well-known '70 or 72' question which is also met in the traditions on the origin of the Septuagint and the mission of Jesus' seventy (two) disciples in Luke 10:1. The letters are again permutations of the Holy Name YHWH and of 'HYH (Ex. 3:14); see n. 27.

39 Why only the right eye has a guardian angel is unclear. In some other versions his name is Rahmiel, 'God is my love'.

40 I rad *shl* (of) instead of the ms.'s *shn* (tooth) which makes no sense.

41 I assume that this name is a paleographically mangled form of Begadhuzya Takhsi (metathesis of *beth* and *gimel*, misreading *daleth* as *resh* and *vav* as *zayin*), the first part of which is obviously constructed on an alphabetic principle (b, g, d, h, v/u, z, being the second through seventh letters of the alphabet, with *ya* added); see Scholem, *Jewish Gnosticism* (n. 3) 37 n. 4. The second part, Takhsi, might be a transcription of the Greek word *taxei*, 'in order', sc. the order of the alphabet.

42 *I.e.*, the names mentioned are to be attributed to the fingers in this order beginning with the thumb.

43 Note the difference with 79-80.

44 See line 82 with note 42.

45 *Sc.* in Deuteronomy 10:17.

46 Deuteronomy 7:9 with a minor variant reading and a major addition, sc. 'Lord of Lords'.

47 *Sc.* Metatron, see note 21.

48 The following two lines make clear that the preceding indications of length are not human but divine measures, which are infinitely larger. Cohen (1983) 108 remarks: 'It seems clear that this conversion table is a fixed literary pericope inserted here by the editor to take some of the sting out of the text (...) by multiplying the dimensions from the merely immense to the incalculably vast'. In the other recensions there are several variants of this conversion table.

49 Read *'mh* instead of the ms.'s *'mr*.

50 Isaiah 40:12.

51 A famous scholar from the 2nd half of the 2nd century C.E.

52 This short sentence is the only *SQ* passage that seems to have a parallel in the Babylonian Talmud, *Bekhorot* 44a, but there in a wholly different context, where the appropriate proportion of nose to little finger indicates the point at which nose-length may be considered a defect of sufficient gravity to invalidate a priest's right to serve in the temple. See Cohen (1983) 218.

53 Read *kl* instead of the ms.'s *kn*.

54 Lines 109-114 are a conspicuously long quote from Song of Songs 5:10-16, with various omissions, metatheses, and mistakes (and an interruption, see n. 56). The 'beloved' of the Biblical text is interpreted as God and the quote functions as a sort of Biblical confirmation of the validity of anthropomorphic mysticism. See the discussion of the use of this passage in *SQ* by Cohen (1983) 111-2.

55 It is unclear of what this figure is a measurement, possibly of the precious stone mentioned in 107-8.

56   Curiously enough, the Biblical quotation is interrupted by the
      warning that the mystic will not attain his goal (for which see line
      126) if he will not conclude his spiritual exercises by reciting
      these verses from Song of Songs.

57   The meaning of 115-116a is unclear. Actually one expects the quote
      from Song of Songs to be the end of the text or at least the
      passage from 117-122 to come before this quote. The order of the
      text in its present state does not seem to me to be the original
      one.

58   Isaiah 6:3, from the prophet's vision of God!

59   The scribe mistakenly repeated the plural of the previous sentence
      (in the Hebrew text the words 'his eyes' and 'his eye(s)' follow
      immediately upon one another).

60   The 10:1 proportion between height and width seems too thin for a
      normal man, as Cohen (1983) 222 n. 22 correctly remarks. It is
      clear that this total figure is not arrived at by adding up the
      previously mentioned measures.

61   'This thing' is the *SQ*.

62   See note 17.

63   For the expression cf. Luke 16:8 and 20:34, with the comments in
      P. Billerbeck, *Kommentar zum Neuen Testament aus Talmud und
      Midrasch* II, München 1924, 219.

64   Here it is clearly stated that the reward of the mystic will be not
      only other-worldly but also this-worldly.

65   The rewards promised by Aqiva will only be realized if there is
      daily exercise by the mystic, although it is not clear what exactly
      is meant by reciting something that is not a *mishnah* as a *mishnah*.
      Cohen (1983) 223 surmises that 'the mystic is being enjoined to
      recite the text in the fashion of a *mishnah*, *i.e.* out loud, orally'.

ON THE GODDESS' "PHASES OF LIFE" IN SOME HINDUISTIC TEXTS

Teun Goudriaan

1. It may be called remarkable, that the recent movement in Christianity which is orienting itself towards a female nature of God seems to be inspired almost completely by women, while the traditional paternalistic idea of God is being defended most emphatically by male authorities. Within Hinduism, the worship of, and speculation about, the feminine conception of the Godhead (afterwards: 'The Goddess') by theologians, philosophers, and mythographers - not to speak of many millions of believers - is a well-known phenomenon. This statement is, however, in need of some qualification at the outset. Although the Goddess is being worshipped by many people as omnipotent, source and ultimate destination of all life, she is often considered in Sanskrit religious literature, especially the literature of Śāktism as the active, self-manifesting and self-transforming part of the bipolar Cosmic Being: Brahman or Śiva. The term Śāktism 'the doctrine of Śakti' is a device for summarizing the ideas and conventions of the followers of the feminine view of God. The concept of Śakti 'power, energy' can hardly be detached from a male counterpart[2]. 'Śakti' can be described as the spontaneous, pulsating, expanding, creative aspect of the Supreme Being, as has for instance been expressed by the eighteenth-century philosopher Bhāskararāya in his work Varivasyārahasya[3] 'Secret of Worship', vs. 4:

'The Śakti is His innate luminous vibration

in the shape of reflection;

only in connection with Her, Śiva creates,

maintains and destroys the world.'

In this view, the male aspect of divine nature is at the same time its innermost core, its primeval base. This core remains unaffected, self-absorbed, and unchanging; the female aspect is moving, changing, erupting in cosmic creativity. In a radically Śākta orientation, the male aspect, being formless and undefinable, stands completely - or almost completely - in the background, while all attention is concentrated on the Goddess Who is alone active. Such a position is found i.a. in the Devī-Bhāgavata Purāna[4] and the Kālikā Purāna[5], medieval texts of a narrative-speculative character and unknown age and place of origin. In sources like these, the reader encounters statements to the extent that the Goddess acts completely autonomous as the ground of existence, and as such is to be equated with the universe.

2. It may happen that mutually differing viewpoints are represented in the same source, so that the author's final view of the nature of God does not become completely clear. A case in point is the Mahānirvāna Tantra (MNT)[6] 'Tantra of the Final Release', a very young text (second half of the 18th century), which, however, managed to obtain an important status among the followers of the Śakti and of Tantrism in Bengal and elsewhere. In its third chapter, a reformistic worship of the impersonal Brahman is expounded, while ch. 5 is devoted to the figure of Ādyā Kālī 'the Primeval Kālī', who seems to be a personally conceived female alternative to Brahman. She can, says the text (5,137f.) be meditated upon in two ways: abstract (arūpa) and concrete (sarūpa). The abstract form is unmanifested and therefore also undescribable, even unknowable: 'Who is able to know Thee ?' (4,15). She can be approached only by expert yogins in meditative trance, is unlimited in time and space, etc. Out of compassion for less talented worshippers, for the well-being of the world in general, and for the destruction of the demons (clearly 'popularizing' motivations), the Goddess has manifested herself in concrete shape in a variety of ways. The meditation on the concrete form has three aims or results:

1) The mind is trained in the concentration upon the
   Goddess' nature.
2) The faculty to comprehend her abstract form is
   stimulated.
3) Desires in the mundane sphere are brought te
   realization.

The meditation on the most sublime concrete manifestation of the Primeval Kālī is described, in accordance with tradition, in a stanza composed after the standards of court poetry in a complicated metre (lost in the translation):

'I worship the Primeval Kālī,
Whose body resembles a (black) cloud;
the Three-eyed One, Who is dressed in red,
Who is standing upon a red lotus.
Who carries the moon in Her crown,
Whose gestures symbolize safety and liberality.
With Her large eyes She watches

Mahākālā (the god of destruction)[7],

who dances in front of Her and drinks

the sweet, spirited mead'.

Her worship can be realized internally, on the spiritual-symbolic plane, as well as in external ritual. Internal worship, seemingly simpler, can be done correctly only by those who are spiritually advanced. In this ceremony, the worshipper offers his own heart-lotus to the Goddess as a seat; he washes her feet with water-of-life emitted from the mystical centre directly above his head (Sahasrāra); his mind is the gift of flowers, he pleases her with a dance consisting of the activities of the senses, and so on.

3. Besides this concrete form, the Goddess has - in consonance with Tantric tradition - still another, even purer form which holds an inter-mediate position between the concrete and the abstract: the phonic, condensed to perceptibility in a mantra of ten syllabes (MNT 5,9f.): *hrīm ṣrīm krīm Paramesvari svāhā*. In this mantra, only the word Paramesvari 'O Supreme Lady' possesses a conventional meaning applica-ble in everyday language. The term *svāhā* has two functions:

a) Its traditional function is to accompany a ritual oblation into the sacrificial fire according to Vedic prescriptions. The use in a Tantric mantra connects that mantra with the hallowed Vedic revelation;

b) it denotes that the mantra is the phonic form of a female power. The first three syllabes (*bīja* or 'seminal units') occur also elsewhere in Tantrism, sometimes in variable meanings. It seems plausible that they denote here the nature of a threefold partial manifestation latently present within the Primeval Kālī. These three secondary manifestations fulfil three specified functions represented by three goddesses. The syllables in question might be considered as the phonic equivalents of these goddesses:

creation, emanation   - hrīm - Māyā

maintenance, confirmation   - ṣrīm - Śrī, Laksmi

destruction, reabsorption   - krīm - Kālī, Kālikā

Instead of Māyā, the delusive power which emits the world of objects from herself and presents them as enjoyable to the experiencing subject ('manifold in form through Māyā', MNT 4,34), we find in the creative function also the name of Sarasvati, goddess of learning and consort of the creator-god Brahmā. This situation may be secondary, but it has a deep meaning: Sarasvati is associated with the Hamsa, literally 'goose',

symbolically rather 'swan', the internal energy of Śva which ascends
within the yogin's body[8].

The three functions are explicitly mentioned in MNT 4,29:

    'Thou, as the great Mistress

      of Yoga, createst and maintainest

      and destroyest in the final phase

      the entire world of creatures,

      the moving and the unmoving'.

In the Śakta presentation, the three partial aspects of the Goddess
delegate these functions to the three male gods who elsewhere in
Hinduism have the final responsibility for them: Brahmā, Visnu and
Rudra (or Mahākala), the so-called Trimūrti.

4. In other Śakta sources, the nomenclature and functional division of
the Goddess and her three aspects can vary. The Saundaryalaharī 'Gulf
of Beauty', a famous poem attributed (probably incorrectly) to the
philosopher Śankara and composed in the best traditions of court poetry, associates the name (Mahā)māyā with the universal form of the
Goddess in stanza 98[9]:

    'The Goddess of speech, Druhina's (Brahmā's) consort,

      call Thee the experts of tradition;

      or Hari's (Visnu's) consort Padmā (Laksmi)

      and the Mountain's Daughter, partner of Hara (Śva);

      while Thou, in Thy greatness which is

      difficult to reach, O Mahāmāyā,

      as an undescribable Fourth settest everything

      into motion, Oh Lady of Parabrahman'.

In the Laksmī Tantra, a text of Visnuite signature, the name Mahāmāyā
is connected with the third or destructive of the Goddess' three partial
functions, while in her supreme form she is identified with Laksmī[10].
These few instances concerning only one of the Goddess' many names
may suffice to give an impression of the abundance of conceptions and
speculations, unhampered by ecclesiastical dogmatism. The Goddess'
threefold activy (originally connected with the philosophical doctrine of
the tree guna 'strings', basic functions or modifications of the primal
nature or Prakrti[11]) is also described with other terms which shed light
on other aspects of her theology. Mention is often made of the triad
Vāmā 'the Lovely', Jyesthā 'the Elder' and Raudrī 'the Terrifying',
which can best be considered as the 'mythologizing' counterpart of the

threefold distinction of cosmical Energy into Icchā 'Intention', Jnāna
'Wisdom' and Kriyā 'Activity' common in speculative context. The
Yoginīhrdaya, a concise but important early Tantric text[12], identifies
(1,36f.) both triads in the mentioned sequence, associating them at the
same time with other concepts which stand for alternative modes of
existence or manifestations of the Goddess, such as:

1) The three basic powers of physical creation known from Vedic
tradition: Soma (moon, water), Sūrya (sun,light) and Agni (fire,
heat);

2) three symbols in which the divine has been reduced or rather
concentrated to primary form: aṅkuśa 'elephant goad' (a hooked stick),
bindu 'drop', and śṛṅgāṭaka 'triangle';

3) the most important alternative, the already mentioned phonic
manifestation. This concept is intimately linked with a doctrine of the
levels of speech developed by the famous philosopher of language,
Bhartrhari: a) the Paśyantī 'Observing', still abstract and undifferen-
tiated; b) the Madhyamā 'Intermediate' in which differentiation is devel-
oping in a still unarticulated form; and c) the Vaikharī 'Concretized',
the linguistic expression which can be heard and understood. These
phases of speech are also, as has been argued elsewhere[13], to be
localized in some of the mystic power centres generally known in
Tantric texts: the 'Observing' in the Svādhisthāna 'Resting-in-itself' in
the lower part of the body, the 'Intermediate' in the heart-lotus
Anāhata 'Unstruck', i.e. 'Unarticulated'; and the 'Concretized' in the
Viśuddha 'the Pure' at the level of the throat which i.a. activates the
organs of speech.

In the light of speculation on the Goddess' supreme form referred to
above (e.g. the 'Primeval Kālī'), it is understandable that also on the
phonic plane a primary, completely unevolved phase has been put
forward. This is Parā 'Highest, Supreme', internally localized in the
lowest mystical centre called Mūlādhāra 'Primary Base'. This is the same
place where the Goddess in her microcosmic manifestation is resting as a
fiery snake or column (Kundalinī), until she is awakened by the yogin
and soars upwards along the power centres in the direction of the
domain of Śiva above the fontanelle. From this last equivalence
(Parā-Kundalinī it follows, that the threefold 'evolution' of the Goddess
can also function as a way to final release. The yogin – identifying
himself with the Kundalinī – rises from the nether world, the 'Fire of
Dissolution' (Varivasyārahasya 20f.), realized in the Mūlādhāra, to the

place where a cool lunar lustre of intense clearness is the scene of the blissful union of Śiva and Śakti.

5. At this moment, the reader might already be somewhat confused by the bewildering variety of speculations and epithets. Nevertheless, one other concept should not be left unmentioned in the present context. In some old Tantras, mention is made of the following three manifestations: Parā 'Supreme, Supramundane', Parāparā 'Intermediate', and Aparā 'Lower, Manifested'. The Mālinīvijaya Tantra (3,30-33) still refers to three *groups* of such Śaktis, in consonance with later Vedic tradition. According to this text, the Parā Śaktis grant access to Śiva's spheres, the Intermediate bring about the results of human endeavour (*karma*), while the lowest cause people to fall (into the cycle of rebirths). The Netra Tantra (19,159f.) goes a step further and associates Aparā (singular) with Raudrī and Kriyāśakti, Parāparā with Vāmā and Jyesthā (resp. Icchā- and Jñānaśakti), while Parā is enthroned above these levels in the lofty solitude where according to the Mahānirvāna Tantra, as we have seen, the Primeval Kālī is situated. Abhinavagupta of Kashmir ($\pm$ 1000 A.D.), the most important exponent of the Trika school of Śaiva philosophy[14], who accepts the Mālinīvijaya and Netra Tantras as authoritative, nevertheless degrades the Parā to the first or creative phase of the threefold course of life, to be equated with Icchā 'Intention'. Parāparā is relegated to the second phase (Jñāna), while Aparā remains on a level with the third phase (Kriyā). Outward appearance and character of these three goddesses are described as follows[15]: Parā in the middle, beautiful and friendly disposed, clear as moonlight, pouring out the water-of-life; Parāparā to her right, red and somewhat irate; Aparā to her left, dark (literally: black-red), very wrathful and terrifying. One should further imagine these Goddesses as seated on the lifeless bodies of their male partners (whose names are unimportant in the present context) on the points of a symbolic trident which rests in the Mūlādhāra and reaches up to the Sahasrāra[16]. Above this triad, Abhinavagupta then postulates, following another *guru* tradition and in accordance with later sources such as the MNT, the goddess Kālī as the universal Fourth Power. She represents 'the pure autonomy of the self, the innermost identity' (Sanderson), the 'virgin consciousness'[17] which the adept realizes within himself as redemptive experience.

6. An interesting, although somewhat standardized, popularization of

the Goddess' threefold manifestation can be found in the already mentioned Kālikā Purāna (KP)[18], which describes appearances of the mother
goddess Kāmākhyā who is especially well-known in Assam. She is often
called Mahāmāyā and identified with Kālī. Her main sanctuary is located
near the former capital Guwahati (Gauhati). Kāmākhyā (as the text
says) can manifest herself in three figures. In lovable appearance, she
wears a garland and daubs her body with red saffron; she is standing
upon a red lotus. In martial appearance, she exchanges the garland for
a sword and stands upon a white corpse. Between these two, in her
liberal nature, she stands upon a lion. The corresponding colour is not
mentioned in this last case (golden? black?). This threefold manifestation is to be associated with the Three Gods, in the following way (vs.
64f.):

lovable	liberal	martial
lotus	lion	corpse
Brahmā	Visnu	Mahādeva (Rudra/Siva)

As we see, instead of the three basic functions we here find three
personal characteristics implicitly connected with the functions, as is
suggested by the association with the three male deities. A somewhat
more intellectual elaboration of the same principle is the threefold
manifestation of the goddess Tripurā 'She of the three fortresses'. Her
representation and worship is intimately connected with her phonic form
which is well-known as the Śrīvidyā: a mantra of fifteen syllables divided into three 'heights' (kūta), as has been described in i.a. the KP[19].
With the three parts of the Śrīvidyā correspond three personal manifestations[20]:

1) Bālā 'the Young Girl', represented as a young lady of about
sixteen years, of fresh beauty. She has the colour of vermillion, three
eyes and four arms; in her hands she holds bow and arrows, both made
of flowers (attributes of the god of love), a book and a rosary (symbols of learning and phonic manifestation). She is also called Vāgvādinī
'the Eloquent'.

2) Kāmeśvarī 'Lady of desire' has the (deep red) colour of the
Bandhūka flower. Her body is full-grown, she loves strong drink and
emits a dazzling radiance. She grants the worshipper a sweet smile. Her
four hands are provided with the attributes book and rosary, and the
gestures of safety and liberality. She also wears a garland of skulls
and resides under a wishing-tree. Her other name is Sundarī 'the
Beautiful', or Candikā 'the Impetuous'.

3) Bhairavī 'the Awe-inspiring' has the (white) colour of a China rose (*japā*), and dishevelled hair (perhaps denoting the status of a widow or a woman living in solitude). She is seated upon a laughing corpse (Sadāśiva, a form of Śiva). Her attributes are the same as those of Kāmeśvarī. Her shapely body is naked; she laughs loudly and is addicted to the enjoyment of streams of blood. She is also called Sammohinī 'the Deluding'. In this variety, besides the functions and psychic characteristics still clearly implied, there seems to be a tendency to apply a threefold age division as another code for the basic threefold manifestation. The idea has, however, not found full expression. As the result of such meditation and worship, all desires are said to be fulfilled and 'the abode of the Goddess reached' (a standard phrase). The Jñānārnava Tantra, which describes a similar (but in details differing) meditation, specifies the results: worship of the first form is commendable for wisdom, of the second for obtaining power over other people, especially women or rulers, and of the third for cure of disease ('destruction of poison', etc.)[22].

7. In the mentioned representations of Tripurā, the Goddess is described as a young girl in the first of her three partial manifestations. More than once, however, in Tantric literature the idea is expressed that the young girl represents the Goddess in her purest, essential, unevolved state. An allusion to this idea has already been encountered in the work of Abhinavagupta (above, note 17). The Yoginī Tantra, a late medieval text from the Northeast of India[23], in this context expresses itself as follows: there are two kinds of yoga (here: concentration upon the Supreme), the divine and the heroic. In the divine yoga, the practiser is advised to imagine the own Ātman as identical with Brahman or with the universe. The heroic yoga in first instance departs from a geometric representation: a triad of circles (bindu) arranged in the form of a triangle, from which emerges

'a female figure aged sixteen

whose luminous glow as of innumerable dawns

brightens the heavenly spheres'.

With this female form, worshipped by Brahmā, Visnu and Śiva, one should then identify one's own body. A good instance of this approach can be found in a text of speculative-narrative character and little literary attractiveness, the Tripurārahasya[24]. The Goddess' deepest essence, it is stated here, is the union of consciousness (*cid*) and bliss (*ānanda*), she exceeds speaking and thinking and is the ground and unaffected witness of the world process. Again it is said that compassion with her worshippers is her motivation for manifesting herself in different ways. She does so in full autonomy (*svātantrya*). In the primal stage of manifestation, she develops within herself a desire to emanate: Icchā, a condensation of her nature which should - says the author - be equated on the mythological plane with the primeval form (introduced already earlier in the text) of a Kumārī 'virgin, young unmarried woman'. In a later chapter (58), the author returns to the subject in the context of the Tantric mystical physiology which has succinctly been alluded to above. Part of this doctrine is the well-known theory of the three ducts (nāḍī) which, mutually intertwining, lead upwards in the human body from the Mūlādhāra to the crown. In the central duct, it is explained (58,40f.) exists the conscious principle in fiery form. Strictly speaking, consciousness is light, but this becomes manifest as fire 'due to the abundance of darkness (which is inherent to the subject-object differentiation)'. This fire of consciousness can be emitted through the third eye which the Goddess and her perfect adepts possess. As we saw, consciousness in intimate coalescence with bliss is the Goddess' essence. In the world, the text says (58,42f.), this is represented as a beautiful female figure on which human beings meditate in order to realize happiness within themselves. A similar consideration underlies *Śivasūtra 1,13 icchāśaktir umā kumārī* 'Umā, the Virgin, is the energy Intention'[25]. The commentator, the learned Kṣemarāja (11th cent.) interprets this statement as referring to the perfect consciousness of the yogin who has attained Śiva-status. He equates this Intention-energy with the supreme female manifestation of the cosmos, here called Parā Parameśvarī, whose nature is perfectly free and independent. Also here, the idea of Kumārī is therefore connected with this basic freedom. In my opinion, 'Kumārī' in this context does not therefore in the first place refer to virginity, but to the unmarried state. In social life, this state - in normal circumstances - was connected in the consciousness of high-caste Hindus with childhood. This is why 'Kumārī' or 'Bālā' can also be - and has been - explained as 'child'.

8. Freedom implies playfulness. The Goddess 'play' expresses itself in the spontaneous creation (and destruction !) of the world process, as Kṣemarāja remarks[26]. The names Bālā and Līlāvinodinī "She who

delights in play" occur in the Lalitāsahasranāma, the "Thousand Names of the Attractive One", a long litany of epithets of the Goddess[27]. The commentator, the abovementioned Bhāskararāya, in this context refers to another text for the statement:

'O Beloved One, as Thou dost play like a child, Thou
art Bālā',

and also to the late Vedic Śvetāśvatara Upaniṣad (4,3) 'Thou art boy or girl'. Unavoidably, the immensely popular figure of the playful toddler Kṛṣṇa comes to the mind.

As to the name Bālā in the Lalitāsahasranāma, a modern commentator holds that one should here think of Bālā Tripurasundarī (mentioned above), whom the meditator should imagine as a playful little girl of between two and nine years of age[28]. It is exactly the unripe young girl who is brought here to the fore as the representant of the Goddess as source of all creation. In the Svacchanda Tantra, one of the oldest, largest and most authoritative Tantras, the Goddess' status as a Kumārī is similarly associated with her supernatural creative power (yogamāyā), by means of which she 'envelops' her essence 'with all sorts of names and forms of (secondary) goddesses'. But in this same form she brings 'the worlds to expansion', in other words, she is a virgin and virtually a mother at the same time. The same paradox is signalled by Michael Allen in his interesting description of the present-day Kumārī worship in Nepal[29]. Basing himself upon statements of knowledgeable Nepalese informants, he argues that the virginal, child-like manifestation should not be interpreted as a negation, but as a representant of potential creativity in its purest forms. This is why the little child-Kumārīs are made up as ripe young women for official occasions. Kumārī worship is not only known from present-day Nepal, but is repeatedly mentioned in Hindu texts of differing age and origin[30]. There are also groups of Kumārīs such as the group of five (Ahalyā etc.) mentioned by Allen (p. 54), functioning as bridesmaids or, on special occasions, as 'assistants' of an official Kumārī. A group of nine Kumārīs is mentioned in the Kulārnava Tantra (10,20-38).

9. Among the many interesting names of the Goddess in the Lalitāsahasranāma features no. 111 Bisatantutanīyasī 'More delicate than a lotus stalk'. In the course of his elaborate commentary on this name, Bhāskararāya discusses a text-place from the Vedic Taittirīya Āraṇyaka[31], where mention is made of three phases of life during which

a woman can commit an offence: 'in which a virgin exceeds the limit (?, Skt. *mandrayate*, translation uncertain), in which a (young) woman, in which a matron (*pativratā*) ... all that Agni puts right'. The whole passage is interpreted by our commentator in the light of Kundaliniyoga, a procedure during which, as remarked above, the Goddess in fiery form wakes up within the yogin's body and ascends towards the place of union with Śiva. One should in this case - Bhāskararāya remarks - imagine the Kumārī as a crying (his interpretation of *mandrayate*) new-born baby at the moment of leaving the Mūlādhāra. The second phase, that of an adolescent, marriageable young woman, is reached by her as soon as she passes the mystical centre at the level of the heart (Anāhata). As soon as she is united with her partner in the Sahasrāra above the head, she has the status of a legally married woman. This latter status of the Goddess is very popular and has found expression in several myths and epithets (Pārvatī, Satī etc.).

It should be noticed, that in this viewpoint no place is available for the terrifying manifestation or for old age as a third phase of life. For a well-known representation of the Goddess as an old woman, we have to turn again to the Mahānirvāna Tantra (5,55f.), where suggestions are made for the so-called *sandhyā* meditation, which is to be performed on the three crucial moments of the day. The starting-point here is the idea that the day is a miniature representation of the vital process, individual as well as cosmic. The Goddess of the Sandhyā is Gāyatrī (in the MNT, a stanza in honour of the Primeval Kālī) who according to the text is a manifestation of the Great Goddess herself. At daybreak, one should meditate on her as a girl of brightly reddish colour, sweetly smiling and seated upon a goose. In this form, she is to be associated with Brahmā. At noon, she is related to Visṇu; her appearance is dark blue (an alternative to black), her figure is that of a young adult woman, and she is seated upon the 'eagle' Garuda. At sunset, one should represent her in one's mind as old, pale and dressed in white, but benevolent and liberal. In this phase, she is associated with Śiva and seated upon a bull.

The representation of the Goddess as an old woman is rare. The name Vrddhamātā 'Old Mother' occurs in the litany of a hundred names of Durgā from the Viśvasāra Tantra[32]. In the Nepalese countryside, 'grandmother goddesses' (Ajimā) are worshipped, especially in connection with children's diseases[33]. Much better known are the

representations of repulsive or terror-inspiring goddesses who as a rule
are not explicitly characterized as 'old'. The most famous of these
figures is Cāmundā, who is described in the Devīmāhātmya (an old and
basic text) as emaciated, with sunken eyes, clad in an elephant hide,
garlanded with skulls, desirous of animal sacrifice (in former times even
of human sacrifice), worshipped on cremation grounds[34]; of others, we
mention Danturā 'She of the teeth', represented as squatting on the
ground, with bare teeth, protruding eyes, meagre pendulous breasts,
and sunken belly[35]. It would seem that the old woman and the emaciated, ghostly being, and perhaps also the beautiful but terrifying de-
stroyer (e.g. Durgā or the Bhairavī, mentioned above, from the Kālikā
Purāna) are alternative representations of the 'third phase' from the
threefold 'course of life' ascribed to the Goddess in manifested form.
Such a opposition should be corroborated or falsified by further research, during which the investigator should be aware that old age as
well as the inspiration of terror can be interpreted as images for the
approach or even the breakthrough of liberating insight.

NOTES

1　　An instance is Jnānārnava Tantra 10, 2f.: Brahman consists of
　　　Śiva and Śakti. Here, the male and female poles are considered to
　　　be equal and their union as the universal Soul.
2　　J. Gonda, Die Religionen Indiens, II. Stuttgart: Kohlhammer,
　　　1963, p. 39f.; C.M. Brown (see Note 11), p. 148.
3　　Varivasyarahasya, ed. Subrahmanya Sastri. Madras: Adyar, 1934.
　　　- English translations in this article are directly from the Sanskrit
　　　originals, unless otherwise indicated.
4　　P.G. Lalye, Studies in Devī Bhāgavata. Poona: Popular Prakashan,
　　　1973, p. 161, 166.
5　　Kālikā Purāna, ed. Biśwanārayan Śastri. Varanasi: Chowkhamba,
　　　1972; K.R. van Kooij, Worship of the Goddess. According to the
　　　Kālika Purāna, Part I: A Translation with an Introduction and
　　　Notes of Chs. 54-69. Leiden 1972 (Thesis Utrecht), p. 10.
6　　Mahānirvāna Tantra, ed. J. Vidyasagar. Calcutta 1884; trsl. A.
　　　Avalon, 'The Great Liberation'. Madras: Ganesh, 3rd ed. 1953.
7　　Mahakala is Kali's servant according to MNT 4,30.
8　　André Padoux, Recherches sur la symbolique et l'énergie de la
　　　parole dans certains textes tantriques. Paris: Inst. de civ.
　　　indienne, 1975, p. 121.
9　　Trsl. after the Dutch translation by Ine E.M. Willems,
　　　'Saundaryalahari, Sanskriettekst met Nederlandse vertaling,
　　　introductie en commentaar'. Paper, submitted for the doctoral
　　　examination Indian and Iranian languages and cultures, Utrecht
　　　1986, p. 90.

10 *Sanjukta Gupta, Laksmī Tantra, A Pañcarātra Text, Translation and Notes.* Leiden: E.J. Brill, 1972 (Thesis Utrecht), p. 27 (LT 5,1-6).

11 See, *e.g.*, J. Gonda, *Inleiding tot het indische denken.* Antwerpen: Standaard 1948, p. 140. - Another description of the Goddess' threefold manifestation can be found in the interesting study by Cheever M. Brown, *God as Mother: A Feminine Theology in India.* An Historical and Theological Study of the Brahmavaivartapurāna. Hartford, Vt.: Claude Stark, 1974, p. 148f.

12 Ed. G. Kaviraj. Varanasi 1963.

13 *E.g.* by Rāghavabhatta (15th cent.), in his commentary on Śaradatilaka 1,110-114, cf. Padoux, o.c., p. 122f.

14 Bruno Nagel, *Herkenning van het Zelf.* Abhinavagupta's Iśvara-pratyabhijñā-vimarśini I,1,2-3 vertaald en nader beschouwd. Amsterdam: Centrale Interfaculteit (Thesis of Univ. of Amsterdam) 1986, p. 3f.

15 The description follows the authorative treatment of the subject by A. Sanderson, 'Mandala and Āgamic Identity in the Trika of Kashmir', in: A. Padoux (ed.), *Mantras et diagrammes rituels dans l'Hindouïsme.* Paris: Centre National de la Recherche Scientifique, 1986, p. 169-214, on p. 189. Sanderson's article is based in the first place on Abhinavagupta's Tantrāloka.

16 Illustration at Sanderson, *o.c.*, p. 187.

17 Skt. kumārikācakram 'virginal circle'; Sanderson, *o.c.*, p. 193, n. 117.

18 Kālikā Purāna 58,57f. (Van Kooij: 60,57f., on p. 96f.). Summary in the useful booklet by B.K. Kakati, *The Mother Goddess Kāmākhyā.* Gauhati 1948, p. 38f.

19 KP 63,51f. (Van Kooij, p. 149: 66,51f.). - With the Śrividyā corresponds the famous Śriyantra, an ingenously constructed geometrical figure replete with symbolism, which consists of intersections of nine triangles. The unevolved nature of the Goddess is to be localized within the central triangle, of which Brahmā, Visnu and Śiva inhabit the corners.

20 KP 63,85f. (Van Kooij, p. 152: 66,85f.).

21 KP 63,158f. (Van Kooij, p. 160: 67,56f.).

22 Jñānarnava Tantra, ed. G.S. Gokhale. Poona: Ānandaśrama Series no. 69; 1952, ch. 19,9f. - There are still other descriptions of threefold manifestations the worship of which is described as conducive to specified results, *e.g.* those of Ugratārā and of Kubjikā (the latter highly mystifying). They are not discussed here in order to avoid further complications.

23 Yoginī Tantra, ed. Kanhaiyalāl Mishra. Bombay 1956 (Samvat 2013), 1,6.

24 Tripurārahasya, Māhātmya Khanda, ed. Mukunda Lāla Shastri. Varanasi: *Kaśi Sanskrit Series*, Vol. 92, 1932, ch. 10,12f.

25 *Śiva Sūtras*, The Yoga of Supreme Identity. Text of the Sūtras and the Commentary Vimarśini of Ksemarāja Translated into English ... by Jaideva Singh. Delhi a.o.: Motilal Banarsidass, 1979, p. 53f.; *S'ivasūtra et Vimarśini de Ksemarāja*, traduction et introduction par Lilian Silburn. Paris: Inst. de civ. indienne, 1980, p. 48f. - The S'ivasūtras are a short collection of aphorisms belonging to the most important revealed texts of "Kashmir" Śaivism. They date from about 800 A.D. or earlier.

26 Ksemarāja, comm. on Śivasūtra 1,13: *sā ca kumārī viśvasargasamhārakrīdāpara.* He gives still other interpretations of this passage, which will not concern us in this article.

27   *Lalitāsahasranāmam with Bhāskararāya's Commentary*, trsl. into
     English by R. Ananthakrishna Sastry. Adyar (Madras:
     Theosophical Publishing House), 1951, 4th ed. 1970, nos. 965 and
     966, p. 366. - The quoted passages in English are by this transla-
     tor.

28   *Sri Lalita Sahasranāmam with introd. and comm.* by Chaganty
     Suryanarayanamurthy. Madras: Ganesh, 1962, p. 161. -
     Bhāskararāya also quotes Śiva Sūtra 1,13 at another of the 1000
     names of Lalitā: Uma (no. 633). The expression *līlā* 'play' further
     occurs in names no. 649 and 865.

29   Michael Allen, *The Cult of Kumārī. Virgin Worship in Nepal.*
     Kathmandu 1975, p. 60.

30   Allen, *o.c.*, p. 2,61; R.N. Nandi, *Religious Institutions and Cults
     in the Deccan (c. A.D. 600 - A.D. 1000).* Delhi 1973, p. 123f.;
     G. Hartmann, *Beiträge zur Verehrung der Göttin Laksmi.* Wertheim
     a.M. 1933, p. 36; *Jñanārnava Tantra* 22; *Yoni 'Tantra*, ed.
     J.A.Schoterman. Delhi: Manoḣar, 1980, etc.

31   *Taittirīya Āranyaka*, ed. in the Anandaśrama Skt. Series, Vol. I.
     Poona 1967, p. 121.

32   Trsl. A. & E. Avalon, *Hymns to the Goddess.* Madras: Ganesh,
     1952, p. 81f.

33   Allen, *o.c.*, p. 51.

34   R.N. Nandi, *o.c.*, p. 132f.; K.K. Handiqui, *Yaśastilaka and Indian
     Culture.* Sholapur 1949, p. 56.

35   R.C. Majumdar, *History of Bengal*, I. Dacca 1943, p. 455 and
     Plate XIV-36.

VISUALIZATIONS IN BUDDHIST MEDITATION

Ria Kloppenborg

Ronald Poelmeyer

'It is all in the mind'

From its very beginning, Buddhism emphasized the vital importance of meditation as a means of attaining insight and liberation from the painful cycle of existence (*samsara*). The canonical scriptures present a great variety of meditations and meditation-techniques, which, during later centuries, have been systematized. They can be traced to roughly two traditions[1]. One of these aimed at the development of insight ('seeing the things as they are'), the other was based on pre-buddhist ascetic and yogic practices, which aimed at the experience of higher states of mind; and which could provide the practitioner with supernatural powers (*siddhi*), which were supposedly produced by these practices.

Visualization has always been recognized as a strong emotional stimulus in meditation. It enables the meditators to create objects and beings, other worlds and paradises by the force of their concentration of mind, and facilitates the transformation of everyday consciousness into that of the higher states.

It is not possible here to elaborate on the early techniques. We may refer to the various meditations on the impermanence of the body and of worldly phenomena by visualizing one's body, after death, in various stages of decay (the 'meditations on the impure', *asubhabhavana*). To facilitate the emergence of the images, and to strengthen the experience of 'reality' of their vision, the meditators could visit cemeteries or use a skeleton as a meditation-object.

Other examples of early visualizations can be found in the 'devotional' meditations: for instance in the 'remembrance of the Buddha' (*buddhanusmrti*), where the meditators imagine the Buddha in front of them, if necessary with the help of an image, to honour and worship the Master and to deepen one's confidence in the Way taught by Him.

The Amitayurdhyanasutra, an early Mahayana work, describes a visualization procedure of this kind as being taught by the Buddha to the Lady Vaidehi, his contemporary. In this *sutra*, the meditation is focussed upon the visualization of Sukhāvati, the western paradise of the Buddha Amitāyus. Repeated practice of this is supposed to lead to rebirth in that paradise[2].

The Sādhanamālā, an 11th century compilation of *sādhanas* or 'evocations' ascribes some *mantras* and *dhāraṇis* to the historical Buddha.

According to orthodox Buddhism, the Buddha rejected the value of popular cults, magical practices and yogic powers. Nevertheless, these have been and still remain important elements in Buddhist meditational and spiritual practices. As early as pre-buddhist times, meditation and asceticism were considered to bestow extraordinary powers upon the practitioners[3]. The buddhist canonical scriptures frequently describe these powers and the miracles which they could produce[4]. In addition to ascetic practices, *mantras, mudrās and dhāraṇis* have always been used as tools which can influence and master the worlds of gods and superhuman beings.

The Mañjusrimūlakalpa, dating from the first century A.D., is the first buddhist text to provide us with a multitude of these formulas and practices, many of which date from earlier times.

Buddhist deities

Although rejecting the concept of a creator-god, buddhist theories of rebirth incorporated the worlds of divine beings as one of the levels of rebirth. By doing so, Buddhism included pre-buddhist deities in its ontology. The world of deities extended when buddhist philosophy systematized the divine abodes and incorporated various levels of meditation as various heavens; including the divine beings belonging to that sphere[5].

Other developments contributed to the extension of the buddhist pantheon. Two of these can be mentioned here, since they were directly influenced by the techniques of visualization.

1. One of the most important of the larger Mahāyānasūtras, the Saddharmapundarika, or 'Lotus'-*sutra*, is an example of a text in which adjectives and epithets of the Buddha are represented and personalized as Buddhas and/or Bodhisattvas. Those names that were to become most popular as separate Buddhas or deities were probably those with an auspicious meaning; or those that could be connected with existing divinities. Examples of this development are, for instance, Amitāyus, 'Immeasurable Life', and adjectives, which were associated with

important events in the Buddha's life[6]: *e.g.* Aksobhya, 'the Unshakable One' for the moment before the enlightenment, when the Bodhisattva defeated Māra's army; and Avalokiteśvara, 'the Lord who looks down (compassionately)', for the Bodhisattva's decision to enter his last life for the welfare of all.

In the course of time, many of these personifications have become prominent members of the Mahāyāna pantheon and have been provided with detailed iconographies, *sādhanas*, *mantras* and 'biographies'.

2. The second development requires a more detailed description. It concerns a change in emphasis in the traditional forms of meditation under the influence of existing yogic practices and of doctrinal changes. It is fortunate that the third German expedition to Turfān (1905-1907) has provided us with a Sanskrit text of the Hīnayāna Sarvāstivāda-school which, according to Bareau[7], flourished between the second century B.C. and the third century A.D.. The text is a manual of buddhist *yoga*[8].

This text describes the meditations that are well-known from the canonical sources, like the *aśubhabhāvanā* and the four 'immeasurable states' (*apramānāni*). Here, however, we see a different kind of practice developping. Instead of meditating on, that is, thinking over, for instance, impermanence, this is being actually and physically experienced by the meditator. And, instead of developping the emotion of, for instance, equanimity (*upeksā*), this is projected by the meditators as a person, a vision, placed in front of them.

Instead of thinking about, meditating on, pondering over doctrinal truths and virtues, the monk/*yogin*/*yogācāra* visualizes these as persons coming out of one's own heart and projecting them in front of oneself. The meditator, that is, one's own body, is the basis (*āśraya*) of the vision.

It might be interesting to quote the descriptions given in the text, since there are many elements in it that will return in the later, more developped, Tantric visualizations.

a. At the beginning of the meditation, the phenomenal world of ordinary perception must be broken down:
'Then knives, coming out of the body (*āśraya*) of the *yogācāra*, separate the whole ocean of living beings by reducing it to the five elements' (160 V 5).

b. Having analysed the elements, the *yogin* becomes convinced of their impermanence: "'This is without Self (*ātman*) or anything belonging to the Self". Then the six pieces, representing the six elements, burn in the fire of his disgust' (160 R 1).

c. The wisdom, resulting from this insight, is visualized as follows: 'Then from drops a body consisting of the six elements is created. A woman with a lamp in her hand, as embodiment of wisdom (*prajñā*) explains: "Destroyed is the body, empty (*śūnya*) ... elements only" ' (160 R 5).

d. Another, similar, way of visualization is that of equanimity: "Then (in his heart) a white-coloured woman appears, dressed in white clothes, seated in meditation-posture, and remains there as the embodiment of equanimity" (160 V 2-3).

e. During this proceeding, the meditator receives a consecration or initiation. One visualizes this *abhiseka*, the ritual of which is based on the Indian royal consecration: "The Lord binds a silk cloth on the *yogin*'s head and says: 'Hail thee, who will be the world's leader in a future period' " (150 R 1).

f. The *abhiseka* means the fulfillment of the meditation. The *yogin*'s body stiffens, when he experiences *nirvāna*. This experience is described in positive terms, contrary to the usual descriptions in Theravāda and Hīnayāna scriptures. It is 'the city of *nirvāna*' (*nirvāna-nagara*) and 'peace and happiness' (*upaśama-sukha*).

g. At the end the visions are withdrawn in the *yogin*'s body. 'Then all that is to be known is hidden in the *yogin*'s body' (127 R 1) and 'At the end all disappears in the *yogin*'s navel. Then is the awakening (from the trance)' (139 R 3).

h. After these overwhelming experiences, the meditators want their own *nirvāna* to be given to the beings (as is done in the traditional Mahāyāna *parināmanā*, 'dedication' of the Bodhisattva). Although a Sarvāstivāda text, the meditators aim at Mahāyāna goals when they dedicate their own liberation to all beings. One solemnly promises (*pranidhāna*) to put oneself in the service of their salvation and therefore one hears the prediction of one's own future Buddhahood.

Thus, the text exemplifies the transition from monk to *yogin*, and from *yogin* to Bodhisattva. It is clear that the modifications of these traditional practices have been made under the influence of doctrinal and philosophical developments. The philosophical theories, on the other hand, have been greatly influenced by the experiences during meditation, and the consequent reflexion on these experiences[9].

Schmithausen has convincingly argued that already in an early stage of the development of Mahāyāna philosophy, spiritual practices have influenced theory and doctrine. Visualization-techniques can be considered as the basis of the Yogācāra conception that all phenomena are only creations of the mind (*cittamātra*), similar to the visions of the meditator. All phenomena are "constructions of thought" (*vikalpa*), they are not different from the mind, for they do not exist outside the recognition of the mind[10].

The visualizations aim, therefore, at the elimination of all objective phenomena, the realization of the essential emptiness of all phenomena, and therefore of their "worthlessness". This realization will free the meditator from the false view of duality. It will then free him from attachment and hence from suffering. Both the spiritual practices and the philosophy function in this perspective of insight and can therefore only be understood when they are seen in the light of their spiritual results.

All these developments have ultimately resulted in an extensive text-tradition of detailed descriptions of the various methods and stages of vizualization in later Mahāyāna and Tantra. On the basis of these descriptions, an outline will be presented of the method of visualization. In this paper, however, variants of different schools or authors are not discussed, nor the different interpretations within the four Tantric systems of Krīya, Caryā, Yoga and Anuttarayoga. A translation of the *sādhana* of Tārā will illustrate the outline.

The stages of visualization

1. The preliminary phase consists of purification-rituals of the site and of the person of the meditator. When visualizing benevolent deities (for instance Tārā), the site is to be made pleasant with flowers and perfumes; but the more awe-inspiring deities demand another kind of preparation, according to their character.

2. The following practices precede the visualization, or follow the "creation" of the chosen deity:
- the taking of refuge
- the confession of sins
- rejoicing in the merit of all beings
- the direction of the mind towards enlightenment; the intention to become a Buddha for the sake of the world
- many descriptions include here the meditation on the four 'divine states' (*brahmavihāra*), viz. friendliness, compassion, sympathetic joy and equanimity.

3. The visualization starts with the generation of the residence of the chosen deity or deities, their paradise, including palaces, gardens, flowers, jewels, gates and all kinds of auspicious symbols, according to the known iconographical descriptions. As in the Buddhist manual on *yoga*, mentioned above, light and bright colours play an important role[11].

4. The process of emanation or creation (of the deity) (*utpattikrama*) starts with the visualization of the chosen deity's seed syllable (*bīja*) in the heart of the meditator[12]. Rays, coming forth from this syllable, enlighten the worlds. Some *sādhanās* state that Buddhas and Bodhisattvas are attracted by these rays and are visualized in front of the meditator and worshipped by him. The rays may "project" the divine being, whose essence is symbolized by the seed syllable in the meditator's heart. He or she is visualized according to a chosen iconographical form. Then also the deity, thus created, is worshipped. A deity, created like this, is called a 'symbolic being' (*samaya-sattva*)[13]. After the projection of the deity, rays of light are envisaged as coming from the deity, enlightening the world and destroying all suffering.

5. Then the meditator is to understand the inherent purity of all phenomena, including oneself. One realizes this by means of the *mantra*: *Om svabhāvaśuddhāh sarvadharmāh svabhāvaśuddho'ham*. The meditator should attain the insight that all phenomena are essentially pure, and therefore that the dual conception of *samsāra* and *nirvāna* is a false construction of thought. The meditation on emptiness (*śūnyatā*) serves the same insight. "He should conceive the entire universe, with its mobile and immobile creations as the clear manifestations of non-duality, when the mind is devoid of all kinds of false reflections and of such thought-categories as the subject and the object". This emptiness *must be realized by the mantra*: *Om śunyatājñānavajrasvabhāv-ātmako'ham*. This also means the realization of the ultimate identity of *nirvāna* and *samsāra*. See *e.g.* Hevajra Tantra I.1.11 (8th century): 'O Wise One, you should conceive of existence in knowledge of its non-existence, and likewise you should conceive of Heruka (the chosen deity) in knowlegde of his non-existence'[14].

6. The visualization may then be concluded by identifying the generated "symbolic being" with the universe and the meditator, by the "process of realization or reabsorption (*sampannakrama*) of the seed-syllable into the meditator's heart. This is the realization of the medita-

tor's essential identity with the deity, the essential non-duality of the divine (*nirvāna*) and the self (*samsāra*).

7. The identification can be actualized ritually by means of a consecration, whereby the seed-syllables *om*, *āh* and *hūm* are placed on the meditator's forehead, throat and heart by touching these places on the deity's visualized image and on the own body of the meditator (*nyāsa*). By this ritual, the deity is reabsorbed. Hevajra Tantra: *Om Herukasvabhāvātmako'ham*, 'Om, I am the essence of Heruka'.

8. The visualization may also be continued by 'drawing in' the eternal or metaphysical aspect of the deity. From the seed-syllable in the heart of the meditator, who has identified himself with the deity, rays of light reach the deity's palace in paradise and touch his 'knowledge' (*jñāna*), to bring it down in front of the meditator as the 'knowledge-being' (*jñānasattva*)[15]. After worship, meditations and *nyāsa*, this being will also be absorbed into the meditator's heart. Tucci[16] rightly points out that this proceeding looks like a descent 'from above'. In fact, as this too is created during the meditation, it actually means the light within, which does not descend, but reveals itself. Finally, the 'symbolic being' and the 'knowledge being' have both been absorbed and united in the meditator's mind.

The two movements in the meditation, of the 'process of emanation or creation' and the 'process of realization or absorption', reenact the likewise illusory processes of cosmic creation and reabsorption of phenomenal existence. They are based on two ideas: The preliminary idea, based on a false conception of the reality of the divine, and the idea, based on the certitude of the knowledge that the divine is nothing else than an emanation of our mind. In the course of the meditation the illusion of reality, with all its transporting experiences and visions, must make place for the insight that these are only conceptions and images of the mind, that these are only creations and games of the uncontrolled thought-processes. In the words of Tucci[17]: 'Das dichotomisierende Denken im seiner unbegrenzten Projektions- und Reflektions- fahigkeit erschöpft sich so in sich selbst und findet schliesslich, jenseits jeder Dualitat, in der Grenzsituation, die Leerheit wieder: es handelt sich dabei tatsachlich um ein Wiederfinden, nicht um ein Erlangen, denn zu erlangen ist da nichts'. And in the words of the Hevajra Tantra: (I.V.1 and 11): 'In reality there is neither form nor seer ..., neither thought nor thinker. There is neither meditator, nor whatso'ever to meditate ...'[18].

The evocation (*sādhana*) of Tārā: an example of a visualisation (*Fig. 1*)[19].

'(1) Hommage to Tārā.

(2) Having made a prostration to the Goddess Tārā, the Great Lady, the Mother of the Buddhas, the Immaculate Lady, for the benefit of the virtuous ones, I will describe here the realization of that Goddess out of my affection for her and in appropriate words, on command of my gurus.' (...)

'(4) To begin with, the *yogin* should, after getting up at dawn, wash his face, feet and so on, and relieve himself. Then he should sit in a comfortable position on a piece of land, where nobody is around, which suits his mind, which smells good and which has nicely smelling flowers scattered upon it. Then he should imagine in his own heart a circle of white rays, emanated from his first sound, with in the middle thereof a beautiful blue lotus, with in the stalk thereof a full moon disk, and he should visualize the yellow syllable *Tām* upon that full moon disk.'
(...) 'appearing from that yellow syllable *Tām* all the worlds in the ten directions are visible through oceans of light, which remove the darkness which obscurates the world,'
(...) and reveal in the sky the end- and numberless Buddhas and Bodhisattvas, (...)
'having sacrifized to those compassionate Buddhas and Bodhisavattes,'
(...) he should confess his sins,
(...) with the appropriate formula: "Every sin I have committed in the cycle of rebirth that has existed since beginningless times, physically or even mentally, that I had committed, am committing or that I take pleasure in, I all confess."
Then the *yogin* should rejoice in virtue, having made a vow not to commit any sin again, by saying: "I rejoice in all the good works, which have been done, are being done and will be done by the Victorious Ones, the Enlighted Ones, who teach (the Buddhas), the Enlighted Ones, who do no teach (the Pratyekuddhas) and the Disciples, who only listen (*śrāvakas*), as well as their spiritual Sons, the Buddhas-to-be (Bodhisattvas), with their gods and their pure worlds."

(8) Then he takes Refuge to the Triple Gem with the formula:
"To the Enlightened One I take refuge until the moment of my own En-
lightenment.
To the Doctine I take refuge until (...)
To the Congregation I take refuge until (...)"

(9) Then he should make a Petition to the *Tathāgatas* (Buddhas) with
the words: "May the Reverend Ones, the *Tathāgatas*, as well as the
Buddhas-to-be, who assist the world as long as the cycle of rebirth
exists, remain in the cycle of rebirth in order to make me attain
nirvāna."

(10) Then the *yogin* should pronounce the Request (*yācanā*), with the
words: "May the Reverend Tathāgatas deliver such an excellent lecture
on the Doctrine, that the beings, who still wander about in the cycle of
rebirth, will be freed from the bondage of phenomenal existence." ...

(11) Immediately thereupon the *yogin* should dedicate the merit resulting from his ritual so far, with the words: "I dedicate all the resulting
potential merit, produced by my excellent sacrifice and my confession to
Supreme Enlightenment." ...

(12) Then the *yogin* should realize-in-his-meditation the four pure
states of mind (*brahmavihāra*) consisting of the concepts of friendliness, compassion, sympathetic joy and equanimity, pronouncing aloud
these virtues one after the other.
a. Question: What is this friendliness?
Answer: It is characterized by loving every being as if it were one's
only son, or to put it in other words: it is characterized by a comportment which leads to wellbeing and happiness.
b. Question: Then, what kind of compassion is meant?
Answer: It is the desire to remove sorrow and the cause of sorrow; it
is the intention or compassion, which is formulated by the words: "I
will save the creatures who have entered the iron house of the cycle of
rebirth, which is set on fire by the storm of suffering, caused by the
three roots of suffering (*i.e.* desire, hatred and delusion)." Or, in
other words: it is the wish to save the beings, who are suffering
because of the three roots of suffering, from the ocean of the cycle of
rebirth.

c. Question: What is sympathetic joy?

Answer: Sympathetic joy (*mudita*) is pleasure, or: sympathetic joy is the intention, which is formulated by the words: "All beings, who are wandering about in the cycle of rebirth, have to be established by me in Buddhahood, which has no real location, as well as in the means to attain it." And, moreover, it is the mentality, which directs itself on the enjoyment ... of good deeds (of others).

d. Question: What is equanimity?

Answer: Equanimity (*upeksa*) is a most useful conduct with regard to the creatures, who are either useful or useless, for the one who has removed the bondage that is connected with resentment. Equanimity means living according to the Law to help others, without being bothered by the shortcomings of affection or a comportment which is guided by one's own taste. Or, in other words, equanimity means to be indifferent towards praise or blame, which rank high among the eight mundane qualities, viz. gain and loss, fame and scandal, praise and blame, happiness and sorrow, and so on.

(13) Immediately after the realization-in-meditation of the four pure states the *yogin* should realize the fact that all elements are pure by nature. He should then bless the purity by nature of the elements with *the following mantra*: "Om svabhāvaśuddhāh sarvadharmāh; svabhāvaśuddho' ham" (Om. All elements are pure by nature; I too am pure by nature.)

Objection: If all the elements of existence are pure by nature, why does the cycle of rebirth continue to turn?

Reaction: It continues to turn because mundane thought is clouded by errors like the thinking in terms of object and subject. The realization-in-meditation of the true Way is the means to erase those errors of thought. The cycle of rebirth may be stopped through this realization. Thus it has been established, that all elements are pure by nature.

(14) Having realized the fact that all elements are pure by nature, the *yogin* should realize the fact that all elements are empty (*sarvadharma-śunyatā*). Emptiness here means: the *yogin* should imagine that the variety of elements, mobile or immobile, is in principle nothing else than the empty sky of nun-duality of his own mind; than the projection of all discursive thinking in terms of object, subject and so on. He should

bless this emptiness with the mantra: "Om śunyatājñanavajrasva-
bhāvātmako'ham". (*Om.* In essence I have the adamantine nature of the
knowledge of emptiness).

(15) Thereupon he should visualize the goddess Tārā from the yellow
syllable *Tam,* (...) the Reverend Lady, the Noble Tārā, with the
deepest green complexion, two arms, a smiling face, (...) adorned with
jewelry (...) with hundreds of lovely garlands, (...) she sits in a
cycle of white rays, on a white lotus, (...) The *yogin* may visualize
the Reverend Lady in this form as long as he wishes.

(16) Thereupon, (...)the Reverend Lady, perfect since beginningless
time, should also be invited from the sky in the form of the
"knowledge-being" (*jñānasattva*) (...)

(18) Having sacrificed and praised her again and again, the *yogin*
should show various signs of hands (*mudrās*) (...)

(19) Having pleased the Reverend Lady in the form of the knowledge-
being with these signs of the hands, the *yogin* should then visualize
the *mantra* of the Reverend Lady in the form of the symbolic being
(*samaya-sattva*). Thus he should present the identity of both forms of
the Goddess.

(20) Thereupon all the Tārā-divinities come forth from the yellow syllable *Tam,* (...) They remove the sorrows of the beings who live there,
like poverty and so on, (...); they satisfy them with the ambrosia of
the teaching of the Doctrine of non-substantiality.

(21) When they have brought all sorts of good to the world, again and
again, and have established various forms of the Goddess Tārā, they
are withdrawn into the yellow syllable *Tam*. Thus one should realize-in-
meditation the Goddess Tārā by means of the process of creation and
absorption of the image as long as the separation that exists between
oneself and Her has not been overcome.

(22) When one breaks away from one's visualization one should recite
the appropriate *mantra*. In this case it is the *mantra:* "Om Tārā tuttāre
ture svāhā" (...) It is said that the *yogin*, when he has risen from his

trance and has seen the world in the form of Tārā, may live as he pleases, because of his identification with the Reverend Lady. Usually the eigth great supernatural powers fall down before the feet of the one who realizes-in-meditation according to this method the Reverend Lady. Then what to say about the other supernatural powers? (...) Even Buddhahood, which is the most difficult to attain, will be in the palm of one's hand. This finishes the slightly elaborated realization of the Goddess Tārā.

Dedication:

May people, through the excellent, immaculate and vast merit I gained in the realization of the godhead, quickly reach the city of the Buddhas, O Tārā, knower of the three worlds, now that I have performed your excellent visualization.

May the world, through the benefit, which has been gained by describing this slightly elaborated visualization of Tārā, reach the city of peace. This is a work of the reverend scholar-elder Anupamaraksita. (Kimcitvi- stara-tārasādhana of the Sādhanāmala.)

NOTES

1   See J. Bronkhorst, *The Two Traditions of Meditation in Ancient India*, Stuttgart 1986.

2   *Amitayurdhyanasutra, in Buddhist Mahāyāna Texts*, tr. by E.B. Cowell, F. Max Müller and J. Takakusu, SBE XLIX, Delhi 1968. Cf. also the visualization-meditations described in the Bhadrapalasutra, which had already been translated into Chinese in 179 A.D., see L. Schmithausen, 'Spirituelle Praxis und philosophische Theorie in Buddhismus', in *Zeitschrift für Missionswissenschaft und Religionswissenschaft*, 3, 1973, pp. 161-187.

3   Cf. Ria Kloppenborg, 'Ascetic Movements in the History of Theravada Buddhism', in *The Young Buddhist*, Singapore 1981, pp. 95-103; and Ria Kloppenborg, *The Buddha's Redefinition of Tapas* (in press).

4   See *e.g.* Catusparisatsutra III, ch. 24, where the Buddha uses miracles to convert a Brahmin teacher, see Ria Kloppenborg, *The Sutra on the Foundation of the Buddhist Order (Catusparisatsutra)*, Leiden 1973, pp. 50-68.

5   See E. Lamotte, *Histoire du Bouddhisme Indien*, Louvain 1976, pp. 34-5.

6   See D.L. Snellgrove, *Buddhist Himalaya*, Oxford 1957, pp. 59-60.

7   A. Bareau, *Die Religionen Indiens* III, Stuttgart 1964.

8   D. Schlingloff, *Ein Buddhistisches Yogalahrbuch*, Berlin 1964.

9   L. Schmithausen, *o.c.*

10 See *e.g.* Samdhinirmocanasutra, ch. VIII, 7 (p. 91, 3), (translation p. 211-2: Vijñaptimatra), ed. and tr. by E. Lamotte,

Louvain-Paris 1935, which dates from the third century A.D., and Schmithausen, o.c., pp. 167-169.

11 Cf. Schlingloff, o.c., p. 41-2, and cp. Bodhicaryāvatāra, Ch. II, ed. P.L. Vaidya, Darbhanga 1960; tr. Ria Kloppenborg, Śantideva. De Weg tot het Inzicht, Amsterdam 1980.

12 Apart from this method, others are described, cf. F.D. Lessing-A. Wayman, Introduction to the Buddhist Tantric Systems, Delhi ²1978, pp. 159 ff.; 175 ff.

13 Cf. Lessing-Wayman, o.c., n. 17 (pp. 162-4), quoting the Sṅags rim chen mo (388a-3, 4): 'The samaya-sattva is the body of the deity graced with face and hands, actually the manifestation of one's own mind, a transfiguration of ordinary ego'.

14 See D.L. Snellgrove, The Hevajra Tantra, I, London 1959.

15 Cf. Lessing-Wayman, o.c., n. 17 (pp. 162-4), quoting the Tantrar- thavatara-vyakhyana: 'The being born from knowledge is the corporeal manifestation of the Lord and retinue arisen from the higher comprehension (adhigama) of the pure Mind of Enlighten-ment'.

16 G. Tucci, The Theory and Practice of the Mandala, London ²1969, p. 96.

17 G. Tucci-W. Heissig, Die Religionen Tibets und der Mongolei, Stuttgart 1970, p. 110.

18 D.L. Snellgrove, The Hevajra Tantra I, London 1959.

19 Sādhanamāla, ed. B. Bhattacharya, 2 vols, Baroda 1925-1928.

Fig. 1

WHO WAS FIRST: THE FOX OR THE LADY?
THE GOD OF FUSHIMI IN KYŌTO

Jacques H. Kamstra

The subject 'effigies dei' or the image of god evokes in several religions sometimes complete opposite attitudes. Some gods seem to forbid to pay any reverence to their images, others, however, just seem to promote the carving of images. So in Judaism and Christianity it is God himself who created man in his own image, but does not allow him to erect images in his honor. In Japan, however, we can observe the opposite. There it seems that gods are not far enough developed yet to have images of their own. This is also stressed by Carmen Blacker who writes: 'The belief that the *kami* have any permanent or 'true' form which they can manifest to human senses is, however, late and derivative from Buddhist iconography. In the early cult a *kami* had no shape of his own, his occasional visionary appearances being temporary disguises only' (Blacker: 38). On the other hand gods are believed to exist only if they become visible in their symbols: the *shintai*, which means the divine body. *Shintai* is a material and visible symbol in which the god is believed to be present. Those *shintai* are: the mirror of Amaterasu, rocks, stones and even whole mountains for many other gods (See Herbert: 192). If a god fails to have a *shintai* of his own, he might be useless and might not exist any more. So the absence of the Christian God in a material and visible *shintai* is an important tool in the Sokagakkai's refutation of the Christian concept of God[1].

In this paper I will discuss this general problem in Japan's history of religion only as far as it appears in a specific cult aimed at a specific god: Inari, goddess of rice, wealth and luck. This divinity very often is visualised as a fox. In Japan the belief in this deity is very popular. In a recent folder of the Fushimo Inari shrine of Kyōto the number of Inari shrines all over Japan is estimated at 32.000. Inari seems to meet the needs of Japan's modern society. M. Czaya points out: 'At present, of course, the daily needs of the people are vastly more complicated than they were in prehistoric times and so the Japanese have systematically expanded the attributes of Inari-sama. In doing so, they have given this deity the power to grant them all kinds of boons unknown to their ancestors: success in business, passing examinations, winning lawsuits, safety on the highways, amassing wealth - good fortune in all its modern contexts and connotations' (Czaya: 262 f.). The variety of purposes of the Inari faithful is also feasable in many types of shrines. The Fushimi Inari shrines of Kyōto are of nation-wide importance: they are large in size and are surrounded by 350 acres of own forests and land. Being the first Inari shrines to be erected in Japan, they named and framed all the other Inari shrines of the country. Other shrines cover an area of a few square meters only. Thousands of those shrines border the streets of villages and cities. Sometimes their reddish features embellish the roofs of department stores or other public buildings. Many Japanese keep tiny Inari shrines in their houses. Typical for all these different types of Inari shrines are the large numbers of red *torii*, Shinto wooden archways, small or large, in a long row in front of the shrine. On the slopes and hills of the Fushimi Inari shrines of Kyōto there are about 10.000 *torii* of all sizes. Being red these distinctive marks of Shintoist architecture point at the five Taoist *hsing* and their deeper implications[2]. Sometimes very tiny *torii* are employed as offerings to Inari. Behind the row of *torii* on both sides of the shrine two statues of white foxes are erected. Every visitor of this shrine will agree with the description of Casal: The foxes 'of whitish stone if large, or formed of white porcelain when small, sit on their haunches, with erected bushy tail which end in a "jewel"; the right one, hold in their teeth a longish cylindrical object, the left one, hold in their teeth or in their jaws a key' (Casal: 47). The cylindrical object is a phallic symbol. This applies also to the key, which is believed to unlock by divine power the godowns and granaries of rice and wealth. Casal explains: 'Since rice, in Japan, as corn with the Europeans, represents the country's wealth, the Inari foxes also procure cash and other property. Their, or their master's shrines are just popular with all classes of people but especially with the traders, geisha, and other "materialistic persons", who generally have a tiny Inari shrine in their own home, complete with the pair of foxes, or sometimes even the foxes alone' (Casal: 47)[3].

Every year tens of millions of Japanese throng to these shrines. Therefore it is quite strange that most of the scholars of Japanese religion do not pay any attention to this cult[4]. W. Gundert might explain why this is the case: 'Das religiöse Bild der Tokugawazeit bliebe unvollständig ohne einen Blick auf die halbfrommen Gebräuche und Anschauungen der breiten Masse, die von der um Ruhe besorgten

Regierung als ungefährlicher Zeitvertreib gerne geduldet, von der buddhistischen und schintoistischen Priesterschaft erfinderisch ausgenützt, doch mit höheren religiösen Motiven so wenig zu tun haben, dass sie weder dem Buddhismus noch dem Schintoismus im strengen Sinne zuzuzählen, sondern eben als Vulgärreligion und Aberglaube zu werten sind' (Gundert: 139f.). Here it would be interesting to discuss the presuppositions of Gundert on the 'compartmentalization' of Japanese religion and of 'superstition'. Perhaps M. Czaya cuts the cackle when he writes down: 'The utilization of the power of human sexual activity for the purpose of effecting a greater yield of crops logically leads to concentrating the attributes of all related deities in one divine being. In Japan, this composite divinity - the triad Saruto-hiko, Uzume, and Ugadama - is known as Inari-sama, or simply as Inari. It represents the religious expression of the integration of sex and food, the most vital forces in nature, in the daily lives of the Japanese people' (Czaya: 262). So this cult occupies the focus of the religious life of the ordinary Japanese people, who care more for the daily bread than for some abstract religious ideals (See Kamstra 2: 57). The question which occupies my mind is: how could the image of a female goddess and of her equivalents develop into that of a sacred and white fox? I suppose that the lady was first not the fox. Some scholars contend the opposite: the belief in animal gods should have preceded and grown into that of a female deity[5]. Buchanan states that in East Asia there has been already belief in sacred foxes. Hence this development (Buchanan: 30ff.). In support of my view is for instance Jolanta Tubielewicz who is of the opinion that the use of foxes in the service of Inari is of a later date than the Heian period. It is not even mentioned in the *Sarashina Nikki*[6] which among others describes the pilgrimage to Fushimi Inari (Tubielewicz: 78). This is also confirmed by Volker, who adds that the idea of the fox god by then has been imported from China (Volker: 76). Earlier reports of foxes in Japan's oldest chronicles do not refer to fox gods but just to fox animals as omina of some events to come. These reports, however, have been copied and derived from Chinese sources.

The Inari cult is an immense subject of research, which compels me to set bounds to this paper[7]. So I will confine myself to the Inari cult of the Fushimi Inari shrine of Kyōto, which is believed to be the main shrine and the starting point of the whole cult. But even here I will have to narrow down my focus by confining myself to the relation of the fox with the goddess of food, Uka no Mitama, only. I will not further discuss the other 8 main deities who are enshrined on the Inari mountain nor do I intend to discuss the demoniacal forms of foxes which in Japan coexist with the sacred white foxes of mount Inari. To this end I will:

1. locate the cult in the Fushimi Inari shrine of Kyōto,

2. discuss the nature of Uka no mitama as far as revered on this mountain,

3. discuss some archaeological and anthropological viewpoints concerning this divinity. I will consider the Chinese and Buddhist aspects of Inari on another occasion.

1 The location of the cult in the Fushimi Inari shrines of Kyōto.

The city of Kyōto has been planned and built in a valley which is surrounded on the West, the North and the East by several mountainous ranges, so even today this city is best accessible from the South. A visitor of this beautiful city will be quite surprised to find most of its famous Buddhist temples and Shintoist shrines on the slopes of these mountainous areas. In Japan this is not so strange for here mountains are believed to be quite sacred being the abodes of the gods and the souls of the deceased. The Fushimi Inari shrines are located on one of these sacred mountains, namely to the South-East of the city on the Higashi-yama (i.e. the eastern mountain) and in the old crown estate of Fukakusa. In 711 A.D. here the Hata Irogu built a shrine for 'what becomes rice': *inenari* or Inari. This fact is covered by the *Fudoki*, the local description, of the province to which this area belongs. Lewin translates this as follows: 'Hata no Kimi Irogu, ein ferner Vorfahr der Hata-no-Nakatsue no Imiki hatte Reis aufgehäuft und besasz Reichtum im Überfluss. Als er aus gestampftem Kochreis eine Zielscheibe (zum Bogenschiessen) machte, verwandelte sich diese in einem weissen Vogel, der emporstieg und sich auf einem Berggipfel niederliess. (Dort) wurde er (wieder) zu Reis und wuchs empor. (Inenari "zu Reis geworden") machte man schliesslich zum Schreinnamen' (Lewin: 175). It is quite logical that this mountain while it borders on Yamato's largest rice area became the dwelling place of this deity. It has a quite impressive history. Here I mention a few items only.

Founded in 711 it was for sure one of the first well organized shrines of the country. In 908 other gods became enshrined on the three peaks (mitsu-ga-mine) of mount Inari: Sada hiko no kami, god of the cross-roads and of procreation and (under his additional names) also of the earth and of the ancestors (Herbert: 77f.; Buchanan: 91), and Omiya no me no mikoto (or: Ame nu Uzume), patron deity of singers, dancers, actors, geisha and prostitutes. In 1072 the Inari shrine was one out of 22 shrines to be visited by the emperor. In 1266 six more major deities were added to the three main deities: two deities under the name of Tanaka no ōkami: gods of the paddy, and four deities under the identical name: Shi no ōkami: four great gods[8]. These nine gods together constitute 'the god Inari' and are as 'one' god the object of worship for most of the faithful. So the god Inari became a god for many purposes. In addition to these nine 'main deities' of this mountain there are ten subsidiary gods worshipped at several places on the mountain. Two of these subsidiary shrines are dedicated to 'Byakko', the white fox, and to Chōja, the wealthy man, i.e. Irogu, the Hata who used rice dumplings as a target for his arrows. In 1871 the shrine of the three main deities was raised to the status of *kampei-taisha*, the highest rank among national shrines. As a *kampei-taisha*, 'a government shrine' it received offerings from the Imperial Household (Creemers: 27). In 1938 it was out of more than 110.000 shrines one of the 58 principle shrines of Shinto in the Japanese empire. The main festivals of course are concerned with the sowing and the harvesting of rice and address the combined god Inari, of whom Uka no mitama is the first and the principle goddess and from whom the other gods derive their importance in their relationship to rice.

2 Uka no mitama and the Inari mountain.
In the first reports on the mountain of the Inari shrine in the *Fudoki* only mention is made of the goddess of rice, not of her name. The name Uka no mitama appears in the following report derived from the *Nijunisha Chushiki*, 'Explanation of ceremonies in 22 shrines': 'In the 8th year of the Eni era (908), Fujiwara Tokihira, Prime minister of Kyōto, built three shrines to Inari, the chief deity being the god of food and clothes. Farmers prayed to her for good crops, merchants for profit, artisans for skill; even officials and military men were not without benefits from her. That being the case, in ancient times, even the Emperor and the nobles sitting down to a meal would first take a little rice and place it aside as an offering to the Inari, deity, "Uga-dama" ("Food spirit") before they themselves tasted the food'

(Buchanan: 60). Who is this Uka no mitama? Japan's oldest holy scriptures contain two different reports about the birth of this deity. In the
Kojiki she appears as a daugher of Susa no o ('impetuous male') and
Kamu o ichi hime ('Divine great majesty princess'). She was born 'when
they were hungry'. The Nihonshoki points to the parents of these two
parent deities namely Izanami and Izanagi as her parents (Buchanan:
87). Neither Buchanan nor Czaya (who quotes Buchanan) wonder why
the names of the parents are different. Has this been the case because
the god of the shrine established by a Hata, or a Korean immigrant,
was also a foreign origin and hence 'sine patre et sine matre'? The same
sources report the violent death of this goddess. Her killers, however,
were different gods. The *Kojiki* ascribes her death to Haya susa no o
no mikoto. The *Nihonshoki* mentions the moongod: Tsuki yomi no
mikoto. The violent death of the deity of food is quite characteristic for
this type of gods all over the world. M. Eder refers to Uka no mitama
when he writes: 'Nun ist bekannt, dass die Vorstellung der pflanzlichen
Nahrung aus dem Leichnam einer Göttin, die von einem anderen Wesen
der Urzeit getötet wurde, zum Weltbild von alten Pflanzern gehört'
(Eder: 242f.; Jensen: 204). The uncertainty about the real identity of
her killer might also point at the Korean descent of Uka no mitama. The
more so because in Korea too rice was believed to be sacred. This is
confirmed by M. Eder, who writes: 'In Korea werden Saatreiskörner das
Jahr über in einem Kruge verwahrt und göttlich verehrt, ebenso ist der
Getreideschober etwas Heiliges. Zu der im Reise verehrten Gottheit
stehen Familien- und Gehöftgeister und Kinderschutzgeister in engem
Zusammenhang' (Eder, 1955: 242). The Korean character of the Inari
goddess might also appear in the number of three shrines which have
been established on the three peaks of mount Inari. S. Gorai points out
that in Shinto unlike in other religions the number three is not believed
to be as sacred as the numbers two or five. Korea, however, is different. So the three shrines, dedicated to the three main deities on the
three peaks of mount Inari might point at the Korean *Sam-shin*, which
means: three- or mountain gods. In the Korean province Kyông-sang
Nam-to these sam-shin are narrowly related to the vessel of rice. They
symbolize conception, birth and education respectively. Life of plants
and of human beings alike depend on these three gods (Eder, 1955:
241). That not only the founders, but also the gods of the shrines
established by them were of foreign descent might explain why Uka no
mitama is known by so many names. Ogura Kōchi in his *Kokutai Jingi*

Jiten analyses and identifies several names of Uka no mitama: Toyo-uke no kami (who is also goddess of the Outer Shrine of Ise), Uke-mochi no kami, Ō-miketsu no kami and Waka uka no me no kami. Motoori Norinaga has pointed out that all these names have in common: *(U)-ka* or *ke*, meaning food (Ogura: 1299-1305). The assumption that this goddess could have been foreign must have been incompatible with Shinto nationalism. This might also explain why even the traces of foreign origin: the original Korean names *e.g.*, completely have been wiped out. The more so because this goddess as bestower of human life also has solid roots in (Korean) ancester worship.

3a The archaeology of the Inari mount and Uka no mitama.

In his lines of the Hata B. Lewin is of the opinion that they in their shrines exerted a strong influence on the development of the ancestorcult of the Japanese (Lewin: 171). Nowhere he points at the Inari mountain as such a place of ancestor worship. Now exactly on the three peaks of the Inari mountain quite a few tumuli have been discovered. According to Hayashiya T. we do not know much yet about the tumulus of the first peak, but from the tumulus of the second peak, where also Uka no nitama is enshrined, a copper mirror has been unearthed, and a *magatama*, a curved jewel, from the tumulus of the third peak. The tumuli date back to the fifth and sixth century and are ascribed to persons of great dignity and influence. In fact the largest 'key hole' tumuli of the whole Kyōto area are found in the Fukakusa district, the area of the Inari mountain and of the Hata clan at the same time. So it seems to be beyond any doubt that these tumuli contain the remains of influential members of the Hata clan. This area was during these centuries the stronghold and center of life of this clan. So we can assume that on this mountain there have been ancestor shrines for the Hata. The more so because on the other mountains in the Kyōto area where the Hata constructed shrines and temples no graves or tumuli have been found which point as clearly at the Hata as here is the case (Hayashiya: 162f.). So far no western author has raised the question: what has been the influence of the ancestor cult on the formation of the Inari cult in general and on the identification process of Uka no mitama in particular. It is quite auspicious that the old mounds not only have been discovered as interesting archaeological artefacta, but that they still occupy a special position and function in the huge variety of shrines and cults on the Inari mountain. The addition of hundreds of other tiny shrines to those still extant on the Inari mountain must have been due to its tumuli and mounds. It was believed that the ancestors could escape their abodes through small holes in the tumuli. So S. Gorai points at the Inari-chronicle of 1332, written by some Seikei, which mentions 49 'kami ana', *i.e.* holes of gods in the mountain (Gorai: 145). Special attention was paid to these holes by turning them into *sengu*, *i.e.* little shrines, adorned with special tiny red *torii* and two white fox messengers. Later on even artificial small mounds were made: the *tsuka*. A modern folder of the Inari mountain estimates the number of *tsuka* on this mountain at more than 20.000. Very often these *tsuka* consist only in boulders and large stones. Many chronicles report that these stones had been bestowed on the deities of the mountain by emperors and high officials.

Here we might encounter one of the principle reasons why on this mountain the cult of the fox became popular. S. Gorai points out that in areas of many tumuli foxes do appear frequently: like ancestor gods they are also capable of appearing and disappearing in holes. As to this they have much in common with the spirits of the dead who can fly away out of their mounds through several holes. So these spirits could become identified with foxes. It is quite questionable, however, whether the Hata clan already paid homage to their ancestor gods in the shape of foxes. Otherwise this cult of foxes also would have been recorded in the many chronicles prior to the eleventh century[9]. So I am inclined to assume that until the eleventh century the gods who were worshipped at the Inari mountain have been ancestor gods and gods of food at once. They were much alike the Sam-shin of Korea. M. Eder: 'Allgemein kann man sagen, dass man sich bei Erntefeiern an die Ahnenseelen oder an die Schutzgötter des Gehöftes und des Hausherren wendet' (Eder, 1955: 241). These gods still did not have shapes of their own. In their vagueness their names and characters still were interchangeable. The first text which considers divine beings in the shape of foxes is the *Ō-u-ki* of 1031.

The fox replaces the lady: Uka no mitama in anthropological vieuw point.

Some Japanese authors repeatedly explain the metamorphosis of Uka no mitama into a fox by stressing the etymological relationship of Miketsu no kami, one of the mythological beings identified with Uka no mitama, with the Japanese word for fox. Mi (=honorificum) Ke (=food) tsu

(=connective word) no(of) kami(god) can also be read as: Mi (three) ketsu (=fox or foxes) no kami. Later on Mi-ketsu was changed into Ō-ketsu, respectful food, or Ō-kitsu: large fox, and the expression hime no mikoto: divine princess, was added to these words. Thus a neutral and impersonal god: food was turned into a divine and female fox-god. I do not believe that the Japanese of those days were so simply minded as to rely only on an etymological mistake which should have made them seeing in a god of food a sacred and large fox. Some more arguments are needed in order to explain this transition. The statement of S. Gorai that the animal fox does not produce the Inari fox is quite logical. Gorai finds it quite typical that in Japan specific animals are ascribed to specific mountains: the monkey *e.g.* to the Hiei mountain and the wild boar to the Aizen mountain, both of Kyoto (Gorai: 144). The fox can be ascribed to the Inari mountain. That this happened is also due to a special relation of animals to food. M. Eder points out why different animals are needed for food: for rice has to be brought from heaven to earth: 'Wie in Indonesien und anderswo neben der altpflanzerischen Erklärung für die Herkunft der Körnerfrüchte, nämlich Diebstahl vom Himmel durch ein listiges, Prometheus-ähnliches Wesen, einhergeht, so finden wir auch in Japan diese Zwiefalt in den Herkunftsagen: einerseits stammt hier der Reis zusammen mit anderen Feldfrüchten aus dem Leichnam der getöteten Nährungsgöttin, andererseits wurde er von fabelhaften Wesen durch Diebstahl aus dem Ausland ins Land gebracht. Als Volbringer dieses Diebstahls werden angegeben der Ackerbaugott (wobei kein Zusammenhang mit heute als Ackerbaugottheiten verehrten Wesen erkennbar ist), der Fuchs (steht heute mit einer Fruchtbarkeitsgottheit als deren Bote in enger Verbindung, wird sogar mit ihr identifiziert), dann die Wildgans. Der Gedanke dass der Reis aus dem Himmel stammt, klingt auch in der japanischen Mythologie an, nämlich in den Worten, die die Sonnengöttin Amaterasu zum Vater des Ninigi, des Ahnen des Kaiserhauses, sagt: 'Auch die Reisähren des reinen Hofes, welche ich im hohen Himmelsgefilde geniesse, will ich meinem Kinde zum Genuss übergeben' (Eder, 1955: 243). It is quite interesting that a trickster fox is needed to guarantee food for mankind. As a prometheusian animal he carries the rice from abroad or from heaven without producing it. Thus he is a rather questionable messenger of the goddess of rice. As her messenger he does not stand alone. In Japan's mythology quite a few animals appear as messengers of gods. So white birds guided the armies of emperor Jimmu and of other emperors against the enemies of the nation. Well known are the deer of the Kasugai shrine, the lobsters of the Matsu no o gods and the monkeys of the Hiĕ shrine (Herbert: 169) under the leadership of prince monkey paddy. Earlier I pointed at other sacred animals as turtles, birds, fire- and dragonflies as messengers of eternal life (Kamstra, 1: 1986, 55f.). But none of these animals are so versatile as the trickster foxes, who cheat the goddess of food by stealing rice and fool human beings in many disguises. They bridge many gaps in human life: not only the need of food and of other commodities but even much deeper. The trickster connects and mediates between life and death, past and future, nature and culture, it reveals not only the clash of different cultures but also of several classes. In this picture of the trickster as characterized *i.a.* by Lévi-Strauss (248) and more recently by Robert D. Pelton, the Inari fox fits in perfectly: it revives dead people and keeps living human beings alive, it cheats men but also gods, it laughs at the difference between the profane and the sacred, sexuality and frigidity. By doing so it continuously transgresses the boundaries set to gods, men and animals[10]. Thus they can appear as real 'Heilbringer', be it of salvation in the terms of common men: daily rice and well being, as the carriers of curse and doom[11], as demoniacal beings, or even of the absolute. This development took place after the eleventh century, *i.e.* after Japan became acquainted with the Chinese belief in foxes endowed with such versatile qualities.

In Japan the first book to mention this kind of a fox is the *Genji Monogatari* (finished in 1004) be it as a fooler or deceiver of men[12]. It describes the metamorphosis (*henge*) of a fox into a beautiful girl (De Visser: 24). This story has been followed by many legends and anecdotes of this type[13]. There is no doubt that these stories have been influenced by and originated in Chinese beliefs. Especially during the T'ang period (713-905) some specimens of fox belief became fully prosperous. So in the *Yŭ Pao tales* 'foxes were believed to change themselves especially into charming ladies, with the object of tempting men to sexual intercourse' (De Groot, V: 582ff.). De Groot remarks: 'The belief in bewitching were-vixens, or, as we find them generally denoted in the books, *hu mei*, "vulpine enchantresses" was especially prominent during the T'ang dynasty' (De Groot, V: 587). The Inari fox, however, has nothing in common with this treacherous fox and animal of darkness (belonging to the principle of *yin*, which explains why they take the shape of women to seduce men (De Visser: 10), though they are thought to be able to transform themselves into men and the most harmful foxes even into Buddhist monks). With the holes of the mounds of the Inari mountain in mind it is worth while to note that in China too foxes by no means could become transformed into men without the use of human skulls and bones. Here the Chinese belief in foxes fits precisely to the holes of the tumuli of the Fushimi Inari mountain tops. This is confirmed by De Groot: 'The fact, that foxes habitually live in old caved-in graves explains why anthropomorphosis is connected particularly in China with these animals. In those haunts, Reynard borrows the human form from the buried corpse by bringing himself in close contact with it, thus instilling into himself the soul-substance contained in those remains' (De Groot, IV: 192). So in China and in Japan the ancestors are thought to be able to damage or to favour their descendants by means of the foxes, their messengers. They might damage their own flesh and blood by means of their own bones and skulls, which became alive in this special type of foxes, for, as we know, 'Reynard as a beast is not ferocious or dangerous' (De Groot, II: 195).

Many other qualities of the Inari foxes are depicted in Chinese literature. Casal quotes the *Shuo-wen encyclopedia* which describes the goblin fox 'as the courses upon which ghostly beings ride', so he could become the mount of Uka no mitama. In the *Li-wei-tsu* he is depicted as one of the four gods of wealth together with the snake, the hedgehog and the weasel (Casal: 2n.). This might lead into the apotheosis of the Inari fox into the 'Lord of the animals', the 'Herr der Tiere' and under Tantristic influence into the bodhisattva lord fox, identical with Buddha Vairocana. Longevity is an attribute of the goblin foxes due to their way of living in holes and rock caverns, despoiled of air and sunlight. In his translation of the *Hüen chung ki* De Groot points out that this quality increases along with the age of the fox spirit: 'When the fox is fifty years old, it can transform itself into a woman; when a hundred years old it becomes a beautiful female, or a *wu* (Chin.: shaman) possessed by a spirit (shen), or a grown-up man who has sexual intercourse with women. Such beings are able to know things - occurring at more than a thousand miles distance... And when a fox is a thousand years old, it penetrates to heaven and becomes a t'ien-hu, a celestial fox' (De Groot, V*;, 586f.). And here we return to the trickster fox. In the Inari foxes the belief in trickster foxes and Chinese goblin foxes became intertwined.

Until now I still left the question unanswered why Uka no mitama or her messenger the fox is believed to be female. M. Eder might explain this: 'Häufig ist der Reisgeist ein weibliches Wesen, das in das Frauengemach gebracht wird. Nur Frauen füllen die Reissaatsäcke und nähen sie zu, pflanzen die Setzlinge' (Eder, 1955: 242). In Japan and in China it is generally believed that foxes can transform themselves into beautiful women. Hence they are named: tōme: bitch-fox, vixen. This argument of Eder, which will be confirmed by everyone who observes quite closely rice cultivation on Japan's countryside, is strengthened by the activities of female shamans, who are quite conspicuous at the Fushimi Inari shrines. They have to free people from the terror of black (demoniacal) foxes. They also take care of people's welfare by practicing every night austerities under the waterfalls of Fushimi Inari or by dancing *kagura* (= sacred dances). Even at Fushimi Inari they still keep alive one of the most ancient forms of Japanese religion: they are remainders of pre-Buddhist times when women occupied a prominent place in Japanese religion.

So far there are so many elements in the Inari cult which point at China: the founders, the belief in foxes and in their qualities. There still are some rituals which stress this fact. Against the opinion of Origuchi Shinobu, who relates Inari to the complex of *marebito*, the supernatural guests who at regular times would arrive at the shores of our world in boats from Tokoyo, the miraculous land across the sea (Blacker: 72ff.), S. Gorai points at the fact that rice too has to be brought to Japan from abroad. For that reason at set times, on the top of the Inari mountain *saitogoma*, fire rituals[14] are held in honor of the divinity coming across the sea. It goes without saying that Uka no mitama also takes care of seafood. The country where the *daimyōjin*[15], the great and famous god, 'regularly' is coming from is China. This is established in the *Inari-ki*, the Inari chronicles, of 1332 (Gorai: 139ff.). So the divinity of food flies across the sky from China to Japan. How is she flying? On the back of a fox, as a fox, or, all by herself? Because the goddess has no shape of her own, she could take the shape of a man, a woman, a child, or even an animal (Gorai: 138). The shape she finally is believed to adopt depends on many beliefs which came across the sea to Japan so SHE TURNS INTO A FOX.

NOTES

1   So Ikeola Daisaku: 191.
2   In the *torii* only two colours out of five remain: black at the base and red as colour of the vertical and horizontal beams of the *torii*. The colour red is considered to be the best preventive of evil. The deeper meaning of the five *hsing* becomes apparent in the following scheme:

organ	virtue		element	direction
liver	love	wood		east
lungs	righteousness	metal	west	
eart	propriety		fire	south
kidneys	wisdom		water	north
spleen	good faith	earth		center

colour	sacred animal	season
green	dragon	spring
white	tiger	autumn
red	sparrow	summer
black	turtle	winter
yellow	general	

The Japanese idea of the *torii* might have been derived from Korea, where similar ideas exist. Here the four sacred animals are replaced by four generals of the sky. In case the general in the center is replaced by the sacred fox, the fox will take the highest rank under its fellow sacred animals and become: 'Herr der Tiere'. I do not know, however, whether this idea which is quite fundamental for the *torii*, was also at work in the development of the fox cult of the Inari mountain. The *torii* itself also seems to be derived from China or from Korea, where the 'Red Arrow Gateway' also marked the entrance to Confucian temples and to imperial tombs. For the five *hsing* see: Toyakawa: 552f.; Buchanan: 105; Fung Yu-lan: 41f. For the origin of the *torii* see Shimonaka 2: 36ff.; Casal: 46 n. 55 (for the relation with Shinto and Amaterasu).
3   See also Volker: 77.
4   No mention whatsoever is made of it in Hori, 1968, 1985; M. Anesaki, 1969; Byron Earhart, 1974 and many others.
5   So Czaya: 256 and Buchanan: 7ff.
6   The diary of Sarashina. Sarashina is told to be a daugher of Sugawara no Takasuya, who is believed to be a descendant in the sixth generation of the famous cultural hero Sugawara no Michizana. She lived under emperor Go Rei-zei (1046-1068). See Aston: 118.
7   So even the monumental work edited by Gorai of almost 1000 pages does not yet cover all the aspects of the Inari cult.
8   For more details about these gods see Buchanan: 85-102.
9   See for some of these chronicles: Buchanan: 59-63.
10 Concerning the role of the trickster-'Heilbringer' fox we are still in need of a thorough comparative study. So it would be interesting to compare the role of the foxes and badgers in Japan with the roles of foxes in other parts of the world. For Africa see Griaule and Dieterlen, 1965. See also Baart: 265-278.
11 For the meaning of this type of salvation see Kamstra 1986, 2: 57.
12 See Casal: I; De Visser: 20ff. mentions some legends from the 8th, 9th, and the 10th centuries, namely the *Ryoiki*, the *Fuso Ryakki* and the *Mizu Kagami*. The *Ryoiki* (about 822) reports Chinese legends only, the *Fuso Ryakki* and the *Mizu Kagami* are of much

later dates, namely 1094-1169, and the second half of the 12th
century respectively.

13 Many of these stories are covered by De Visser and Buchanan. See
    De Visser; Buchanan: 39-58.

14 Nowadays *saitogoma* is an ascetic practice of Japan's mountain
    ascetics: the yamabushi. By walking through the hot ashes of a
    huge bonfire they try to get rid of all kinds of spiritual defile-
    ments. See the description of Blacker: 250ff.

15 See Eder, 1935: 331: 'Ausser der Unterscheidung von Schreinen
    mit "grösseren" oder "kleineren" Göttern gab es Schreine, deren
    Götter den auszeichnenden Namen *myojin* ("berühmte Götter")
    verliehen bekamen. Das waren Götter, denen der Volksglauben
    besondere Kraft und Bedeutung zuerkannte. Sie zeichneten sich
    durch Erhörung von Bittgebeten besonders aus. Dem wurde
    Rechnung getragen, als die Schreine von der Regierung in ein
    System gebracht wurden. Dabei erhielten eine Anzahl von
    Lokalgöttern amtlicherseits besondere Anerkennung. Es wurden 285
    Götter als *myojin* registriert'; *daimyojin* points at the excellent
    place of Inari under the *myojin*.

USED LITERATURE

Anesaki M.
1969
 History of Japanese Religion
  Tokyo

Aston W.G.
1972
 Nihongi;
  Tokyo

Baart W.J.H.
1982
 'De trickster opnieuw bezien' in *N.T.T.*,
 p.265-278;

Blacker C.
1975
 The Catalpa Bow;
  London

Buchanan D.C.
1935
 'Inari: its origin, development, and
 nature',in: *The transactions of the Asiatic
 society of Japan*, second series, vol. XII,
 p.1-102

Casal U.A.
1959
 'The goblin fox and badger and other witch
 animals of Japan' in *Folklore Studies*, 18, 1-94

Creemers W.H.M.
1968
 Shrine Shinto after World War II
  Leiden

Czaja M.
1974
 Gods of myth and stone
  New York

Earhart H.B.
1974
 Japanese Religion: Unity and Diversity
  Encino, Cal. U.S.A.

Eder M.
1955
 'Die Reisseele in Japan und Korea', in
 Folklore Studies, 14:215-244

1978
 Geschichte der japanischen Religion, 1 Band
  Nagoya

Fung Yu-lan
1953
 A History of Chinese Philosophy
  Leiden

Gorai S.
1985
 'Inari shinko to Bukkyo' in: S. Gorai ed.
 Inari shinko no kenkyu, 75-150.
  Tokyo

Griaule M., Dieterlen G. *Le renard pâle*
1965
  Paris

de Groot J.J.M.
1976
 The Religious System of China, vol.II, IV, V
  Taipei

Gundert W.
1935
 Japanische Religionsgeschichte
  Tokyo

Hayashiya T.
 Momoyama

1976   Kyoto
Herbert J.   *Aux sources du Japan Le Shinto*
1964   Paris
Hori I.   *Folk Religion of Japan*
1968   Chicago
                              Waga kuni minkan shukyo no kenkyu, 2 vol.
1985   Tokyo

Ikeda D.   *Shakubuku Kyoten*
1969   Tokyo
Jensen A.E.   *Mythos und Kult bei Naturvölkern*
1951   Wiesbaden
Kamstra J.H. 1:   'Unidentifiable Buddhas and Bodhisattvas
1986   of1986the Asuka period (592-697)' in: *Visible
                              Religion*, 4-5:50-62

1986   2:   *Een moeilijke keuze: de godsdienst van gewone
                              mensen*
                              Bolsward
Lévi-Strauss C.   *Anthropologie structurale*
1958   Paris
Lewin B.   *Aya und Hata*
1962   Wiesbaden
Ogura K.   *Kokutai Jingi jiten*
1940   Tokyo
Pelton R.D.   *The trickster in West Africa*
1980   Berkeley
Shimonaka Y.   *Shinto Daijiten*, 3 vol.s
1940   Tokyo
Toyakawa R.   'Zenshujiin to Inarishinko' in: S. Gorai ed.:
1985   *Inari shinko no kenkyu*
                              Tokyo
Tubielewicz J.   *Superstitions magic and mantic practices in
1980   Heian period*
                              Warszawa
de Visser M.W.   'The fox and the badger in Japanese
1909   folklore'in: *The transactions of the Asiatic
                              Society of Japan*, vol. 36, part 3
                              Yokohama
Volker T.   *The animal in Far Eastern art*
1950   Leiden

IMAGES IN ISLAM
DISCUSSION OF A PARADOX

Kees Wagtendonk

None of the three monotheistic religions permits images of God. Moreover, the Bible and Islamic tradition explicitly prohibit the making of images of living beings (men or animals) for the purpose of worship. God is incomparable to anything that exists. He is the only One that deserves worship.

But in a way monotheism does have images. The image does not necessarily have to be a graven one to be an 'image'. Naturally, only as long as the godhead is conceived of as a person, one can call up him/her before one's mind. The believer needs to think of God as a person because a god that is totally different cannot be known and cannot be approached[1]. Significant in this respect is an observation by the Muslim theologian Djâhiz (d. 864), who remarked that the Christians were more zealous in their worship of God than others because of their incarnation dogma[2]. Therefore, no matter how transcendent the conception of the deity is, the godhead may at the same time be visualized as a person. In other words, certain ideas form an image. In this sense Islam evidently has images of God though it shuns graven and other palpable images. Though on every page the Koran is aware that God cannot be seen, yet, just like the Bible, it speaks about God in clearly anthropomorphic terms.

It is my aim to review some of the anthropomorphic 'images' of God that can be found in Islam. These images usually are descriptions in books or other writings and they live in the hearts and the minds of the believers. They are not palpable nor are they located in holy places like graven images in temples, and they can therefore not be worshiped as 'Kultbilder'. With the latter, however, they share their 'visibility', at least for the mind's eye and, in many cases, their anthropomorphism. Both kinds of images are expressions of human thinking about the divine. And the conceptions of gods determine statues as much as the statues determine people's ideas about the gods[3]. Both re-present the deity, while on the other hand, the deity never coincides with the statue. The graven image always remains an image and never *is* the deity[4].

We shall discuss anthropomorphic 'images' of God in Koran, Tradition, theology and mysticism. *Visual substitutions* can be found in the mosque and in related Islamic art. Because of the significance of Muhammad for Islam we shall also have a brief look at the way he is portrayed.

The image of God in the Koran.

In the Koran there is a certain tension between two notions concerning God: God is far above what men think, and at the same time men can approach Him. Though the Koran does not mention the Second Commandment, it contains the story of Ibrahim who destroys the man-made idols. Because God is totally different, all visual representation of Him is implicitly condemned. Some 'images' of God, such as the heavenly triad, are rejected. The image of God as a father or as a mother is abhorrent to the Koran (Cf. Sura 112). The Koran carefully avoids all figurative speech on this point as too suggestive. Not only the image of God as father of all people is lacking, also the image of love for mankind is almost absent. Resemblances that are all too human, are avoided.

The idea that God would be tired or would need sleep is expressly denied in the famous throne verse: 'slumber affects Him not, nor sleep', to guard the heavens and the earth 'wearies Him not' (2:255). After the creation God seated Himself on the Throne (7:54), but it is not said that He *rested* on the seventh day as Muslims never fail to comment (as if this were said in Genesis).

Though man was created in a beautiful shape (64:3) and 'in the best of moulds' (95:4), and though he was infused with God's spirit, it is not said that man was created in God's image and after His likeness (Gen. 1:26). There is nothing like Him (42:11), He is the exalted (20:114). He is also the Concealed One, nobody knows His mysteries (*ghaybihi*) (72:26), 'sight reaches Him not' (6:103). God 'taught man what he did not know' only by revelation (96:5). God seems to be far away, the distance to Him is possibly great.

But other verses of the Koran stress Allâh's nearness to man: 'I am indeed close (to them): I listen to the prayer of every suppliant when he calls on Me' (2:186) and 'We are nearer to him than his jugular vein' (50:16).

And though Allâh is incomparable and undescribable the Koran is not lacking in descriptions. Allâh is called 'the light of the heavens and the earth' and His light is compared to 'a lamp in a niche' (24:35). Most prominent are His divine qualities, His all-embracing knowledge, His power and His will. He is the Eternal, the First and the Last, the Sovereign. He is also the Merciful and Compassionate. And He bestows daily sustenance. He wants to guide man to eternal bliss. Man is asked to call upon Allâh by His (99) most beautiful names (7:180). These names, derived from the Koran, describe Allâh's qualities not only in abstract terms like al-Haqq (the Reality), al-`Alî (the Most High), al-Ahad (the One), but also in clearly anthropomorphic terms like al-Samî` (the Hearer), al-Basîr (the Seer), al-Mudjîb (the Answerer). The Koran uses some more anthropomorphic descriptions like God's hands or his seating himself on the throne (7:54). When it is said that the idols have neither hands nor feet, eyes nor ears (7:195) the implication is that Allâh does have all those four parts of the body. Whether we understand this as power or life is irrelevant.

In verses like 'everything perishes but his *face*' (28:88), or 'whichever way you turn, the *face* of Allâh is there' (2:115) the notion of limitation that is implied in anthropomorphism is effaced. But the paradox between the undescribable and the descriptions remains, the same paradox as we find in the Bible.

Anthropomorphisms in Tradition.

In Tradition, when compared to the Koran, some new anthropomorphisms can be found. I shall mention three of them. It is true that, differently from the Old and New Testaments, in the Koran God's weeping 'to see faithless man reject his love (...) would be inconceivable coming from the master of the worlds'[5]. This also holds for Islamic Tradition, but another of the very human emotions - laughing - , said of God, is present in at least thirteen *hadiths*. We read that God laughed about how a poor couple of the Ansâr found a way when they had to put up a Muhâdjir and treat him as a guest, while they had nothing to eat themselves[6]. Another story is of the perseverance-is-rewarded type. It tells us about a man who was saved from hell and led into paradise only because he cried so persistently that in the end God laughed and let him in[7]. This resembles a popular Turkish legend that tells how God laughed when a sinner who was referred to hell, pleaded that according to his knowledge God would refrain from punishing in hell aged Muslims[8].

Another tradition even speaks about God's girth [9]. Tradition is also

acquainted with the praying of God, witness the wellknown eulogy
sallà'llâhu `alayhi wa sallam. Both can also be found in Jewish tradi-
tion[10].

The uninhibited use of (some) anthropomorphisms is strongly resist-
ed by the theologians but sometimes it meets with their understanding.
Rûmî lets the shepherd say to God:

'O Lord (...) where art Thou, that I may serve Thee and
sew Thy shoon and comb Thy hair? That I may wash Thy
clothes and kill Thy lice and bring milk to Thee, O
worshipful One; That I may kiss Thy little hand and rub
Thy little feet and sweep Thy little room at bed-time'.

And when, in Rûmî's story, Moses reproaches him - 'Man, to whom are
you speaking?' -, it is God Himself who reproaches Moses: 'Thou hast
parted My servant from Me'[12].

God's image in Islamic theology.

The paradox of the Koranic imagery has led to different theological
views. The Mu`tazila stressed Allâh's unity. Therefore they considered
qualities like knowledge, will, power, etc. as indistinguishable from His
being. They would rather prefer to say no more than that 'God is'.
This stand was called *tanzîh* (deanthropomorphism). Moreover, the
clearly human qualities of *hearing, sight and speech* were not to be
understood as implying ears, eyes and tongue. *Hands* and *face* were to
be considered as figures of speech. Allâh's hands stand for His power
or bounty. This was called *ta`tîl* (denying of attributes).

The Hanbalites stuck to the verbal meaning of the Koranic terms.
And does the Koran not say: 'Faces that day will beam, looking towards
their Lord' (75:22). This implies the *visio beatifica*. This earned for
them the name of *mudjassimûn* or *mushabbihûn* (anthropomorphists).

For the common people the intellectual abstractions of the Mu`tazila
were not attractive. But al-Ash`arî (d. 935), himself a former
Mu`tazilite, found a compromise. According to the Ash`arite creed *Fiqh
Akbar II* (middle of the tenth century) Allâh has been from eternity
with His qualities and His names. None of His qualities or names has
come into being; from eternity He knows by virtue of his knowledge,
knowledge being an eternal quality, etc. His qualities are different from
those of the creatures. He knows, but not in the way of our knowledge, He hears, but not in the way of our hearing, etc. Allâh is an
entity but without body, without substance, without accidens. He has

no limit. He has hand and face as the Koran says and they belong to His qualities, but they are 'without how' (bilâ kayfa). Allâh will be seen in the Hereafter. The faithful will see Him, being in Paradise, with their bodily eyes, without comparison or modality (bilâ kayfa wa'l-tashbih). And there will be no distance between Him and His creatures[13].

The formula which the Ash'arite mutakallimûn developed as a compromise about God's attributes in its negation resembles the christological definition of Chalcedon. 'Allâh's attributes are eternal, inhere in His essence, are not He and not other than He'[14]. In referring to this very formula in a chapter on the rise of Sufism, Gibb dryly remarked: 'a strong religious sentiment is not likely to be roused - or if it exists, to be moved to enthusiasm - by the orthodox solution of the problem of the Divine Attributes'[15]. A strong personal relation between God and Man can only exist when God is conceived as a person. In the Koran such a conception is found.

Looking at beardless youths.

In Sufi circles, apart from *theologia negativa*, God is seen in human form. The tradition that God created Adam in His image, that can be found in the classical compilations[16], is a favourite in Sufi circles. Its intention, however, is to point to the high position of man, rather than to the human appearance of God.

Here we are concerned with a tradition that is explicitly anthropomorphic. Hellmut Ritter has drawn attention to it in discussing the *nazar ilâ'l-murd*-phenomenon among the Sufis, the looking towards (beardless) youths, the experience of God through the experience of human beauty[17]. According to the *hadith al-ru'ya* Muhammad saw God in a dream or during the *mi'râdj* as a beardless youth. According to one variant Muhammad saw his Lord as a beardless youth with luxuriant hair, in a green robe (or with his feet in green), with golden shoes or amidst a golden tapis. This probably, as Ritter has observed, goes back to Plato's Phaedros which stated that in the beautiful face or form of a young man the beauty of God himself is experienced *as if in an image*[18].

Ritter discerned three types of Sufis in this connection: 1) the anthropomorphists, 2) the ascetics, 3) the pantheists[19]. Under the influence of Ibn 'Arabi's pantheistic monism the first group tended to fuse with the third. It is no accident that the writings of the extreme

anthropomorphists are generally lost and that we have to rely on information from their opponents, orthodox non-Sufis or moderate Sufis. Of
course, the strict `ulamâ' could not tolerate any anthropomorphism that
went further than the Koran.

Ghazâli's comment on this and similar dream-visions is that they are
not real, because *real beauty* has no shape. The same holds true for
the Koranic comparison of God's light to a lamp (24:35) or the tradition
that Adam was created in God's image[20]. Even Ibn Hazm rejects the
literal interpretation of the anthropomorphisms of the Koran. God's
image is to be understood as *God's House*, the Ka`ba. As all houses
belong to God, all images belong to Him. He simply selected one for
Adam[21].

The opponents of the anthropomorphists called them *hulûlis*
('incarnists'), people who, like the Christians, believed in the incarnation of God in a human being. Ibn al-Djawzî (d. 1200) mentions
people who say that one can see with one's own eyes, 'God walking in
the street, one can shake hands with him or touch him ...'[22]. One
doubts the reliability of this information when one compares how Muslims
who visited churches of the Franks during the Crusades claimed that
these contained pictures of 'God as a child' sitting in Mary's lap[23].

Whatever their distorted views, it is a fact that in certain Sufi
circles - up to this century - the practice of *nazar ilâ'l-murd* occurred.
The youth that was the object of the beauty-staring was called
shâhid[24]. The exact intention of the word *shâhid* ((eye)witness) here
fluctuates. One meaning was: *who re-presents God/God's beauty*. Rûmî
and other moderate Sufis objected to calling the youth 'God' and spoke
about 'hypocrisy'[25]. The orthodox Ibn Taymiyya accused the practitioners of *nazar ilâ'l-murd* of sensuality exclaiming , 'God damns the *umma*
that sleeps on those they worship as God'[26]. It seems that (some?)
Sufis have expressed themselves more carefully, trying to avoid scandal, saying that they only contemplated God's creative art in contem-
plating boys, or were only reminded of God's face without any
anthropomorphism[27].

For the ascetics the contemplation of youths was a test in self-con-
trol to suppres sensuality. Djâmî, the Persian poet and mystic (d.
1492), relates how an admirer of a slave who was as beautiful as Yûsuf,
passed a night with him and on discovering his own feelings died rather
than sinned, holding chastity for even more beautiful than the slave[28].

For the pantheists the absolute beauty of God reveals itself in all

earthly things. They are the concretisation of God's attributes. By this
time (13th century) Ibn ʾArabî (d. 1240) taught that all of creation is
the self-revelation of God. God has created the world in order to
admire Himself therein as in a *mirror* and to make love with Himself. He
appears in various concealments. The notion of the mirror is the best
indication of what is meant: the places of His appearance are at the
same time the screens that hide Him.

Man is the most perfect mirror of God, the robe that suits Him best.
But because God appears in *any* beautiful form, and only as if in a
mirror, we can no longer speak of anthropomorphism[29]. We are here in
the sphere of pantheist monism. The entire world is created in His
image and in it God contemplates His own reflection. For Djâmî all the
atoms of the world reflect God as mirrors. And for ʾIrâqî (d. 1287) it
is God's creative Word 'Kun' (be!) which caused that He is in everything (*wayakûn* - 'and it was', cf. Koran 2:117). Also his own heart is
a mirror as much as the face of the *shâhid*.

And here again asceticism appears as ʾIrâqî adds 'Keep your heart
clean, in order that the face appears in its entirety. Offering *dhikr*
with one's tongue for Djâmî is polishing the mirror in order to reflect
God's beauty'[30]. And because God is in love with Himself - Adam is the
mirror in which He looks - man has to free himself of his self so that
God can see Himself. The mirror of the heart has to be polished by
constant asceticism until it can reflect the primordial divine light[31].
Light might indeed be the most appropriate name for God[32]. For man
God in the end remains transcendent. When ʾAttâr's thirty birds
reached Simurgh they found that they were *simurgh* = *thirty birds*, or
'the identity of the soul with the divine essence'[33].

But mysticism is only part of Islam. Until now we have not yet
looked at the Islamic cult and its relation to the image of God. Though
mysticism gives the Islamic cult an extra dimension, the latter should
also be viewed in its own right.

The image or non-image of God in the Islamic cult.
The mosque is an empty space. It is not a temple or a holy place. In
prayer to Allâh the Muslims do not turn to an image but to an empty
niche, the *mihrâb*. The *mihrâb* is indicating the *qibla*, the direction of
prayer, which is the Kaʾba in Mekka. According to a well known tradition the whole earth is *masdjid* (mosque). The Kaʾba is the central
mosque of Islam only as the center of the rites of the Pilgrimage. The

interior of the Ka'ba is empty. Mohammad is reported to have destroyed
the idols that the heathen Arabs kept there.

In the Koran the Ka`ba is called the 'House of God' and it continues
to be called so, but this is only in a figurative sense. Though the
black stone in one of its corners is called 'the hand of God' in a tradition, and pilgrims try to kiss it, `Umar is reported to have already
been sceptical about this.

The emptiness of the mosque goes back to the Islamic interdiction of
making images of living creatures, men and animals alike. The
Old-Testamentary fear that man would worship others apart from God is
also present in the Islamic injunction, as well as the fear that man
might think himself to be God. This happens when he tries to imitate
the Creator.

A *hadith qudsî* makes clear that 'there is no worse wrong-doer than
he who tries to create what I (God) create. If only they could create
an ant or a corn of wheat or barley'[34]. Making images means creating
what is the work of God. The makers of images on the Last Day will be
asked to infuse life into these images and, failing to do this, will be
sent to hell. Houses that contain them will not be visited by the angels.
Muhammad is said to have reproached `A'isha for having curtains with
representations of animals on it.

The law books, in line with the *hadiths*, prohibit images of living
beings (*hayawân*) on walls or curtains, but images on cushions or
carpets (on which one sits or walks) are permitted as are also the
images from which the head is missing or that have holes in their
bodies (*e.g.* Wayang puppets)[35]. The ancient Egyptians also thought
that the person or the animal that is represented by the image was
present in the image, only not if the head was lacking[36].

The Byzantine iconoclasm of the 8th century - the same period as
the above mentioned *hadiths* - might have been of influence on the
Islamic attitude, though there is a difference. The Christian struggle
was directed against *worshiping* images whereas the Muslims went further by prohibiting the *making* of images altogether.

Religious art in the mosque.
The Islamic interdiction had a great influence on religious art. The
consequences for Islamic art in general have not everywhere been the
same, witness Persian miniature painting and Indian Mughal painting.
Saying, that in Persian miniature painting the *intention* of the

interdiction of images is followed because the artists purposely did not use perspective, sounds like a justification after the event[37].

As far as religious art in the mosque is concerned, calligraphy, the arabesque and the geometric ornaments, including the use of colors, can be seen as the positive by-products of the interdiction of images. Like Islam's *Qibla*, the Ka`ba, is decorated by the *kiswa*, the black brocade cover with its splendid golden embroidered Koranic calligraphies, the *qibla*-wall in many mosques, especially the *mihrâb*, and sometimes the whole interior of the mosque contains calligraphed Koranic texts. The *mihrâb* is empty, but through these holy texts that indicate its function as prayer-niche, God Himself is speaking, is *present*. Whether one can read and understand these calligraphed words is irrelevant. It is enough to know that they are God's words.

In simple mosques calligraphies may be absent, but we can often find two medallions at the right and the left over the *mihrâb* containing the names *Allâh* and **Mohammad** respectively. Sometimes a third and bigger one in the middle contains the name *Allâh* again, clearly indicating that the *salât* is for Allâh, not for Muhammad. It serves as a substitute for a Kultbild. In Sufism even one letter, the h - the last letter of the word Allâh and the first letter of *huwa*, 'He', can visualize the divine[38].

God's name - Allâh - , though freely pronounced, when written is so holy that pious Muslims, from fear that the name may be trodden upon, remove any printed paper they find on the surface of the streets. This should be compared to the images of animals that are only allowed on the floor where they are trodden upon. On amulets Allâh's name has a very important apotropaic power.

The Koranic calligraphies play an equally big role as the images of Christ and the saints in churches[39]. They represent God's Word. They are moreover to be recited in prayer and in litanies. In their ornamental function they grant an extra dimension to architecture. 'The decoration (scl. with calligraphy) is added to architecture proper like a rich cloth, which covers the walls of the building. Without this cover Islamic architecture is often reduced to simple and static forms like the cube and the sphere'[40]. That calligraphy in Islam is as old as the interdiction of images is witnessed by the calligraphies on the Dome of the Rock that was built in 691 by Caliph `Abdelmalik. The same caliph replaced the human image on coins by the *shahâda* in 697.

The geometric decoration and the arabesque (stylized vegetal ornament) closely follow the calligraphy as supreme forms of art in Islam. They fill the void that was left by the interdiction of images. Though interwoven with Koranic calligraphy their language is not the language of Revelation, yet their function may transcend the merely ornamental.

Though Ernst Kühnel asserts: 'the arabesque never has any symbolic significance but is merely one ornament from a large stock which includes other vegetal forms'[41] or: 'massgebend ist immer nur die schmuckende Absicht ohne jeden gegenständlichen Gehalt' by the substantiation of these statements he at least claims a negative symbolical meaning. This is apparent from his explanation: 'Die Vorstellung dass die Natur nicht aus sich selber schafft, sondern dass das Wirken des göttlichen Schöpfers sich in allen Vorgängen und Erscheinungen kundtut, dass diese immer nur vorübergehende Bedeutung haben und von vorn herein zum Vergehen bestimmt sind, führt zu der Auffassung, dass es nicht Aufgabe des Künstler sein kann, optisch wahrgenommene oder erlebte Wirklichkeit im Bilde festzuhalten, d.h. vergänglichen, irdischen Formen gleichsam entgegen dem göttlichen Ratschluss Dauer geben zu wollen. Er muss im Gegenteil versuchen, sich von der Natur der Dinge zu entfernen, rein aus der Phantasie seine Eingebungen zu gewinnen'[42]. This 'fantasy' is governed by strict rules. Moreover Kühnel himself also speaks about 'ornamentaler Meditation' and 'Versenkung in die lineare Spekulation mit abstrakter Tendenz'[43]. This approaches a mystic sense.

Titus Burckhardt, denying that the arabesque has a compensatory function stresses that it is rather the very negation of figurative art: 'By transforming a surface into a tissue of colors or into a vibration of light and shadows, the ornament hinders the mind from fixing itself on any particular form saying 'I', as an image says 'I'. The center of an arabesque is everywhere and nowhere, each 'affirmation' is followed by its 'negation' and vice versa'[44].

The geometrical interlacing he mystically understands as the 'Unity in multiplicity and multiplicity in Unity' and for him 'the circle is an evident symbol of the Unity of Being' and 'Islamic art in its perfection can be a *mirror* of God'[45]. The absence of the anthropomorphic means the absence of the subjective element. Architecture and abstract decoration stem from qualitative geometry of pythagoran origin with a harmony and a 'memory of the music of the spheres'. Not individual artistic creation is the aim but the idea of the unity and the immensity of God as reflected in the cosmic order, shaped not according to imagination alone, but also according to inherent laws and qualities[46].

In a similar way Ignaz Maybaum contrasts arabesque and geometrical decoration as well as litany with creative aesthetic religion or illusion that by-passes the one Creator. They do not lure away the eye and the ear from the One God[47]. Positively, they have a supporting function. As witnesses of His unity they direct man's thinking towards God, similarly as the image does.

Images in the non-religious domain and images of Muhammad.
Mughal and miniature painting are well-known examples that show the limits of the interdiction of images. But under fundamentalist influence nowadays Iranian miniature painters, contrary to their own tradition, may paint men and angels without faces[48]. In Saudi Arabia's capital Ryad not long ago one could see road signs for pedestrians on which were depicted human figures without a head[49]. Dolls can still not be brought into the country. Photography and tv on the other hand, by special intercession of king ʿAbd al-ʿAzîz, were introduced rather smoothly. In Holland, those especially, who have recenty converted to Islam may be rather puritanical. One woman, as the author noticed, even removed a picture of a horse from the wall of her sitting-room.

In the central countries of Islam, in pre-modern times, sculptural representations of man are totally lacking. But animal sculptures some-times do occur (*e.g.* watch lions)[50]. In modern times portraits of the dead can be found in many Islamic graveyards even in fundamentalist Iran.

In one respect the Islamic interdiction of images is still generally honored, even outside the mosque. Though other prophets are normally portrayed on religious prints (*e.g.* Ibrâhîm slaughtering Ismâʿil) Muhammad is not, and in miniatures where he does appear, his face is provided with a veil[51]. How strictly orthodox Muslims stick to this is shown by the difficulties that were encountered by Mustafâ al-ʿAqqâd when, in 1976, he brought out a film about the life of Muhammad. Though Muhammad, the principal character, was completely absent from the film, as were his voice, and also his wives, daughters and sons-in-law, religious objections against the shooting of the film in Morocco obliged al-ʿAqqâd to move to Libya. Three days before the première in England, under pressure of the local Muslims, he had to change the title of the film from 'The messenger of God' into 'The message'.

Though originally frowned upon by the `ulamâ', from the late 9th century onward, under the influence of popular preachers precise descriptions of Muhammad's appearance are given. They apparently met the demand of devout Muslims wishing to follow the Prophet's example as well as to meditate about the ideal bodily qualities of Muhammad, including the mole between his shoulders[52], indicators of his prophethood[53].

Ghazâlî for example gives many details: Muhammad is said to have been of moderate stature, his complexion is said to have been 'neither brown nor very white', his beautiful curly hair was 'neither lank nor short and woolly. It touched his shoulders. Muhammad used to make four plaits with each ear exposed between two plaits. The number of white hairs did not exceed seventeen. His eyes were very wide and black. His nose was hooked. He had a broad chest. Between his navel and upper chest there was a single hair. He had three belly folds, etc. etc.'[54].

So-called hilyas, descriptions like this, combined with Muhammad's moral qualities, can be found from the time of the traditionist al-Tirmidhî (d. 892) until the present day[55]. They have no individual traits but give an ideal type of male beauty. Tor Andrae referred to similar descriptions of Buddha and of Jesus, and to the images of both that were modelled after these descriptions: 'Wie das antike Christusbild in seiner jugendlichen schönheit, wie die gestalt Buddhas (...), wie die holdseligen madonnas (...), so zeugt auch das bild, das sich die muslimen von ihren propheten gezeichnet haben, von dem bedürfnis, die geistige hoheit in der schönheit der körperliche hülle verklärt zu sehen'[56].

Annemarie Schimmel proposes a direct connection between the Islamic interdiction of making images of man, let alone of prophets, and the composition of hilyas, the descriptions of Muhammad's good moral and bodily qualities. Famous calligraphed hilyas[57] are still sold in the courtyards of Turkish mosques 'damit sie die Zimmer der Gläubigen smücken und segnen, wie es in der christlichen Welt etwa ein Madonnenbild tun würde'[58]. She refers to an important tradition of Tirmidhî: 'Who after my death will see my hilya, he is as if he had seen me, and who will see it, longing after me, God will for him forbid hell-fire'[59].

All this looks like a transgression of the interdiction of making images. This, however, is not the case because of the formal difference between an image and a description. Though to our modern mind they are very much alike, the former can be objects of devotion, the latter cannot. When calligraphies are made into faces, *e.g.* the face of ʿAli[60], this could be meant as a circumvention, but probably is not because animals and all kind of objects, *e.g.* boats, were also 'drawn' in this way. It rather looks like a form of artful playing.

Magic and images.

On apotropaic amulets all kinds of religious texts are found, from the word *Allâh* to God's 99 beautiful names, Koranic quotations, etc. Often magical squares are added as well as drawings of hands and animals like scorpions, snakes or fishes. It is clear that these animals are thought to be present and to grant protection and bliss. This comes very near the cult of images in which the power of the represented deity is sought.

Conclusion.

Our conclusion can be short. Muslims do not have graven images of God nor of Muhammad. Though pictures of Muhammad do exist, they are rare and often Muhammad's face is hidden behind a veil. More important are the (calligraphed) descriptions of Muhammad that recall the object of their veneration and denote a mysterious beneficial presence of the Prophet.

God, who in the Koran is above all descriptions, in this same book meets man who cannot comprehend Him unless depicted in human form. The anthropomorphisms, in theology half-heartedly accepted, are expanded in Tradition and even in Sufism, but a strong sense of transcendence always remains. And with that, the paradox remains. The mosque is empty, but... God's presence is (only) indicated by His calligraphed Words or His name over the *mihrâb*. Also arabesques and geometrical ornaments have a double function, helping the mind not to be led away from what is not God and directing man's thinking towards God.

NOTES

1   Th.P. van Baaren, *NRC Handelsblad*, 6-7-1985.
2   Hellmut Ritter, *Das Meer des Seele*. Leiden: Brill, 1955, p. 441.

3 Cf. B. Gladigow, 'Präsenz der Bilder - Präsenz der Götter. Kultbilder und Bilder der Götter in griechischer Religion'. In: *Visible Religion*, Vol. IV-V (1985-6), pp. 119f.

4 Cf. Dieter Metzler, 'Anikonische Darstellungen'. In: *Visible Religion* Vol. IV-V (1985-6), p. 96.

5 Maxime Rodinson, *Mohammed*. London, 1971, p. 235.

6 Bukhârî, *Manâqib al-Ansâr*, 10.

7 Bukhârî, *Tawhîd*, 24.

8 Abdulkadir W. Haas, *Türkische Volksfrommigkeit*. Frankfurt: Lembeck, 1986, p. 29. The same story can be found in Abû'l-Layth al-Samarqandî, *Tanbih al-ghâfilin*, 38a, but there it is not mentioned that Allah laughed. Cf. H. Ritter, *Das Meer des Seele*, p. 270.

9 Cf. I. Goldziher, *Die Zâhiriten. Ihr Lehrsystem und ihre Geschichte*. Leipzig, 1884, p. 168.

10 Ezekiel 1:27 speaks about God's loins; Talm. *Ber.* 6a: God applying the phylacteries and, 7a praying.

11 Goldziher, *Ibid*.

12 *Mathnawî* II, 1720, cf. R.A. Nicholson, *The Mathnawi of Jelálu'ddin Rûmî*. London, 1924-40. The translation can also be found in R.A. Nicholson, *Rûmî, poet and mystic*. London: Allen and Unwin, 1956, p. 170.

13 A.J. Wensinck, *The Muslim Creed*. London: Frank Cass & Co., 1965, pp. 188, 193f.

14 A.S. Tritton, *Muslim Theology*. London, Luzac, 1947, p. 168. The two natures of Christ are 'without confusion, without change, without division, without separation'. Cf. J.N.D. Kelly, *Early Christian Doctrines*. London A & C Black, 1977⁵.

15 H.A.R. Gibb, *Islam*. Oxford: Oxf.Un.Press, 1980, p. 86.

16 Bukh., *Isti'dhân*, 1; Muslim, *45*, 115; *51*, 68; Ahm. b. Hanbal, *2*, 244, 251, 315, 323, 434, 463, 519.

17 H. Ritter, *Das Meer des Seele*. Leiden: Brill, 1955, pp. 434-503.

18 Ritter, *o.c.*, pp. 352, 435, 445, 458.

19 Ritter, *o.c.*, pp. 471f.

20 *Risâla fî tahqîq*, 29-32, so Ritter, *o.c.* pp. 448f.

21 Cf. I. Goldhizer, *o.c.*, pp. 116f.

22 *Talbîs Iblîs*, p. 184. Transl. D.S. Margoliouth, 'The Devil's Delusion'. In: *Islamic Culture* 12 (1938), pp. 108-18, 235-240, 352-65, 447-58.

23 *Memoirs of an Arab-Syrian Gentlemen or an Arab Knight in the Crusades. Memoirs of Usama ibn Munqidh (Kitâb al-I`tibâr)*. Translated from the Unique Manuscript by Philip K. Hitti. Beirut: Khayat, repr. 1964, p. 164.

24 Ritter, *o.c.*, p. 470.

25 *Mathnawî* I, 1872.

26 Cf. Ritter, *o.c.*, p. 459.

27 Cf. Ritter, *o.c.* p. 461.

28 Cf. Ritter, *o.c.*, pp. 468f.

29 Ritter, *o.c.*, pp. 477f.

30 Annemarie Schimmel, *Mystical Dimensions of Islam*. Chapel Hill: Un. of North Carolina Press, 1975, p. 171.

31 Schimmel, *o.c.*, p. 190.

32 Schimmel, *o.c.*, p. 376.

33 Schimmel, *o.c.*, p. 307. Ritter, *o.c.*, p. 17.

34 Bukh., *Tawhîd*, 56; Ahm. b. Hanbal, *II*, 391; for complete references, also for the traditions that will be mentioned in the next few lines, see Rudi Paret, 'Die Entstehungszeit des islamischen Bilderverbots' in his *Schriften zum Islam*. Stuttgart: Kohlhammer, 1981, p. 181.

35   Cf. Rudi Paret, 'Textbelege zum islamischen Bilderverbot' in his
     Schriften zum Islam, pp. 218ff.
36   In ancient Egypt images were made harmless in the same way, cf.
     H. te Velde, 'Egyptian hieroglyphs as signs, symbols and gods',
     in: *Visible Religion*, Vol. IV-V (1985-6), pp. 66f.; O. Loretz
     (ed.), *Die Gottebenbildlichkeit des Menschen*. München:
     Kösel-Verlag, 1967, pp. 154.
37   Titus Burckhardt, 'Perennial values in Islamic art'. In: *God and
     Man in Comtemporary Islamic Thought*. Beirut: AUB Centennial
     Publications, 1972, pp. 123f.
38   Annemarie Schimmel, *Mystical Dimensions*, p. 240 refers to Ibn
     `Arabi's visualization of the divine *huwiyya* 'in the shape of the
     letter *h*, in brilliant light, on a carpet of red, the two letters *hu*
     shining between the two arms of the *h*, which sends ist rays in all
     four directions'. She adds: 'Such a vision of the divine in the form
     of a letter is characteristic of a religion that prohibits representa-
     tion, particularly representation of the divine'.
39   A. Schimmel, *Islamic Calligraphy*, Leiden: Brill, 1970, pp. 3f.
40   Titus Burckhardt, 'Introduction to Islamic Art'. in: *The Arts of
     Islam*. Catalogue Hayward Gallery 8 April-4 July 1976. London: The
     Arts Council of Great Britain, 1976, p. 34.
41   *E.I.*, 2, *s.v.* Arabesque.
42   Ernst Kühnel, *Die Arabeske*. Sinn und Wandlung eines Ornaments.
     Graz: Verlag fur Sammler, 1977^2, pp. 7,4.
43   *Idem*, p. 5.
44   Titus Burckhardt, *Perennial Values*, p. 128.
45   *Idem*, pp. 128f. Italics mine (KW).
46   Titus Burckhardt, *Introduction*, p. 32.
47   Ignaz Maybaum, *Trialogue between Jew, Christian und Muslim*.
     London: Routledge & Kegan Paul, 1973, p. 21.
48   *Volkskrant*, 10 december 1986.
49   Thomas J. Abercrombie, 'Saudi Arabia, beyond the sands of Mecca'.
     In: *National Geograpic*, Vol. 129, nr. 1 (Jan. 1966), p. 13.
50   In marginal areas Islamic art might have undergone more foreign
     influences. Cf. René A. Bravmann, *Islam and Tribal Art in West
     Africa*. London: Cambridge University Press, 1974.
51   A veil over the face of Muhammad and sometimes over the face of
     other prophets as well, a concession to orthodox sentiment, occurs
     since the sixteenth century. Pictures of earlier times without a veil
     are rare. See Thomas W. Arnold, *Painting in Islam*, New York,
     1965, p. 98.
52   'Seal of the prophets' after popular interpretation of sura 33:40.
     During a so-called *Sirat*-conference in Pakistan in 1976 a
     medical-doctor devoted a serious paper to this mole.
53   The *shamâ'il al-Mustafâ*, Muhammed's good character qualities, and
     the *dalâ'il al-nubuwwa*, the signs of prophethood. Cf. Annemarie
     Schimmel, *Und Muhammad ist sein Prophet. Die Verehrung des
     Propheten in der islamischen Frömmigkeit*. Düsseldorf-Köln:
     Diederichs Verlag, 1981, pp. 28ff.
54   *Ihyâ' `'ulûm al-Dìn*, VII, 146-149. Cf. Leo Zolondek, *Book XX of
     al-Ghazzali's, Ihyâ 'ulum al-dìn*. Leiden: Brill, 1963, pp. 41ff.
55   Cf. al-Tirmidhì, Abû `Isâ, *Shamâ'il al-Mustafâ*; Jakup Üstun,
     Mohammed the Prophet. Ankara: Turkish Foundation for Religion,
     1975, p. 43.
56   Tor Andrae, *Die Person Muhammeds in Lehre und Glauben seiner
     Gemeinde*. Stockholm, 1918, pp. 119f.
57   For example: see the article of M. Ugur Derman, 'The Hilye about
     the prophet in Turkish calligraphic art'. In: *ILGI*, 28 (Dec. 1979),
     pp. 32-39. The illustration (*Fig. 1*) I owe to Mr Derman's
     helpfulness.

58 *Und Muhammad ist seine Prophet*, p. 33.
59 *Ibidem*. Unfortunately Schimmel did not indicate her source. I could not trace this tradition.
60 Cf. Schimmel, *Islamic Calligraphy*, pp. 11f.

ILLUSTRATIONS

Fig. 1   *Hilya* by Hasan Riza Efendi, dated 1294 A.H. (1877).

Fig. 2   Top of mihrāb in Kocatepe Mosque Rotterdam. The small medaillions carry the names of Allah and Mohammed, the big one Allah.

Fig. 3   Beheaded traffic symbol in Riyadh, Saudi Arabia (courtesy *National Geographic* 129, 1 (Jan. 1966).

Fig. 4   Early Islamic coin with creed instead of image.

Fig. 1

Fig. 2

Fig. 3

Fig. 4

IMAGES OF A YORUBA WATER-SPIRIT

Hans Witte

For Theo and Gertrude
van Baaren

The study of west-african 'effigies dei' has to take into account the dynamic and pragmatic character of west-african religious world-views. In these world-views[1] gods, divinities and spirits are not viewed as persons or static entities that function in theological discourse or as objects of devotion. West-african gods are active forces that are the object of human concern only in as far as the impact of their activity on the world is considered dangerous or useful for human society. The west-african answer to the manifestation of superhuman forces is not in the first place contemplative devotion, but ritual activity in order to manipulate these forces and divert or use them for the benefit of society. This means that west-african 'effigies dei' do not refer to gods in their inalterable essence, they symbolize aspects of active forces that manifest themselves to human society. It also means that west-african religious iconography should not consider material images in themselves as complete symbolic forms that can be analyzed in their morphological detail outside their ritual context. Material images have first of all meaning as requisites for a religious performance, instruments of traditional interaction between cosmic forces and human society. West-african religious sculpture (90% of which consists of wooden statues and masks) only comes to life when it is used in ritual perfomance, *e.g.* when it is danced through the crowd on the head of devotees, washed, dressed, and repainted or when it receives sacrifice. West-african rituals all have this character of manipulation of cosmic forces and they contain the same elements of song and dance, sacrifice and procession. Outside the context of ritual performance the images are often kept in dark shrines or stay covered with sacrificial matter and in general they are hardly visible. They are seldom displayed for their physical form.

As instruments for a certain type of performance and as symbolic references to gods that are seen not as eternal essences but as types of cosmic activity, west-african symbolic images seem to lose their individual meaning and their individuality as signifier. The same type of object can be used in different cults and it is often impossible to deduct the cultual use from the material form.

This 'cultual indifference' of ritual images has, of course, its consequences for west-african iconography. It is very often impossible to deduct cultual use from morphological detail. On the other hand, general physical features such as colour or choice of material, may indicate the cultual context. In general cultual differentiation is not indicated in the first place by material objects, but by the songs, the style of dancing, symbolic colours, and the type of musical instruments that are used.

The Yoruba offer an excellent opportunity to study the importance of contextual interpretation in west-african iconography. Among all the peoples of West-Africa - with the possible exception of the neighbouring Fon and Edo - the Yoruba have created the only religious system which provides for an extensive pantheon with a profusion of cults for the different divinities. Moreover the Yoruba sculptural tradition is, perhaps, the most prolific of the whole vast region. In this wealth of iconographic material the Yoruba use a whole range of different ways of symbolization, from direct, (almost) univocal emblematic references like the double-axe of the god of thunder to the figure of a kneeling woman offering a kola-bowl, that can virtually be used in every Yoruba cult.

The Yoruba territory in Southwestern Nigeria and the Southeast of the Democratic Republic of Benin, is divided into a great number of city- states, each with their own political, social and religious traditions. The cult of most divinities and the activities of religious societies is in most cases concentrated in certain regions and only a few cults have gained importance over the whole of Yoruba territory.

I would like to demonstrate that west-african symbolism expressed in sculpture, colours, choice of material, etc., is not based on a fixed correspondence between traditional forms and univocal meanings. The reference of sign to meaning is determined by a multi-layered, ever shifting context and not by lexicographical univocity.

The cultmaterial of the rivergod Erinle seems a good example for my purpose, because, as Thompson (1969: 134) remarked, he pertains to three symbol-families that are clustered around 1. iron, 2. herbalism, and 3. water-spirits. Erinle, 'one of the major gods of the Oyo Yoruba' (Tompson, o.c.: 130), is called Eyinle in Egbado country. His cult has spread over the whole of western and central Yoruba groups, especially

in Egbado, Aworri, Anago and Ketu. I will briefly examine the mythology of Erinle, before passing on the ritual objects used in his cult and
the interpretation of the symbolism of this complex deity.

The mythology of Erinle

In most of the mythological stories about Erinle we are told that he
was a hunter living in the forest (Johnson, 1921: 37; Abraham, 1946:
164; Bascom, 1969: 88; Thompson, 1969: 130, n. 19; Williams, 1974:
91). In other versions we learn that Erinle was a farmer (Thompson,
1969: 136), or a herbalist (Thompson, 1969: 137). In all stories but one
Erinle sinks at a certain moment into the earth and changes into a
river. This would have happened, according to Beier (1957: 6), in the
neighbourhood of the town of Ilobu.

The reasons given for this transformation from man into water are
very diverse: it happened because Erinle lost a fight with Sango over
the latter's wife Oba (Bascom, *l.c.*); or because he wanted to save his
children who became very thirsty after eating dried beans and maize
(Thompson, 1969: 136); or because his foot struck a poisonous stone
(Thompson, 1969: 139). Johnson (*l.c.*) and Abraham (*l.c.*) state that
Erinle simply drowned.

Williams (1974: 91) relates that Erinle changed into an elephant and
sank into the earth like a wild animal into a covered pit. Williams want
to underline the symbolic elements that link Erinle with Osanyin, the
orisa (divinity) of herbalism, and Ogun, *orisa* of iron. This author does
not go on to relate Erinle's transformation into water, althought this
explains the origin of his cult. On the other hand Williams offers an
explanation of Erinle's name, which he reads as a contraction of *erin*
(elephant) and *ile* (house).

Thompson (1969: 137) mentions a version of the myth in which Erinle
was a powerful herbalist who was called Abatan before his transformation. He was nicknamed Erin 'because of his size'. After he died he
changed into a flowing stream and his name changed form Erin to Erinle
'which means Elephant-Into-Earth' (*erin* + *ile*). It does not seem improbable that Erinle as a hunter or a herbalist who are at home in the
forest, was nicknamed or honoured with the name of the king of the
animals, the king of the wilderness.

After his transformation (or disappearance) into a river, Erinle
founded the kingdom of Ode Kobaye, his underwater capital which,
according to Thompson (1969: 139) must be considered an extension of

the imperial capital of Old Oyo, where his cult may have originated.

Morton-Williams (1964) has indicated that the Yoruba cosmos is divided into two primordial elements: the heavens and the muddy waters. The primordial waters are symbolized under two aspects: that of earth as the untamed wilderness or jungle, and that of rivers and the sea (cf. Witte, 1982a: 21-22; 78-83). Before his transformation Erinle is associated as a hunter or a herbalist with the first aspect (earth), afterwards he is more or less identified with the second (river).

It must be underlined that Erinle's transformation is really an apotheosis. Although a myth, reconstructed from praise poetry, cannot be treated as a biography, it seems that Erinle is consolidated in divine importance through his transformation. Moreover in his cult, which closely resembles that of rivergoddesses, it seems that he is essentially venerated as a water-spirit. On the other hand, the fact that as a water-spirit he does not change into a female being (all the other important river-spirits of the Yoruba are goddessess, who, admittedly, all have definite masculine traits, cf. Witte 1982a: 88-102), and that, on the contrary, his masculinity is underlined in his cult - as we shall see - by the reminiscences of his previous existence as a hunter or herbalist, demonstrates that Erinle's apotheosis did not wipe out his former life and that, even as a water-spirit, he maintains his association with the forest.

The cult material of Erinle

Worshippers will come with all their needs to 'their' deity, but Erinle is renowned for his ability to assure the birth of children and the cure sickness. In the first eventuality one appeals first of all to his qualities as a water-spirit, in the second he is seen as a herbalist. As a herbalist, and also as a mythological hunter, Erinle belongs to a group of deities that is closely linked with the cosmic forces of nature symbolized by the jungle. Herbalists and hunters can only survive amidst the dangers of the wilderness if they are protected by the iron tools and weapons provided by the *orisa* of iron Ogun. Indeed, the cult emblems of Erinle as a herbalist and as a hunter, although they are distinct, belong to the same symbolic cluster that concentrates on iron and on survival in the jungle (cf. Williams, 1974: 87-92; Beier, 1980: 38-41, 75; Witte, 1982a: 105-106).

The main cult object and emblem of Erinle as a water-spirit is the *awo ota Erinle*, an earthenware vessel with a characteristically decorated lid. In this pot fresh water from the river is kept, together with polished stones from the river-bed. Two of these stones are placed on the head of each cult member during his initiation, 'their force is believed to penetrate his character and fortune and to protect him in a fundamental way' (Thompson, 1969: 140). These pebbles are kept in the pot, and others are added during festivals and special occasions, as a token of love and affection for Erinle's continuous protection and as a symbol of his fertilizing powers. However, stones and fresh water from the river are not only to be found in the shrines for Erinle, they are the central cult objects of every water-spirit of the Yoruba.

Worshippers of Erinle are recognized by an iron-chain bracelet worn on the right wrist. This bracelet refers to 'the iron bangles worn by the hunters of Yoruba antiquity' (Thompson, 1969: 130). Some followers of Erinle also wear a chain of iron or brass around the neck (Johnson, 1921: 37). Among the main dance emblems of the cult we find a fly whisk (an attribute of hunters) and a fan. Brass fans refers to the cult of Osun, the most important water-goddess of the Yoruba.

The scope of this article does not allow for a full description of all the objects used in the cult of Erinle. I do like to draw attention to the fact that none of these objects seems specific for Erinle, apart from the characteristic form of the lids of the earthenware vessels and, perhaps, some iconographical details of the wrought iron staffs that stand before his shrines and that on closer study may show subtle differences from the staffs of Osanyin, the deity of medicine. Each object in itself (pots, bracelets, fans, fly whisks, staffs) belongs to a general symbolic context of fertilizing water or protective iron. It is their specific combination that is chracteristic of Erinle.

I would like to demonstrate my point first of all with two superb statues from the Ilapade shrine of Erinle in Ilobu (Beier, 1957: fig. 9, 10d and 12b), representing a rider on horseback (85 cm, fig. 1) and a woman carrying a child on her back (89 cm, fig. 2).

The only indication that the male figure has to do with Erinle lies in the fly whisk that he carries in his right hand, but this attribute marks him as a hunter and not specifically as a (follower of) Erinle. The figure has bracelets on both wrists and not only on his right like the cult members of Erinle.

Female figures with a bowl in their hands and carrying a child on their back are very common in Yoruba sculpture. The distinct feature in our case is the hair-tail with amulets which would mark her on first sight as an Eshu figure. In the context of the Erinle cult it seems to indicate a (male) attribute of hunter-warriors. As a 'projection from the top' (Margaret Thompson Drewal, 1977) the hair-tail with amulets refers to the spiritual powers of the initiate.

But most of all the hair-tail recalls a story about Erinle's hair told by Denis Williams (1974: 90-91): 'All the hunters of the forest one day revolted against Erinle, assailed him, and left him wandering helpless. When found by his wife he requested her to plait his hair into a coxcomb or crest. Then, changing himself into an elephant, he sank into the earth'. One could speculate about the meaning of this story. Does Erinle receive (female) spiritual powers from his wife, that make him strong as an elephant before he is assimilated to the (female) forces of the earth? Again we find in these statues, as in most of Erinle's cultmaterial, only oblique references to the deity.

The combination of a male figure on horseback and a statue of a woman with bowl belongs to the standard repertoire of Yoruba cult material (Beier, 1957; Pemberton, 1975) and does not refer to a particular cult. Specification of the intended symbolism is only obtained within the context of the cult-ritual.

I would like to conclude this brief summary of the complex iconography of Erinle by examining the references to his cult on an Ifa bowl (fig. 3 and 4). The bowl (h. 34,5 cm) was carved in the workshop of the Falade family in Iseyin, perhaps by Ogundeji who was active between 1930 and 1950 (cf. Witte, 1984: pl. 58). The lid of the bowl is decorated with the figure of an elephant who seems to sink, as Williams (l.c.) mentioned, into the earth. On a lower plane beneath the elephant we see a male figure with outstretched arms typical of many Iseyin bowls from the same workshop. The elephant touches the head of this figure with its trunk.

Going clockwise from this figure around the lid, we see an opele divining chain, a standing female figure with a bowl or pot in her hands, a tortoise, another male figure whose hat is touched by the tail of the elephant, a mudfish, another standing female and other opele chain.

The male figure underneath the elephant's trunk holds a fan in his right hand and, probably, a sacrificial cock in his left. Bascom (1969: 88) mentions that the sacrificial food for Erinle includes 'dogs, he-goats, cocks, pigeons, white steamed beans, and yam loaf'. The very prominent coxcomb of the bird may refer to Erinle's plaited hair before his transformation into an elephant. The combination of the fan, the cock and the physical contact with the elephant's trunk indicate that we have to do with a follower of Erinle. The figure wears a thick bracelet on his left wrist, although as a cult member of Erinle he should wear an (iron) bracelet on his right.

The other male figure - underneath the elephant's tail - must also be a follower of Erinle, in view of the fly-whisk in his right hand and his physical contact with the elephant. In his left hand he holds, perhaps, a pigeon.

The fact that the elephant actually touches the two male figures suggests that this most important part of the decoration forms one single symbolic unity referring to Erinle. The two female figures half-way between the male figures, although neutral symbols in themselves, should, because of their symmetrical position with regard to the males, in this case be interpreted as other references to the cult of Erinle, in which women carry pots with water to and from the river (cf. also *fig. 2*).

The rest of the decoration: 2 *opele* chains, a tortoise (the diviner among the animals) and a mudfish, refers to Ifa divination. The mudfish, of course, also symbolize Erinle, but in this case its parallel position to the tortoise suggests a more general interpretation in accordance with Ifa, in which the mudfish symbolizes the ancestral forces of the earth. On the other hand the multiple symbolic meanings of the mudfish are cleverly exploited to link the symbolic complexes of Ifa and Erinle.

The figuration of the bowl is literally dominated by the figure of the elephant. Without this clear indication it would have been difficult to discover the references to Erinle. This is even more true of the figures from Ilobu. Without knowledge of their provenance it would have been impossible to identify them as shrine-furniture for Erinle.

Very often the symbolic meaning of religious sculpture of the Yoruba is not indicated at all by its morphology. In those cases the objects in themselves suggest a very general symbolism that only gets a precise meaning and efficacy in ritual performance.

Reviewing the cult material of Erinle it is after all strange that the deity is never symbolized in the form of an elephant. Such a symbol could be easily recognized and - because of Erinle's name and mythology - it would refer directly to him. Outside the immediate context of his own cult, however, Erinle is represented as an elephant and this fact makes the absence of these symbols in his own cult even more surprising. Just as the forest-and-iron-complex in his symbolism seems to prevent him from turning into a woman (a not uncommon event in Yoruba mythology) to become a river deity like the others, in the same way the water component of his symbolism seems to prevent him from being symbolized as a creature from the wilderness. The delicate equilibrium between the herbalist/hunter and the water-spirit should bot be disturbed by unambiguous symbols.

Outside his own cult Erinle can be appreciated for only one among the many aspects of his character and then he is depicted either as a water-spirit or as king of the forest. We find an example of the first case in the representations of Erinle as a mudfish in the cult-material of Sango (cf. Frobenius, 1912: 206, 209, 217; Thompson, 1969: 131, n. 21; Fraser, 1972: 272; Witte, 1982a: 108-111; Witte, 1982b). As elephant, king of the forest Erinle is represented *e.g.* on mirror-cases (cf. Witte, 1982a: fig. 34) and on wooden bowls (*opon igede Ifa*) in which the utensils for Ifa divination are stored.

NOTE

1   The question whether we should underline the differences between west-african cultures or their unity and consequently whether we should speak of world-views or of the world-view in the singular, is in my opinion a question of perspective. I have dealt with this problem elsewhere (in: Eliade, Histoire des croyances et idées religieuse, tome IV, forthcoming).

BIBLIOGRAPHY

Abraham, R.C.
1946 *Dictionary of Modern Yoruba*. Repr. 1978[6], Hodder and Stoughts, London.
Bascom, William
1969 *The Yoruba of Western Nigeria*. Holt, Rinehart and Winston, New York.
Beier, H. Ulli
1957 *The Story of Sacred Wood Carvings from one small Yoruba town*. Nigeria Magazine, Lagos.
1980 *Yoruba Myths*. Cambridge Univ. Press, London.
Drewal, Margaret Thompson
1977 'Projections from the Top in Yoruba Art', in: *African Arts*, XI-1, 43 s.
Fraser, Douglas
1972 'The Fish-Legged Figure in Benin and Yoruba Art', in: *African Art and Leadership*, ed. Douglas Fraser and Herbert M. Cole, The Univ. of Wisconsin Press, Madison, 261-294.
Frobenius, Leo
1912 *Und Afrika sprach* ... Vita, Berlin-Charlottenburg.
Johnson, Samuel
1921 *The History of the Yorubas From the Earliest Times to the Beginning of the British Protectorate*. Routledge and Kegan Paul, repr. 1973, London.
Morton-Williams, Peter
1964 'Cult Organization of the Oyo Yoruba', in: *Africa*, 34-3, 243-260.
Pemberton, John
1975 Eshu-Elegba: 'The Yoruba Trickster God', in: *African Arts*, IX-1, 20 s.
Thompson, Robert Farris
1969 Abatan: 'A Master Potter of the Egbado Yoruba', in: *Tradition and Creativity in Tribal Art*, ed. D. Biebuyck, Univ. of California Press, 120-182.
Williams, Dennis
1974 *Icon and Image*. A Study of Sacred and Secular Forms of African Classical Art. Allen Lane, London.
Witte, H.A.
1982a *Symboliek van de aarde bij de Yoruba*. U.M.I., Ann Arbor.
1982b 'Fishes of the Earth. Mud-fish symbolism in Yoruba Iconography', in: *Visible Religion*, I, 154-174.
1984 *Ifa and Esu*. Iconography of Order and Disorder. Luttik, Soest.

ILLUSTRATIONS

Fig . 1

Fig. 2

Fig. 3

Fig. 4

STARRING: JESUS[*]

John G. Hahn

'There will never be a greater picture, because there is no greater subject'[1]

SUGGESTED RECONSTRUCTION OF REALITY

In this article we will focus on films 'starring Jesus' i.e. an audio-visual version of the story of Jesus of Nazareth. The difference between pictorial and cinematographic portrayal of Jesus lies in the motionlessness of the former and the movement and action of the latter. The cinematographic portrayal results in the impression that the events shown in the films are more realistic, that the camera was at hand at the very moment things happened. Viewers of a film get the impression, that they see a filmed eyewitness-report of the story that is being told. Films showing a historical reconstruction of a past reality have to deal with the general problem of suggesting a documentary-like reconstruction of reality, whereas fantasy is given. Whereas the holy books in most religions do not present eyewitness-reports at all, films 'starring Jesus', as well as any other 'biblefilm', meet this problem of suggested reconstructed reality where there can be no reconstruction of reality at all because the basic text from which the film is taken - the biblical story - is anything but a reconstructible report. Our first point to stress is, that a 'Jesus-film' is nothing but a dramatized version of a faithful testimony that was written down some 1900 years ago. Even if the film-maker gets the assistance of historians, theologians, archeologists and whosoever, there can only be drama on the screen and never camera-documented, eyewitnessed or reconstructed reality at all[2].

BIBLEFILMS VERSUS RELIGIOUS FILMS

There are many films that can be called 'religious' because they try to tell a story that is indirectly taken from the so called truth of a holy book such as the Christian bible. In a more general way we can say that 'religious films' meet general questions of human existence such as 'love and hate', 'hope and despair', 'life and death' and so forth. In this article we will exclude the kind of general religious films that do illustrate a religious story or which contain general themes of the

Christian faith on a so called nonhistorical basis. In this way we exclude films of famous filmmakers as Ingmar Bergmann, Carlos Saura, Andrej Tarkovski, Luis Bunuel etc. These filmmakers produce films telling general stories that in any way can be related to stories that are originally told in the bible. Films that actualize the gospel by telling stories in accordance with main themes of Christianity are of no interest to our theme. In our article we do look for the typical ways in which the character of Jesus is visualized in films from the time of the invention of the cinema on. We will focus on films 'starring Jesus' only. The question is how to differentiate between films 'starring Jesus' and films 'co-starring Jesus'.

BIBLEFILMS VERSUS JESUSFILMS

If we exclude here all the films based on other parts of the biblical story[3], the remaining films based on (parts of) the new testament can be divided into two groups. The first group comprising all the films that are said to be taken directly from the gospel, such as 'King of Kings' (Nicholas Ray 1961), 'Il Vangelo secondo Matteo' (Pier Paolo Pasolini 1961) 'Jesus of Nazareth' (Franco Zeffirelli 1976) 'Jesus' (John Heyman 1978). The other group comprising all the more or less historical films situated in the beginning of our era in or around the so called 'holy land'. Among these films there is a great number of films of which we can say that they are 'co-starring Jesus', being films about events or persons living in or supposed to have lived in the days of Jesus. Films like The Robe (Henry Koster USA 1953) Ben Hur (William Wyler, USA 1959), Pontius Pilate (G.P. Callegari, Italy/France 1961), Barabbas (Richard Fleischer, Italy 1961), and others, use the character of Jesus as a dramatic instrument to focus on the leading characters of the film. The names of these characters may be taken from the biblical story, but the character of Jesus does not really play a central role in the drama. Jesus just serves as an important auxiliary character, sometimes only just as a symbol for the time in which the film is situated, sometimes as a catalyst for the action in the story of the film. It seems obvious, that this sort of typical Hollywood-films were produced and very well sold in the fifties and early sixties but are increasingly forgotten in our days, except in some small mostly fundamentalist evangelical Christian groups. The way these films and the more recent Jesus-films are used in these circles is of considerable importance to our theme.

THE USE OF THE JESUSFILMS

Most of the Jesus films, we are dealing with, were made in recent times, when Hollywood discovered that themes from the bible could also be sold to the masses. But some of the more recent Jesus films were made to be used as an important instrument for missionary activities all over the world. John Heyman's 'Jesus' is a good example of a film, that is used to spread the Christian faith in over 70 countries by mainly USA-based fundamentalistic Christian organizations such as Youth for Christ, Campus Crusade for Christ, etc.[4]. It is very interesting to see, that this film was but an episode in a far more sophisticated project by the producer/director to make a series of films in which the entire bible would be filmed in order to make the bible accessible even to the illiterate. The general idea of this so called 'Genesis Project' was to produce a 'New Media Bible'. As a matter of fact only a small part of the project could be realized because of lack of finances. 'Jesus', based on the gospel of Luke, was filmed on location in Israel with only one professional actor (Brain Deacon starring Jesus). The copies could easily be made in over 70 languages because the amateur actors speak Hebrew, Aramaeic and Greek and the text of the Gospel according to Luke can just be read by voice-over in any language wanted[5]. As a way of turning the written bible into an audiovisual instrument 'Jesus' was a rather controversial product. The producers, a rather fundamental evangelical breed, stated that their product did not interpret the biblical story but reconstructed it in the most objective way possible, thus creating a film, that shows Jesus as he had really been. The general idea was that if in 0 A.D. the camera had been invented, Heyman's 'Jesus' could have served as an eyewitness-report of the life and death of Jesus. This fundamentalistic position was widely attacked by the Christian churches which could have been one of the reasons of the financial breakdown of the whole project. In short we can say, that the bulk of the films 'starring Jesus' are just produced as any other film about a well-selling story: life and death of a famous historical figure is shown with all the special effects the film-industries have available. Consequently when discussing the character of Jesus as shown on the white screen we have to take in mind, that most of these films were made for purely commercial reasons and that only a small part of these films are explicitly derived from the Christian religion, but that nearly all of them are used within the Christian churches. That means for instance, that a very specific picture and view on Jesus is spread by those who use this kind of films for evangelization in areas with widespread illiteracy is widely spread. It is interesting for several reasons to do research of the more or less codified way Jesus is depicted in these films. One of these reasons being the fact that the audiovisual media become more and more a worldwide instrument of (religious) communication, thus spreading a culturally fixed view on how Jesus has to look and impose a very specific looking Jesus in the minds of millions of people all over the world.

THE ARTHISTORICAL TRADITION

If we look at the age-old tradition of pictorial representation of Jesus in the art we find that there not only exists a certain consistency in the way of depicting Jesus, but also that every picture of Jesus can be placed in the time in which it was made and to the general theological positions in those days. The latter point makes the Jesus paintings of Michelangelo and Rembrandt quite different from each other but it becomes also obvious that both artists do stand in the same western tradition of art and that the differences between their work and for example that of the eastern orthodox icon-tradition is even more obvious. The same can be said of paintings from renaissance painters and modern painters. There also we see a very obvious number of differences but also elements that remained more or less the same throughout the ages[6]. Especially this traditional consistency makes it interesting to trace the way in which not only artists but also film producers have tried to portray and reconstruct the historical life of Jesus, some using one (part of a) single gospel as their basic material ('Il Vangelo secondo Matteo', Pier Paolo Pasolini 1961), others using a romanticized story based on all the gospels as well as on apocryphal and pure fiction together ('The Messiah', Roberto Rosselini 1975; 'The Passover Plot', Michael Campus 1976, etc). Most of the Jesus films depict Jesus in a way, which is highly reminiscent of the way Jesus is traditionally depicted in western art through the ages. In this regard, the important problem is that Jesus is also believed to be divine and naturally this aspect of the historical Jesus cannot be filmed in a tangible way.

WRITTEN OR ORAL TRADITION

Films can only depict reality in front of the moviecamera. Every film that wants to show more than an auditive and visual reality has to make symbolic representation of that non-visual and non-auditive reality. The professed divinity of Jesus of Nazareth is such a non-filmable reality, but also the theological question of the nature of angels. To theologians anno 1987 this last question may seem outdated, to filmmakers it is the very core of their *métier*. But this is not the real problem. If we formulate the problem we are faced with in a more general way we can say, that the Christian tradition has become mainly a written tradition and only partially remained an oral or a pictorial tradition, whereas the medium film can be looked upon as part of the oral and the pictorial tradition[7]. Making a film about the gospel means to translate the written story into some kind of generally understood audiovisual language. But if the translation from one language into another already means some kind of interpretation, then the transposition of the story of the gospel into a totally different medium means far more than that. So we can say, that every Jesus film contains some kind of cinematographic and more or less theological interpretation of the stories the film is based on. But if that is the case, we have to ask how this interpretation directs the way we look at the character of Jesus. The main problem here is twofold. First there is the problem of the professed double nature of Jesus, being both man and god in one, of which one, his divine nature, cannot be made visible in any direct way. The second being the way this double nature is dramatized to create an acceptable cinematographic product that is worth to be looked at.

JESUS AS MAN AND AS GOD

The main problem of the Jesus films is, that the actor who is playing the part of Jesus, can only play the part of the historical Jesus and not the part of the Son of God, as Jesus called himself according to the bible. Every Jesus film is in our opinion first of all a film about the life and death of 'the Son of Man'. Every attempt to interpret the filmed Jesus as the so called 'Son of God', as the Christian Messiah, or as any divinity is the result of an internal Christian understanding and confession and lacks any basis in the film itself. Especially evangelical organizations such as mentioned above tend to make us believe, that the Jesus in the Jesus films is more than just a part played by a human actor. The way these films are used in evangelical circles support these suppositions. Jesus films are actually films, 'based upon the gospel' which means, that any Jesusfilm is related to the Gospel as any other film, based on a novel, is related to that novel even if Christian filmcritics want to believe that bible films are more than that[8]. In concurrence with the results of our research we want to stress that these films are nothing more than visualized reproductions of the confession of the filmmakers and their religious culture i.e. the cultural heritage in which these kind of films are produced[9].

A SHORT HISTORICAL REMARK

Since 1895 - the year in which cinema was made publicly known for the first time - over two hundred films based on (parts of) the bible, both the old and the new testament have been made, including a number of films about the life of Jesus of Nazareth[10]. The first attempts to make a film on a biblical story were undertaken only two years after the first films where shown to the public[11]. The very first Jesus films of which only some photographic reproductions are left[12] were meant to serve the same purpose as Sunday school posters: to help the public in memorizing the holy stories told in the bible. The stories were actually told while the posters or in a given case the film was shown. So it is not surprising that we can discover a great resemblance between the Jesus in these Jesus films and the Jesus shown in devotional and art historical material from the end of the nineteenth century.

THE ICONOGRAPHICAL GAP

Jesusfilms can be taken as iconographical material. It is worth trying to find out in which way the film makers since 1895 have depicted the figure of Jesus. The first point to stress is, that there does not exist a historically reliable or contemporary picture of Jesus of Nazareth. Not only because the artistic skills *anno* 0 C.E. were insufficient for that purpose, but also because of the way in which a human being was depicted in those days was too schematic to give us any clue to the way Jesus really looked like. Even the 'Clothing of Turin' does not really give a clue to this point[13]. Every picture showing Jesus, from the beginning of our era up to our days is a pictures showing the faith of the artist in an aesthetic way. As a matter of fact the traditional religious values of the public dictate the way Jesus has to look to make the artist's product recognizable. If the public cannot for whatever reason recognize Jesus in the artist's product there will be no successful communication between the artist and the public[14]. To reach this basic communication the artist has to use standard formulas to depict Jesus, on canvas as well as on film[15]. That means, that every film maker has to do iconological research, to find out what Jesus has to look like, according to the contemporary iconography. Because we do not know the way Jesus really looked, it is obvious that the results of a filmmakers iconological research results in dependency upon the christian pictorial tradition. This causes any filmed Jesus to stand in an art-historical tradition as well as in the tradition of the simple devotional mass-cards that are being used in the Roman Catholic Church, in the tradition of E.S.Hardy's Sunday school plates, of Shield's 19th century Jesus and so forth. If we study the pictures of Jesus used towards the end of the last century we can find the elements that were used in those days to visualize Jesus of Nazareth. We believe these elements are also used in the more recent Jesus films. The limited length of this article does not allow us to use all the film material we have available. With the help of some typical examples we will try to make clear which elements compose the ideal filmed Jesus.

PAST CENTURIES JESUS

It seems obvious, that in the early days of the cinema the film makers looked for pictorial material that was at hand to represent their Jesus. The very popular Doré-drawings, the Hardy-, the Shields-, the Constable-paintings etcetera show us Jesus as a tall, gentle looking man, with light-dark shoulder-long gleaming and wavy hear and an almost mysterious smile on his mouth. His beard is neatly trimmed and his light colored eyes look at the public around him in a mysteriously touching way. His frozen movements often make the traditional gesture of redemptive salute and there is often a halo over his head. He is very often depicted as a real un-Jewish man(!) dressed in something like a long kaftan and wearing an Arabic headdress to suggest a Middle Eastern appearance. He looks like an ideal man for identification and projection: the son every mother wishes, the son-in-law every father wishes for his daughter, the ideal older brother to both men and women, the bosom-friend we all wish to have. These pictures of Jesus use strongly codified symbols for recognition and identification, symbols that are taught to the christian public to belong to Jesus, symbols that make the pictures generally accepted.

SOME EXAMPLES FROM ART HISTORY

By comparing the appearance of Jesus on devotional pictures, works of art and in films we meet the problem of the lack of motion in pictures and works of art. We therefore exclude the action and focus on the person of Jesus and the context he is shown in. The first thing we see is that the setting of main actions of Jesus seems to be rather traditional. When we compare the famous fresco of the Last Supper by Leonardo Da Vinci (Milan 1495/98) with drawings of the same story from later times and with filmed episodes of the same event, we find, that most of them show a Jesus in a setting that is derived from Leonardo's masterpiece. For character-positions, inventory and background artist and film makers still take Leonardo as their example[16]. If we focus on the way Jesus was painted and drawn both in 'high art' and in devotional pictures at the end of the last century we see a Jesus that has certain traits in common even if most of the details differ from painter to painter. This kind of Jesus we can trace back in a series of Jesus films.

SOME EXAMPLES FROM FILMS.
In a short fragment of a Gaumont's film from 1906 as well as in a Pathé-fragment from 1907 we meet a typical 19th century Jesus. In both fragments the figure of Jesus looks almost identical. Also the 1935 produced French film 'Golgotha' (Jean Duvivier) shows us a Jesus that could easily have been copied from a devotional picture from those days, but that also has many traits in common with his thirty years older predecessors. The same can be said of Nicolas Ray's King of Kings (1961), of Rosselini's Jesus (1975), of Michael Campus' Jesus (1976) of Zeffirelli's Jesus (1976) and so forth but in a certain way also of Norman Jewison's 'Jesus Christ Superstar'. The actors playing the role of Jesus fit perfectly in the picture we drew of the typical filmed and more or less devotional Jesus. Even a film that tries to tell the story of Jesus with the forms and means of the modern musical, which means a rather 'abnormal' sort of Jesus film runs along the lines of the way in which Jesus is traditionally depicted. It is obvious, that if we speak of certain traditional 'rules' concerning the way Jesus has to be depicted in films, that there are also exceptions. But even these exceptions tend to depend on the traditional 'values'. The Jesus from the musical Godspell (USA 1972), Pasolini's Jesus (Italy 1961), the Jesus in Gareth Davies 'Son Of Man' (GB 1969) and Life of Brian's Jesus (Terry Jones GB) seem to be different from the standardized Jesus we described above, but despite the differences there remains a kind of overall harmony. It is impossible to go here any deeper into the multitude of questions concerning the Jesusfilms. A thorough analysis of a

great number of (parts of) Jesusfilms formed the basis of this short
article in which I wanted to show briefly the possibilities of iconological
analysis of modern iconographical material. This kind of research is
only a small part of the audiovisual iconology of religion that becomes
more and more important with the growing distribution of audiovisual
media also for religious communication[17]. The study and research into
these media as a means of religious and interreligious communication is a
rather modern variety of the study of the History of Religion. I do
hope that it will be a variety that can be elaborated in the next 40
years of the Nederlands Genootschap van Godsdiensthistorici (NGG).

NOTES

*) I'd like to thank Prof.Dr.Frits Tillmans. Drs.Jan Besemer, Rolf Deen
and a number of student at the Katholieke Theologische Hogeschool
Amsterdam for their helpfull suggestions on the theme of this article.
1   Will Rogers' comment on The King of Kings, Cecil B. De Mille USA
     1929. Cited after D.Blum, *A Pictorial History of the Silent Screen*,
     New York (Grosset & Dunlap) 1953, p.314.
2   Cf. D.Thomas, *The Face of Christ*, London 1974, Chapter 1.
3   Films such as 'The Ten Commandments' (Cecil B. De Mille, USA
     1929 & 1956), 'Samson and Delilah' (Cecil B.De Mille, USA 1950),
     'Salomé' (William Dieterle, USA 1953), 'David and Goliath' (R.Potter
     & F.Baldi, Italy 1959) 'The Book of Ruth' (Henry Koster, USA
     1960) 'Sodom and Gomorrha' (Robert Aldrich, Italy/France 1961)
     'The Bible' (John Huston 1965), etc.
4   Cf. *Uitdaging*, 1981/10 1982/12, 1983/7-8 In this evangelical journal
     the success of the film is counted in 'souls that give their lives to
     Jesus' after having seen the film. Articles give examples from
     India, Pakistan, Nigeria, Bahrein etc.
5   It is remarkable that satellite broadcasted 'Europe TV' showed the
     film in their program at Good Friday 1986 (Europe TV, 28.3.1986,
     21.25h - 23.15h, with an 'introduction' the day before 27.3.1986,
     22.50h - 23.20h).
6   Cf. D.Thomas, *o.c.*, and G.Rombold & H.Schwebel, *Christus in der
     Kunst des 20. Jahrhunderts*, Freiburg i.B. 1983.
7   Film and Television can be seen for the time being as final stage of
     a development that begins at Altamira's and Lascaux' cave paint-
     ings. Cf. My dissertation to be published in 1988.
8   Cf. R.Joos, 'Lichtspiel und Glaubensverdunkelung', in: a*Medien
     praktisch*, 2/81.
9   More elaborated arguments to this position are being published in
     my dissertation in 1988.
10   Cf. R.H.Campbell & M.R.Pitts, *The Bible on Film. A Checklist 1897
     - 1980*, New York 1981
11   The first pieces of Jesusfilms we could discover where made in 1906
     in France in the Gaumont studios. By 1910 over 30 Jesus films were
     made.
12   A photo of a 'last supper scene' of one of the first Jesusfilms can
     be seen at the French Filmmuseum in Paris.
13   As the originality of the Clothing is still uncertain, we can not rely

on it as an arthistorical useful picture of Jesus.

14 Cf. My dissertation to be published in 1988.

15 For 20th century paintings showing Jesus even in a non-pictorial way see G.Rombold & H. Schwebel *o.c.*

16 Even in films like Viridiana (Luis Bunuel, Mexico 1961) and La Ultima Cena (Tomas Guttiérez Alea, Cuba 1976) and others we meet scenes, directly taken from Leonardo's Milanese fresco. We meet Leonardo even in cartoonlike and cynical drawings and paintings like Matthias Koeppel's Last Supper (FRG 1982). See: *Stern* (a German weekly), April 25th, 1984, p. 128 - 137.

17 Cf. Johan Hahn, 'Religieuze Communicatie: bouwstenen voor een theorie', in: J.Hemels & H.Hoekstra, *Media en Religieuze communicatie*, Gooi & Sticht, Hilversum 1985, p.26 - 36.

Photocomposition A

ICONOGRAPHIC DEPENDENCY

Sources:

1   Reint de Jonge, drawings for a TV-series 'The Gospel according to John', *Evangelische Omroep*, Netherlands 1985
2   The genesis Project, Jesus - The Gospel according to Luke, GB 1976
3   Drawing by Gustave Dore, 1832-1883
4   Gerard van Honthorst, *The unbelieving Thomas*, ca. 1617
5   Nicolas Ray, *King of Kings*, USA 1961
6   Shaw's Bible plates (drawn by E.S.Hardy) (detail), Gr.Br. 19th century
7   Roberto Rosselini, *The Messiah*, Italy 1975
8   Devotional mass-card: The Holy hart of Jesus (detail), Netherlands about 1950

(Photographs - taken from reproductions and a color televisionscreen with frozen videotaped pictures - and composition by the author)

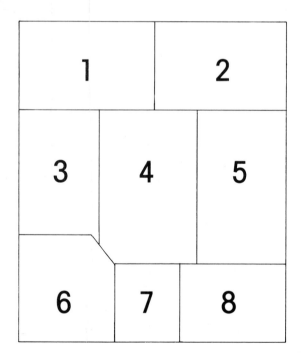

PHOTOCOMPOSITION A

Photocomposition B

ICONOGRAPHIC DEPENDENCY

Sources:

1   Alexandar Petrovic, *The Master and Margarita*, Yougoslavia/Italy
    1975
2   F.J.Shields, *The Good Sheperd* (detail), City of Art Gallery
    Manchester, 19th century
3   Devotional Mass-card found in a nuns-covent in Paris 1986
4   Pier Paolo Pasolini, *Il vangelo secondo Matteo*, Italy 1961
5   Jesus face as 'printed' on the Clothing of Turin, said to be the
    clothing Jesus' dead body was wrapped in for his funeral
6   Jean Duvivier, *Golgotha*, France 1935
7   G.P.Callegari, *Pontius Pilate*, Italy/France 1961
8   Gaumont, *La Vie du Christ*, France 1906
9   Illustration from J.H.Gunning JHzn, *The bible for Children*,
    Netherlands 1894
10 Pathe, *La Vie de Jesus*, France 1907
11 Franco Zeffirelli, *Jesus of Nazareth*, USA/GB/Italy 1976

(Photographs - taken from reproductions and a color televisionscreen
with frozen videotaped pictures - and composition by the author)

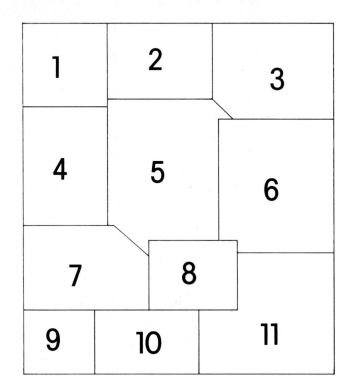

PHOTOCOMPOSITION B

'EFFIGIES DEI' AND THE RELIGIOUS IMAGINATION
A PSYCHOLOGICAL PERSPECTIVE

Coenraad A.J. van Ouwerkerk

Confronted with the immense variety of images of God as they occur within the context of many religions, a psychology of religion is forced to search for a perspective on these images which is at the same time relevant and manageable. Such a perspective may be opened up by fixing the position of God images within a psychological theory of religion. Such a theory must be able to explain and interpret *all* central religious phenomena; images of God however must be counted as one such phenomenon.

1 Images of God in a psychological perspective. Some introductory questions.

There exist various psychological theories of religion, some of which have acquired a certain authority and have the advantage of a certain consensus. On the level of a more general approach, two main trends can be identified, which may be roughly distinguished as 'functional' over against 'symbolic' theories. Until further elaboration suffice it for the moment to characterize a functional theory of religion as one, which views religion predominantly as a response to and a solution of the fundamental psychologial (existential?) predicament of man (cf. Yinger 1970, 5 ff.); and a 'symbolic' theory as one which sees religion primarily as a (presumed) manifestation (epiphany) of some 'out-of-the-ordinary' reality or dimension of reality (the ultimate, the beyond, the numinous, the sacred, gods, God). This reality evokes or presents itself in an experience of a special quality - a religious experience (cf. O'Dea 1966, 19 ff; Berger 1974). This rather precarious distinction between two theoretical conceptions of religion within the psychology of religion is here introduced in the assumption that a quite different function and significance will be assigned to images of God depending on divergent theoretical options with respect to religion.

Psychology of religion however is psychology and so, whatever conception of religion it may favour, it cannot but take into account the psychology of images and imagination. The study of religious imagery

therefore requires the combination and integration of two lines of inquiry, one unfolding a theory of religion, the other working out a theory
of the imagination. It is no caprice to suppose both lines being
connected, because in our view the imagination is at the heart of
religion (cf. van Ouwerkerk 1986, 101 ff). In a psychological analysis
however, images and the imagination prove to be complex phenomena.
Let us for the moment notice, that in the confusing usage with respect
to image and imagination two major shades of meaning of these terms
can be distinguished: the term imagination designates the *representation
of* an existing object in an image, which compensates for its absence
(reproductive imagination) or it refers to the production of an image,
which recreates an object by the way of fiction (productive
imagination).

Two theoretical conceptions of religion, a functional and a symbolic
one; two modalities of the imagination, reproductive and productive
imagination. The question then arises, if any insight in the psychological function and structure of images of God may be gained by the way
of finding a connection between a certain view on religion and a certain
form of imagination. The paper proposes some tentative answers to this
question. The question however is so complex, that we will be forced to
extend our investigation beyond the limits of psychology.

2 Images of God and two psychological perspectives on religion.

There are certainly many questions psychology of religion may ask
about the complex phenomenon of religion, but in our view they all in
the end come down to the basic question: why and in what way does
man pass beyond reality as it urges itself upon him? Or in Freud's
phrasing: how does man arrive at religious ideas 'which ... are not
precipitates of experience and end results of thinking?' (Freud 1927 ch.
VI). We take this question as our guideline; it introduces most directly
the problem of the religious imagination, while it at the same time
causes the diversity of psychological interpretations of religion.

This fundamental question, thus formulated, is not necessarily or
primarily one about the origin of religion(s) or, for that matter, about
the original creation or production of images of God. One does not
witness the emergence of images of God but finds them as already
constituted. But these images as they present themselves in certain
religious symbolic systems, suppose and imply certain psychological
processes, and contain a certain psychological significance or meaning.

In actually relating to such images, in appropriating them, man passes through these processes, tries to adopt, internalize the meaning of which these images are the precipitates and reflection. Thus psychological theories of religion and of religious imagery can be considered and used as expositions of their psychological structure and meaning without sharing their interest in origins. Not psychic origin, but originality of religion and religious imagery is under dispute.

Let us see, which results psychology of religion may yield in studying images of God as precipitates, reflections or expressions of the process in which *homo religiosus* is engaged.

In the introductory paragraph, this process has already been briefly described as it is interpreted by functional and symbolic theories of religion. Both theories interpret this process as consisting in two moments or phases: they assume that the religious process presents a 'breaking point' in the round of ordinary experience *and* a 'breaking beyond' ordinary experience (cf. O'Dea 1966, 5). These pregnant metaphors of 'breaking point' and 'breaking beyond' are very appropriate to point out the marked differences between the two conceptions of religion.

In a functional theory the experience at the breaking point is itself an a-religious (and rather negative) experience. Up to this point, such a theory seems rather plausible: nobody would deny the existence of limit-situations, acting as breaking points. But what about 'breaking beyond'? What does confer to the 'movement' of breaking beyond its direction and object? The answer, rather naively proposed by the theory is: religion. But how does the theory conceive religion? As a creative product of man's search for a solution for his predicament, or as phenomenon (already available) to which man feels attracted because of his critical situation?

Symbolic theories understand religion *itself* as *the* 'breaking point'. It is religion itself which breaches as it were the course of ordinary experience, eliciting a specific experience, because religion presents, manifests a (dimension of) reality, which induces man to 'move beyond'. To such a conception of religion adhere theories like those of R. Otto and M. Eliade; theories which introduce the category of the sacred, the numinous in order to define religion as breaking point.

Considering both theories, one wonders if there is not so much question of two different theories about religion, but of two types of religion or religious options which are under discussion in the respective theories. Is it feasible to distinguish between a type of religion (a more psychological type?) centered around the problem of 'man becoming himself', of man searching for a solution of the predicament of life, and a form of religion (a more cosmological type) centered around the riddle, the mystery of 'reality', exemplified by the cosmos and its various aspects? Ricoeur (1960, 18ff.) has proposed to relate both types of religion by seeing in cosmos and psyche two poles of the same expressivity. Religious symbols refer to the cosmic manifestations of the sacred, but it is not the cosmos out there, in its quasi objective appearance, which manifests the sacred. It is the cosmos in as far as the subject relates to it and so discovers and expresses its own desires and expresses its own desires, conflicts and crises, and its attempt to become itself as a subject. In the formula of Ricoeur (*ibidem*): 'I express myself in expressing the world (the cosmos); I explore my own sacrality in deciphering the sacrality of the world'. It is in the context of religious symbols, that Ricoeur relates the two modalities of religion, the sacred and the religious experience; the topic of symbol however introduces the issue of the religious imagination.

We introduced already implicitly the issue of the religious imagination by discussing the two psychological theories of religion. The process of 'moving beyond ordinary reality', as proposed by the two theories, involves at least partially an imaginative process, the imagination being exactly the psychological function of 'going beyond the real field of behaviour, namely the field of behaviour as determined by perception and effective behaviour' (Linschoten 1961, 118). It is evident that symbolic theories cannot but engage in the topic of religious imagination. But one has only to mention Freud's theory of religion as illusion (representative of a functional theory) to become aware how also functional theories of religion are confronted with the issue of the religious imagination.

One may surmise that different conceptions of the religious process of 'moving beyond' (functional and symbolic) will selectively use different aspects or moments of the imagination in order to understand the religious process.

3 Images of God: representation and presence.
For a beginning, let us analyze a simple and obvious phenomenon: God is represented in an image. Such an image can be a purely mental representation, it can also assume the concrete form of a most of the

time optic image, a portrait, a picture. Representation designates a specific imaginative phenomenon, which cannot be reduced to perception as if a representation were a weakened form of perception. A simple representation pertains already to the imaginative order in that it does not *present* an object in its real and physical objectivity, but re-presents it, irrealizing the object, as it is not any longer present in its physical density, not any longer defined by the parameters of real pace and time. Image as representation has the function to render present objects which exist elsewhere but are absent; it *substitutes* for things in case of their absence (cf. Sartre 1940). As a function of absence, a representation is however dependent on the things it irrealizes and derives its material from things perceived, remembered or expected. Representations are consequently isomorphic images like pictures and portraits.

When looking at the structure and function of images as representations such as described, one wonders what it means to speak of images, representing God. At this stage of our analysis, it does not trouble us, that images of God as representations seem to suppose the existence and reality of God - a supposition a psychology of religion as a science cannot take over. But if a psychology sees it as its first task to study religion as it is adhered to by religious man (the believer), it cannot avoid a question like: do images of God occur in religion, which intend to be representations of God? If there is some awareness of God as transcendent, it will likely prohibit the believer to take images as simple representations of God. Even when the gods share with man one common world, it is questionable if their images can be interpreted as pure and simple representations, depictions of the gods. But let us wait and see, where further analysis will lead us.

Why then discuss image as representation, when an interpretation of images of God as representations in the proper sense is at least questionable? Apart from showing how even such a selfevident phenomenon as images of God is more complex than the uncritical usage of such an expression would suggest, the discussion introduces the problem of tension between presence and absence, intimately connected with image as representation. Not apparently tolerating the absence of an object, man is capable to make, keep the object present by the way of representation. Imaginative representation is 'presentification', not as effective behaviour, but as psychic performance. One discovers however, that there are different modes and situations of absence, of which up

till now only physical absence came up; there are seemingly also different forms of presence and not for all 'objects' (things, persons) the
same form of presence is relevant. A more accurate analysis of the
presence-absence polarity might broaden the concept of imaginative
presentification beyond its representative form. God is absent, not (for
the believer) in the sense of nonexistent, but in the sense of not
manifest, not accessible the way a mundane entity is. Religion therefore
may be seen as a massive attempt to render God present in the way of
presenting, proposing, creating ways of access, of relating to God.

Further analysis of a portrait as an example of an image as representation might teach us more about the significance of the absence-
presence polarity and of imaginative presence. Without denying that a
portrait is a substitute for an absent object, existing physically
elsewhere, *the mere fact* of representing something or somebody seems
to have a peculiar meaning. Reinterpreting Gadamer's thesis, that a
representation enhances the ontological reality of what is represented
(Gadamer 1960) , one might say, that a representation in its imaginative
freedom and mobility and by the way of imaginative variations, could
not only reveal and throw into relief certain aspects of an object,
otherwise hidden or unobserved, but could also make personal and
intimate, what in reality is distant and alien. Rendering an object
present in a representation, is a specific way of having access and
relating to it.

The form and structure of a portrait confirms this interpretation. A
portrait is supposed to bear a resemblance to the object. The likeness
in a portrait is however hardly ever similitude pure and simple. In a
portrait perceptuel material is fashioned into a composition, in which by
the way of elimination, accentuation, combination and similar procedures
the object is reshaped and transformed, reinterpreted. Portrait as
composition suggests that its function cannot be reduced to one of
merely compensating for physical absence. Representation as the most
simple and basic form of imagination, already brings up the matter of
specific ways of relating to reality and even the question of reality
itself and its modalities (presence, absence, physical existence and
inexistence, imaginative, fictive existence and the like). The discussion
of this matter and the answer to this question cannot but have reper-
cussions on the issue of images of God, as ways of relating to God.

In further analysis we observe, that a simple representation like a
portrait, at the moment it manifest itself as a composition, can be

placed at the starting point of a continuum or line, on which images move according to their increasing creative capacity, loosing along the line their dependency on 'objects of the world', and their character of resemblance, and becoming more and more figurative and fictional, up to the point of representing 'nonexistent things' (cf. Ricoeur 1976, 209). It is as if the imagination follows a trajectory, along which it comes more and more into its own, in the end gathering its full imaginative momentum, creating a fictive world of myth, fairy tale, dream, poetry, narrative ficton. In the context of fiction the fonction of images with respect to presence and absence can be expected to be quite different from the one representations perform.

Now it has been found that images of God hardly make sense when understood as representations, the question arises if they may be qualified as fictional, figurative images. On the one hand a positive answer to this question seems rather plausible; figurative images hint at symbol, metaphor, simile, which undoubtedly are found in most religions. On the other hand, at the moment one admits images of God as figurative, be it in the form of symbol and metaphor, one may in the end be forced to view religion as fiction. Does however such a conception do justice to religion (some religions) as it presents itself or even as it is theoretically reconstructed? The answer to the question, if and how a connection can be established between religion and fiction, depends on a difference of view on both religion *and* fiction.

Referring back to the two psychological interpretations of religion (functional and symbolic), we observe how they imply a different relation to fiction, but also make use of different forms of dimensions of fiction. Functional theories tend to conceive religion as the substitution of 'something' beyond reality, something not experienced in reality. This at least suggests that what cannot be achieved or reached in reality, is substituted by an activity, a relation, an object *in imagination*. But when the term 'in imagination' with respect to religion means 'substitution for reality', religion is suggested to be an *imaginary, fantastic* world. It is however well to remember that 'imaginary' here designates a rather arbitrary recomposition or decomposition of reality, with all its connotations of irreality, of neglect of or contradiction with reality. One can speak here of fiction; such fictions exist and are in fact expressions of the imagination, of the imagination however in only one of its dimensions, or manifestations, which commonly is indicated by the term *fantasy*.

A symbolic view of religion leads to a quite different concept of fiction and brings out an other dimension of the imagination. Viewing religion as a manifestation of the sacred, symbolic theories recur to images as the media of this manifestation, the sacred as 'beyond ordinary experience', not being immediately accessible. Religious images acquire the character of symbols; symbolic images however do not so much represent or substitute for an object, as rather *refer to* bringing out certain of its qualities or dimensions, otherwise hidden or unnoted. Symbols are clearly of the order of fiction, but while irrealizing 'reality', symbols are referring to reality, are bound to it: fiction here does not denote denial or neglect of reality, but rather its re-affirmation by the way of disclosure, In the symbolic imagination a process is operative, different from the one which is active in fantasy. Symbolic images express a new vision in an image (or imagery) , which is not a pure representation or fantastic replica of reality but a creative variation on and alteration of reality.

Fantasy versus creative imagination: we will now further investigate two interpretations of religious imagination and images of God in the context of the two theories of religion.

4 Images of God, God as image.

We think to be justified in taking Freud's theory of religion as representative of functional theories. In a dynamic psychology like the freudian, it is the thrust of desire which moves beyond all real objects, producing *fantastic* objects. Desire has lost its original blissful object, is unacceptable in its vital overpowering thrust, is frustrated by the harsh reality of nature and human society. An imaginary world is created, in which desire finds fulfilment. It would be too simple saying, that such imagery represents an other (real?) object, which substitutes for an unattainable object by the way of compensation. If there is substitution or compensation, then in this sense, that an *image* is substituted for *reality* and so substitution marks the peculiar process, in which reality is *irrealized* and a transition takes place from one order (of reality) to another (of irreality). In that sense the image itself is an *object*, desired, experienced, handled and cultivated for its own sake. Therefore in a freudian conception, which discovered the figurative potential of desire, the image would be ill-defined, when understood as a creative re-interpretation of reality, presenting new, deeper or latent dimensions of reality or a new reality for that matter. What such an image represents is *desire itself*, or rather the desiring subject, or rather the situation of the subject, its precarious position of attempting to become, to be a self. The imagery of desire represents not a desired object, but rather a *scene* (cf. Lorenzer 1970) like for instance the Oedipus-scene, in which the subject itself is involved in a struggle for its own integrity, for self-acceptance, self-fulfilment *etcetera*; it is this struggle, which the image expresses.

Nevertheless, one is throughout Freud's work confronted with the question how desire is represented in the fantastic imagery of desire. Freud qualifies the images in which desire expresses itself regularly as symbolic. And in the case of dream images this qualification 'symbolic' seems appropriate. They express indirectly, figuratively, the latent dreamthoughts, which are not allowed to be expressed directly, because they refer to unacceptable or repressed desires. In this way dream images have a double meaning, a literal and a figurative one, the one referring to the other. But they are symbolic in a particular way: they are symbolic in the way not of manifestation, but in the way of dissimulation. So the oneiric symbol 'boat' may refer to 'woman', not however in order to express in a more pregnant way - made possible by an image - what her erotic attractiveness in essence means, but rather in order to cover up the overpowering or unacceptable conflict of sexual desire (cf. Ricoeur 1965, 19-28).

This idea of dissimulation and distortion dominates Freud's theory of the imagination. But when Freud's analysis of images switches from dream-imagery to religious images, images of God loose their seemingly specific symbolic character. Is the father a symbolic image of God? And is 'father', as used here, really an image? There are clearly two lines of argument in Freud's discussion of the God-father image. First there is a simple line (Freud 1927). In its predicament of being threatened by the harsh reality of nature and society, man is in search for consolation. As reality does not grant consolation, man 'imagines' a 'magnified father' as a grandiose consoling figure. One might conclude, that desire is allowed to express itself *directly*, in searching for fulfilment. But why in the form of a father figure? And here the line of argument crosses a second more psychoanalytical one. Man's situation of desolation reminds him of his childhood, in which he looked up to his father as his help and stay. The infantile relation to the father, as soon as remembered, evokes the conflictual, oedipal situation (consolation, but also rejection, authority, guilt, cf. Freud 1930). So the magnified father assumes all the complex characteristics of the oedipal father. But why this fantastic magnification? Not even desire, in the end, or the oedipal conflict are seemingly powerful and creative enough to account for it. Freud has to resort to a historical fact, the murder of the primaeval father of the prehistoric horde, killed by his sons, feared and admired, mourned for and celebrated.

And God-father? Let us be clear about one thing: in no way Freud is questioning the *idea* God; he accepts it as it is found in religions. Neither the reality of God does concern him;God does not exist. His entire speculation is about a fantasma, a fantastic imagery, which in the end finds its origin in a myth, taken as historical reality.

Freud's meandering argument leads to some important conclusions. In any case, there is in Freud's view no image *of* God, but *God is an image*. But more interesting is the fact, that Freud has tried to understand and give substance to the 'going beyond' which in most functional theories remains a movement into a void which can be filled in every way imaginable. The going beyond is an imaginative performance, but its transcending momentum asks for more than pure desire in its fantastic virulence; myth under the guise of history had to be introduced to explain this momentum and thrust. The father-image refers however back to an archaic origin, reiterated in the oedipal conflict of the individual. It does not even hypothetically refer to any reality with which man is confronted, as it were, *in front of him*. Where reality 'imaginatively' is intended, it is an illusory reality, a fantastic one. In no way Freud would consider an alternative interpretation in which God is *seen as* 'father' - 'father' being precisely an *image* of God, whatever the reality of God might be. Imagination (at least the religious imagination) is in Freud's opinion a fascination which excludes critical conscience. Consequently the imagination produces only a pseudo-presence (cf. Ricoeur 1976). Is there another view of religious imagery and images of God, which in the context of creative imagination arrives at a quite different interpretation of imaginative presence and irreality?

5 *Images of God and the creative imagination.*

In order to arrive in the end to apparently some understanding of symbolic images of God, to which symbolic theories of religion show affinities, we will now briefly discuss of the creative, productive imagination. Thereby we adopt Ricoeur's idea, that the literary image (the metaphor) is a paradigmatic case, in which the imagination fully unfolds its potential and manifests its specific nature (Ricoeur 1976, 267 ff.).

In proposing images in their poetic variety, one dissociates oneself from the idea of an image as a perceptual derivative and sees it primarily as a phenomenon of language. It is no caprice to classify images with linguistic phenomena, because in Ricoeur's idea images (even cosmic symbols) are 'spoken' ('parlées') before they are seen (Ricoeur 1960, 18). The first thing thus made clear is, that images are of the order of significations and their relations, and not of the order of things and their connections. Let us then take the metaphor as the prototype of poetic image. Metaphor is a figure of language, a strategy of language by the way of which new significations are created, 'semantic innovation' is produced (Ricoeur 1975).
What does 'semantic innovation' mean and how does it come about?

We take as an example Gerard Manley Hopkins' poetic phrase `Mind, o the mind has mountains'. In such a poetic expression there is a tension between two meanings in two interpretations, a literal and a figurative one (mountain as a geographic constellation and mountain as a predicate of the mind, the mind being a spiritual, mental phenomenon). In a literal interpretation, the proposition leads to absurdity, and produces as it were a 'collusion' between different semantic fields. In the metaphor the absurdity is removed and solved and the challenge of the 'collusion' met with, in that 'mountain' as a predicate of the mind is forced to extend and widen its original meaning, assimilating it to 'mind', but in doing so brings out in the meaning of mind new aspects, new meaning, whereby `mind` is assimilated to the new meaning of 'mountain'. A new meaning complex, a new semantic field is uncovered, in which both meanings (mind and mountain) converge. Metaphor makes one see something as ... ; in seeing something as ... , one sees it in a new way.

Contrary to current opinion, Ricoeur (1975, 273) asserts that a metaphorical enunciation does not only present new, innovative meaning (sense), but has also a *referent*; metaphors refer to reality. This assertion seems in contradiction with the precisely fictional character of figurative, metaphorical language. Fiction clearly abolishes the reference of ordinary language, in creating a fictive world, which consists of an interplay of significations, and not of real 'objects'. It is evident, that fiction suspends the primary reference to 'ordinary reality', but this suspension is the condition for a reference of the second order, in which reality is indirectly intended, namely in so far as is seen and uncovered in the way proposed by the metaphor. In the last resort the tension between two meanings (literal and figurative) in two interpretations and the absurdity of a literal interpretation cannot be resolved until a new level or dimension of reality is discovered, which justifies the new interpretation. In Ricoeur's view fiction is heuristic in that it redescribes reality and presents reality remade.

What is however this reality remade by the way of fiction? In no way the existence of a mysterious reality beyond reality is suggested. First the fictive world is not a denial of the world. Fiction means a *suspension* of the world, in the sense of a neutralization with respect to the world as 'Lebenswelt', the world of man's pragmatic interests, concerns, exploits; the world objecified in service of control, manipulation, adaptation. Fictive irrealization has to be understood as depragmatization and non-engagement with respect to every day life. It is more difficult to concretely define the fictive world in itself. It is not an objective world, but rather the world as a texture of meanings which expresses and makes possible man's profound belonging to and participation in the world (Ricoeur), his 'being in the world'. It is therefore fallacious to speak of fiction as evoking inexisting things. A symbolic image like centaur for example is not an (inexistent) thing; its physical existence is not relevant at all, because a centaur is a set of meanings in a pictorial composition. If it were a thing, it would be a thing, said, spoken rather than a thing seen or perceived.

It is however evident, that fiction comprehends more than poetic metaphor and that there are more ways in which man might experience and express his 'being in the world' than that of his 'appartenance profonde au monde de la vie' (Ricoeur 1976, 214), which poetry makes possible. Thus in a fictive narrative not belonging to and participation in the world are celebrated, but rather his involvement in the actions and passions of life is imagined and figured in a dramatic fictive world, which, in tension with ordinary reality, presents what really and essentially matters in life. The idea of different ways of 'being in the world', figuratively presented in different forms of the world of fiction, could prove to be important, because it might allow us to extend fiction beyond the field of fictive, artistic literature into the sphere of religion. Religion as a fictive world inducing and expressing the specifically religious mode of 'being in the world'?

6 Images of God: the precarious status of the religious imagination.

Religion, conceived as an imaginative world or an imaginative project, inducing and expressing the religious mode of 'being in the world'; a question, not a thesis. In my opinion such a conception of religion does exist and in symbolic theories of religion this conception in some way or another is advocated. These *functional* theories of religion seem to land the discussion of images of God in a deadlock. We turn to *symbolic* theories for a hopefully better understanding of such images. In centering around the idea of *disclosure* (of the sacred) these theories seem to refer to a conception of the religious imagination at least affinitive to the creative imagination discussed in the previous paragraph. In introducing however the idea of the sacred, one gets entangled in a confused discussion about such an ambiguous concept. Does the sacred designate a transcendent reality or a special quality of the cosmos and the human world? The fact that the classical science of religion has made the sacred into its central scientific construct, and the fact that the psychology of religion has seen the sacred as *the* adequate object of religious experience, suggest that they at least see the sacred as a mundane reality (of a special quality and constitution), open to observation and experience, amenable to scientific analysis. But even a science of religion in reconstructing religion has to ask the question, what in reality corresponds to this concept of the sacred. I find Vergote's analysis of the construct 'the sacred' most plausible (cf. Vergote 1974, 471 ff). For brevity's sake, I mention only here the distinction he makes between the adjective and the substantive 'sacred', the substantive being a hazardous construct, suggesting a separate reality. To the adjective a definite and specific meaning can be attributed. The adjective 'sacred' might designate a certain sacred quality of 'the world' (cosmic and human), referring to its mystery, to the origin and end of reality, in the sense of its original fundament and final completion. It has nothing transcendent about it in the traditional religious sense of the term; the sacred is a mundane phenomenon, a dimension of the cosmic and human world.

Why this digression about the sacred? It is in my opinion the sacred quality of the world, which symbolic theories of religion have in mind. But in a perspective of the sacred, religious imagination can be given a central and adequate place and function. And although most of the symbolic theories do not pay explicit attention to the religious imagination, they cannot found and develop their theories, without implicitly supposing the imagination operative. Otherwise a disclosure of the sacred remains a rather mysterious affair.

The basic structural components of the metaphorical process (irrealization, tension between profane and sacred, literal and figurative, imaginative reference) can easily be discovered in religion, as an imaginative vision of the sacrality of the world. This form of religion in its diverse modalities really is fiction, but in the positive sense of metaphorical transformation. Fiction here, does not conjure up pseudo-presence. Presence is imaginative presence in the way of referring to; irrealization is neutralization and non-engagement with respect to the 'thèse du monde' (Ricoeur 1976, 216).

There is however one crucial problem. Could one name this imaginative vision of the world religion? Or does a proper definition of religion implies a God, radically transcendent with respect to reality, accessible to man? The outcome of the discussion about what religion really is, need not to be anticipated in order to discover that something peculiar about religion and the religious imagination is the matter, at the moment one introduces the idea of God. Images of God are in discussion, but how to understand images of God in the light of the religious imagination, when he cannot be assigned a place, role or function in an imaginative vision of the sacred dimension of the world.

When for the believer God is a reality, is it the student of religion permitted to classify God with imaginative fiction? And besides, how can God, *Deus invisibilis and absconditus*, be represented in an imagery, caught up in an interplay of significations, with referring to the world? Theistic religions propose a real relationship with a real God, even on the level of religion as representation and not only on the level of religion as conduct, as a way of life. One may observe already in mythical religions how they break through the boundaries of fiction; for mythical consciousness myth is not any longer merely enacted on the level of significations, only figuratively presenting origin and end. Myth is lived in many cases as presenting and inducing a *real* movement or process, through which mythical man has real access to a founding reality, participating realistically in it.

This tendency towards a quasi-realistic interpretation of the religious symbolic order seems rather inevitable. One finds also outside theology the thesis according to which an additional value of reality is conferred especially to symbols in the form of objects and action, which linguistic metaphors are lacking. Thus Vergote (1980) speaks of the symbolic presence of God in a rather realistic way and throughout the *opus magnum* of Gadamer similar expressions can be found (Gadamer 1960).

A psychology of religion, seeing religion from the point of view of man, might be of some help in clarifying the opposition between real and imaginative, without reducing the imaginative process to a psychological one. Seen from the perspective of man, reaching out to the God in whom he believes, religious imagination could be conceived as evoking and presenting an intentional movement, and expressing an intended experience (a virtual experience) (Ricoeur 1960). So images of God would figuratively express and present a 'moving beyond' rather than the 'beyond itself'. Explaining how God does come to the attention of man, and how the movement to God ever does start, is beyond the grasp of psychology. The movement itself however, can be interpreted in terms of an imaginative process. Without however a text, an imaginative text, in which God is spoken of as a referent of this movement, there is no religious imagination possible or operative (cf. van Ouwerkerk 1986).

Images of God as topic of the study of religion prove to be more complex than the current usage of the term would suggest. That further study of the religious imagination is an urgent task, this paper has hopefully demonstrated, in an attempt to indicate the direction for such a study.

BIBLIOGRAPHY

Frank, M., *Was ist Neostrukturalismus?*, Frankfurt a.M. 1983
Freud, S., *Die Zukunft einer Illusion*, 1927
Freud, S., *Das Unbehagen in der Kultur*, 1930
Gadamer, H.-G., *Wahrheit und Methode*, Tübingen 1960
Klinger, E., *Structure and functions of fantasy*, New York etc., 1971
Linschoten, J., 'Algemene functieleer', in: Langeveld, M.J., *Inleiding in de psychologie*, Groningen 1961
Lorenzer, M., *Kritik des psychoanalytischen Symbolbegriffes*, Frankfurt a.M. 1970
O'Dea, Th., F., *The sociology of religion*, Englewood Cliffs N.J., 1966
Ouwerkerk, C.A.J. van, *In afwezigheid van God*. Voorstudies tot een psychologie van het geloof, 's-Gravenhage 1986
Ricoeur, P., *La métaphore vive*, Paris 1975
Ricoeur, P., 'L'imagination dans le discours et dans l'action', in: *Savoir, faire, espérer*. Les limites de la raison, Bruxelles 1976
Sartre, J.-P., *L'imaginaire*. Psychologie et phénoménologie de l'imagination, Paris 1940
Vergote, A., 'Equivoques et articulation du sacré', in: E. Castelli (ed), *Le sacré*, Paris 1974, 471-492
Vergote, A., 'The chiasm of subjective and objective function in the symbol', *Kerygma* 14 (1980) 27-49
Yinger, J. Milton, *The scientific study of religion*, London 1970

LIST OF AUTHORS

J. N. BREMMER, Senior Lecturer of Ancient History, Faculty of Letters, State University of Utrecht.

T. GOUDRIAAN, Senior Lecturer of the History of Indian Culture, Faculty of Letters, State University of Utrecht.

J. G. HAHN, Lecturer of Communication Studies, Amsterdam Catholic University of Theology.

P. W. VAN DER HORST, Lecturer of New Testament Exegesis and Early Judaïsm, Faculty of Theology, State University of Utrecht.

PH. H. J. HOUWINK TEN CATE, Professor of Ancient Near Eastern History and Hittitology, Faculty of Letters, University of Amsterdam.

J. H. KAMSTRA, Professor of the History of Religions, Faculty of Theology, University of Amsterdam.

R. KLOPPENBORG, Senior Lecturer of the History of Religions and Buddhist Studies, Faculty of Theology, State University of Utrecht.

C. A. J. VAN OUWERKERK, Professor of the Psychology of Religion, Faculty of Theology, State University of Leiden.

D. VAN DER PLAS, Lecturer of the History of Ancient Religions and Egyptology, Faculty of Theology, State University of Utrecht.

R. POELMEYER, Buddhist Studies, Amsterdam.

H. S. VERSNEL, Professor of Ancient History, Faculty of Letters, State University of Leiden.

K. WAGTENDONK, Senior Lecturer of the History of Religions and Islamic Studies, Faculty of Theology, University of Amsterdam.

H. WITTE, Senior Lecturer of the History of African Religions, Faculty of Theology, State University of Groningen.